"I thank God for Sheila Wray Gregoire. Literally. She speaks bluntly and honestly about sex but disarms with transparency, humor, and grace. This a must-read for every woman who has questions about sex. Which means this is a must-read for every woman. She goes where the rest of us fear to tread! I will be recommending this book over and over and over again."

— SHAROL JOSEPHSON
director with FamilyLife Canada

"I could not put this book down! Sheila Wray Gregoire's fantastic new book, *The Good Girl's Guide to Great Sex*, is a gift to wives of all ages. It looks at the subject of sex from every conceivable angle, reminding us that it's okay to be a good girl. In fact, good girls enjoy sex more! With honest testimonies, funny stories, and sobering statistics, Sheila conveys desperately needed truth and clarifies the mixed messages sent by today's culture. Whether you're newly engaged or have been married for years, you will connect with Sheila's honesty and transparency and wonderful sense of humor. Every bride I know is getting this book. Thank you, Sheila, for giving us such a wonderful and honest resource."

— KATE BATTISTELLI
author of *Growing Great Kids*

"Sheila forthrightly debunks myths and taboos about good girls and sex. A must-read for any woman (and husband too) wanting liberation and headache-free bliss in the bedroom, as God intended."

— CHRISTINE WILLIAMS
journalist, columnist, and
award-winning TV producer/host

the good girl's guide to great sex

(and you thought bad girls have all the fun)

SHEILA WRAY GREGOIRE

ZONDERVAN®

ZONDERVAN.com/
AUTHORTRACKER
follow your favorite authors

ZONDERVAN

The Good Girl's Guide to Great Sex
Copyright © 2012 by Sheila Wray Gregoire

This title is also available as a Zondervan ebook. Visit www.zondervan.com/ebooks.

This title is also available in a Zondervan audio edition. Visit www.zondervan.fm.

Requests for information should be addressed to:

Zondervan, *Grand Rapids, Michigan 49530*

Library of Congress Cataloging-in-Publication Data

Gregoire, Sheila Wray, 1970 –
    The good girl's guide to great sex : (and you thought bad girls have all the fun) /
    Sheila Wray Gregoire.
        p.   cm.
    Includes bibliographical references.
    ISBN 978-0-310-33409-5 (softcover)
        1. Sex counseling. 2. Sex – Religious aspects – Christianity. 3. Women – Sexual
    behavior. I. Title.
    HQ63.G66   2012
    306.7082 – dc23   2011048411

The author is represented by MacGregor Literary.

Cover design: Connie Gabbert
Cover photography: iStockphoto.com®
Interior photography: iStockphoto.com®
Interior design: Beth Shagene

Printed in the United States of America

To Keith
I love you

Contents

Foreword

I was introduced to Sheila Wray Gregoire's words long before I met her in person — and I loved them! I was on the *Hearts at Home* blog, researching a topic for moms, and I started following the bread-crumb trail of mommy blog to mommy blog at light speed. I hit Sheila's *To Love, Honor and Vacuum* and stopped ... and paused ... and read ... and stayed and read more ... and more ... Still hungry for more of her wisdom, I signed up for the RSS feed! I couldn't get enough of Sheila's common-sense advice, which is sprinkled with humor, wisdom, and always, always, always honest — very honest — extremely honest words. Sheila is candid, sincere, frank, straight-forward, and courageous. She is like fresh air on a clear, snowy Canadian day. I am not the only one who feels this way about Sheila's writing. Her blog is one of Canada's most popular. I think it might be because she courageously calls things like she sees them.

I know she is gutsy, because I, too, made the brave and bold (and maybe half-crazy) decision to join the small handful of women willing to write a book about sex! Actually, I have penned a few books on sex and romance, so perhaps that is why Sheila and her publisher, Zondervan, had the wild idea that I might have something nice to say in a foreword for this exciting, much-needed, new book! I have some idea how it feels to be in Sheila's shoes as she sought to create a love-changing resource to add the spark and sizzle to your sex life.

Why a Good Girl's Guide on Sex?

Pure Pleasure: Making Your Marriage a Great Affair was our (my amazing husband, Bill, and my) first book — and writing a book about sex is not how most people start their writing careers! That book is now out of print, so we created one that was much more honest, straightforward, and spirited to replace it: *Red Hot Monogamy*. Are you wondering what causes a seemingly sane, conservative woman to write a book about sex? I am pretty sure if you ask Sheila and me that same question, you will get the same answer — WE HAD TO!

Broken hearts, a myriad of questions, and a landslide of emails from precious women, much like you, beckoned us to jump in the deep end of the human relationship pool. We both try to answer (dare we say *advise?*) women on matters that happen behind locked bedroom doors (or maybe other doors!). As you read *The Good Girl's Guide to Great Sex*, I will give you the same advice I give those in the audience of our events. At conferences, I hold up a copy of *Red Hot Monogamy*, a black Sharpie™ marker, and a bright-pink highlighter and say, "This is your sex life. You design it. God will lead each of us to our own comfort level with our spouse. So when you read, if you love the idea, highlight it with an enthusiastic, 'Wow! Awesome! Let's try that!' If you hit something that makes a chill go up your spine, simply draw a line through it with a, 'Hmm, not ready for that one yet!'"

Too Hot to Handle?

Before you get out a brown-paper wrapper to cover up the fact that you are reading a book on sex, stop and consider the evidence that God is applauding your choice! After all, he placed an entire book in the Bible dedicated to marital intimacy. So stand tall as you echo the words of the wife in Song of Songs, "… when I found the one my heart loves. I held him and would not let him go." (Song 3:4).

It is a challenge as a writer to pen something on a topic as controversial as sex and make everyone happy, so give Sheila some grace as you read (like a Good Girl should). If you hit a steamy section, just turn up the air-conditioning, grab an iced tea or a snow cone, and fan away — but KEEP READING! If you read and all this talk of why and how to be a good girl makes you roll your eyes — KEEP READING! Sheila's top-notch extensive research will convince you that Good Girls really do have more red hot monogamy — and they love it — and so do their husbands! Follow Sheila's great example and be brave enough to read all the way through — clear through every well-documented and educational footnote! You will be glad you did — and so will your guy!

Maybe you are still struggling with the why of reading a book like this. I think you are reading *The Good Girl's Guide to Great Sex* because you want something out of it:

- Help for your marriage
- Humor to spark up a long-term love life
- Healing from the baggage and pain of your past
- Hard facts to counsel a friend or yourself
- Hope for an orgasm or multiples ones!

Maybe you are in the majority group of women who say, "Why should *I* read a book about sex — shouldn't my man? What about me?" I will tell you what I share with every woman who has heard me speak on *52 Ways to Wow Your Husband*:

Step out. Take a risk and "wow" your husband. There is no downside. As you gain new tools and ideas to wow your mate, God will be changing you — and you are going to like the woman you will be at the end of this book. Sure, implementing the wonderful, insightful, practical *Good Girl's Guide* ideas will please your husband. It will also change his heart so he becomes easier to live with, easier to love — but so will you! Your desire to enrich your sex life will likely transform your marriage and your man, and he may want to boomerang some of that love, some of those sizzling, sexy ideas, right back to you!

To "wow" your man, to really become what Sheila calls a Good Girl (and great lover), keep this simple acrostic in mind.

BE ...

Willing:

If you are not quite excited about this adventure in *The Good Girl's Guide to Great Sex*, simply pray, "God give me the desire to care about my Good Guy." We have seen that women who pray about better sex in their marriage often become the answer to their own prayers!

Observant:

Clue into your sex life, into your husband, and into what's going on in your own heart, mind, and body. Sheila will challenge and cheer you on as you tap into the sexy Good Girl inside. Some of your preconceptions will take a new slant, and many of your fears or frustrations will vanish if you put your whole heart and mind (and body) into this hands-on homework!

Watching:

Go get some girlfriends and challenge them to buy *The Good Girl's Guide to Great Sex* and pray for each other as you daringly seek to enhance your marriage. See how God will help you become a better wife and more confident lover. God will add some "wow" to the intimate times you have with your man because he set this whole sex thing in motion:

That is why a man leaves his father and mother and is united to his wife, and they become one flesh.

GENESIS 2:24

You can trust him and Sheila's *Good Girl* practical recommendations to fan the flame of your sex life.

What's So Different about a Good Girl?

In the first book of the Bible, God spelled it out — we are different, "male and female he created them" (Gen. 1:27). Good Girls are wired differently than Good Guys. In our bestseller, *Men Are Like Waffles,*

Women Are Like Spaghetti, we share a quote that captures these differences in the bedroom in a very simple, clear-cut way:

HOW TO IMPRESS A WOMAN:
    compliment her, cuddle her, kiss her, caress her, love her, stroke her, tease her, comfort her, protect her, hug her, hold her, spend money on her, dine her, buy things for her, listen to her, care for her, stand by her, support her, go to the ends of the earth for her.

HOW TO IMPRESS A MAN:
    show up naked!

So all you Good Girls (and you former Bad Girls going good), read every word on every page of *The Good Girl's Guide to Great Sex.* After you complete this task, my smart, savvy, sexy friend, show up naked!

Grab *The Good Girl's Guide* and find a quiet place to settle in. My guess is this book will be the page-turner it was for me. I read it straight through, pausing just long enough to plan some Good Girl sex with my great guy! (Heavy, happy sigh!) We have been happily married for over thirty-two years, and we have been marriage educators almost all of those thirty-plus years — and Sheila still managed to enlighten me on some things! She also confirmed many of the things Bill and I have seen work for couples and their intimate lives, so I found myself saying, "That's right, Sheila! Amen! You got it, girl!" The best part of reading *The Good Girl's Guide to Great Sex* is that you will find yourself, with the turn of every page, anticipating your next time with your Good Guy. (Wahoo! Oh, yeah!)

Now, be a Good Girl and flip the page and begin — you will be so glad you did! Sheila's terrific tools, awesome advice, and intriguing ideas will empower, encourage, and enrich your love life — and it is my guess that all the love you lavish on your husband will boomerang back and bless you!

Thank you, Sheila! Lead all of us Good Girls to God's true erogenous zone!

From one Good Girl to another — enjoy listening to our Good Girl guide, Sheila — and have FUN being the sexy Good Girl you were created to be!

Pam Farrel — international speaker; author of over thirty-five books on relationships, including the bestselling *Men Are Like Waffles, Women Are Like Spaghetti*; cofounder, with her husband, Bill, of Love-Wise: www.Love-Wise.com

Who's a Good Girl?

With their silicone-injected lips and their Botox-injected faces, they pout seductively up at us from the covers of *Cosmopolitan*, enticing us to buy their magazine with promises of "7 New Sex Tricks that Will Leave Him Begging for More." As if there were any new tricks. We've been at this for millennia, and personally, I think we've got it all figured out. And we really don't need silicone to do it right.

But the message won't go away. It blares at us from television screens, billboards, movies, and more: *Bad girls have more fun!* They have more sex and better sex than you boring Good Girls who play games on Facebook, volunteer at church, or cuddle up on your couch to spend Friday night watching a quiet chick flick. Bad girls don't have time for any of that. They're out making conquests!

Here's a news flash for you: bad girls actually aren't having that much fun. Those magazines and movies that sell the bad-girl mystique are like the bullies that taunt you on the playground, telling you how stupid you are, even though their IQ is only slightly north of a weasel's. At the time, though, it feels like they own the world and you own the dirt.

My husband was bullied in school. He was a smart kid and a sweet kid (which is probably why he's a smart and sweet man), and kids used to hassle him for his homework. He went on from public school to excel in med school, and he returned to his hometown as a pediatrician. When he walked into one of his first deliveries, the prospective dad took one look at him and turned pale. "Please don't hurt my baby," he said. For there, before Keith, was the bully who had taken a swing at him fifteen years earlier. Now the tables were turned.

Keith had mercy on both the baby and the dad, and the day ended happily. But while Keith once felt like a weakling, that didn't mean he *was* a weakling. He had brains, he had motivation, and he had God to help him make it through med school (and an awesome wife who paid the bills). He may not have realized all his assets during his public-school days, but he was actually better off than the bully who acted so tough.

That's how it is when it comes to Good Girls and bad girls too. Those extolling the bad-girl lifestyle claim that bad girls know how to have sex best. The media features bad girls flaunting their bodies and bragging about their conquests. Indeed, our culture is based on this bad-girl idea that women are sex obsessed in the exact same way fourteen-year-old boys are. And yet none of it's true.

A Family Research Council study of 1,100 married couples revealed that the women who had the most fun in the bedroom were not the Paris Hiltons of the world.[1] The prototypical sexually happy woman better resembled that middle-aged secretary who lives down your street, puttering around in her garden, packing an extra twenty-five pounds. Gravity has taken its toll, but she's the one who's the tiger in the bedroom. She's the one having fun, because she has the secret to sexual success: she's been married to the same man for the last twenty-two years, and they're totally and utterly committed to one another.

Just because someone dresses provocatively does not mean that her sex life is satisfying. Sex doesn't work that way, because sex was designed to be something private, between two committed people. And *designed* is the key word. Sex isn't an animal instinct; it's something beautiful that God created us for, at our core.

Our culture celebrates sex only as instinct — we have a drive that needs to be met. I don't understand why this is supposed to be so marvelous, though. After all, animals operate on instinct too. Their goals in life — in as much as they're able to make goals — are to get all their physical needs met. And by and large, they instinctually know how to do that.

People, on the other hand, have to be taught what to do. Then, even when we are taught, we have the capacity to refuse. We can act in ways diametrically opposed to our well-being. We can be stupid. We can be selfish. And what's more, we can even be noble, something most animals, with the exception of a few dogs, aren't able to be. That's what makes us essentially human: we have a choice. And because of that, we have the capacity to actually be good and to choose to do what's right. In other words, people aren't simply animals. We're higher than that. To think that operating solely on animal instinct is progressive is exactly backwards. It's regressive.

That bad-girl cultural icon with her stash of flavored condoms and a closet of clubwear isn't more in touch with her sex drive or more authentic about her sexuality than a Good Girl is; she's less in touch, because she's treating sex as something purely instinctual and not something sacred.

That's why bad girls may talk about it more, flaunt it more, and laugh about it more, but Good Girls actually have more fun!

What Kind of Girl Are You?

Perhaps you're beginning to have your doubts about whether you're actually a Good Girl, because you've been married for a few years now, but you're not having any of this fun we're talking about. You've lived a good life, and you've been faithful to your husband, but there are no bells and whistles in the bedroom. It's rather ho-hum. My prayer is that this book can open up some sexual discovery and help you find that oneness you crave.

Or maybe you're reading this book and you're about to get married. You've grown up in a Christian home, and you're wondering how this whole sex thing works. You're a Good Girl too, and you're going to enjoy this book!

But what if you don't have a pristine past? Does that mean that you're a bad girl?

I think it's more likely that you're a sad girl. Our culture, which has spread this horrid lie that sex should be both anonymous and idolized, is the real culprit here. And I think most girls who buy this line of thinking are hurting because they've been sold a bill of goods. They've been told that if they sleep around, they'll be popular and fulfilled. They've been lectured to by our media that the path to fulfillment lies in beauty and sexual prowess, not in commitment.

And so they have handed over what is most precious to them to gain in return a broken heart and a deep sense of loneliness. The hooking-up culture isn't helping; it's hurting.

Maybe you've been through that. Maybe you've been a "bad girl," doing things that you know you shouldn't. That's okay. The Bible is full of bad girls — former prostitutes, adulteresses, lewd women. Or perhaps you feel like a bad girl because of what others have done to you. Remember Tamar, King David's daughter, whose ugly story is told in 2 Samuel 13? She was a victim of incest from her half brother Amnon, and she lived out her days in shame. She felt "bad," even though she hadn't done anything bad to deserve it. Are you like that?

Or perhaps you feel more like a Good Girl wannabe. You want to have a great sex life with your husband, but you struggle with porn. You find yourself fantasizing about strange things or about strange men.

Jesus came to redeem women just like that — just like you. No matter what you're struggling with, once you've accepted Jesus' sacrifice for all the ugly stuff in your life, now, when God looks at you, he doesn't see the sin. He doesn't see the drunken parties or the groping in the backseat of someone's car when you did what you didn't want to do. He doesn't see your quest for the next guy to make you feel alive. He doesn't even see you through the lens of what your uncle did to you. What God sees, when he looks at you, is Jesus. He sees Jesus' love, Jesus' sacrifice, and Jesus' goodness. He sees that you are now a Good Girl, because you've embraced the truly Good One.

That is good news! You can be a Good Girl even if you weren't a virgin on your wedding night. You can be a Good Girl if you're struggling with sexual problems, if you're haunted by your past, or if you're just simply trying to get over this deep-seated fear that sex is somehow dirty. Being a Good Girl is not based on what you do; it's based on whose you are. And if you choose to follow God, and his design for sex, you're a Good Girl.

Maybe none of this makes sense to you, though. You have no interest in being a Good Girl; you're happy the way you are, and you think this emphasis on sex with one person for life is just a way of ensuring everyone feels guilty and no one has any fun. May I just ask you to hear me out? I think you're missing out on the amazing aphrodisiac that comes from true intimacy — an intimacy you were specifically designed for.

And I want you to experience that, because I want your marriage to thrive. In fact, I've always been rather passionate about healthy families. While most little girls daydream about their wedding, my daydreams as a child weren't nearly as focused on lace and satin. I tended to dream about being happily married with three or five or seventeen children. I didn't want the romance; I wanted the stability.

I was raised by a single mom after my dad left, and I was so adamant that I would do the opposite of my father that I went running into God's arms very early. In university I did postgraduate work in sociology, focusing on the family specifically, just to verify that God's design for marriage really was the best. When I was still young, I married a man equally devoted to God.

And even though our marriage had a very rocky start — as you'll hear about in these pages — I never doubted my commitment, because I saw marriage as the most important thing on earth. I had witnessed firsthand what divorce did, and I wasn't going to be a statistic. When my children were small and a window opened up for me to write for parenting magazines, I jumped through it. Within a few years, I was writing books on parenting, sex, and marriage, trying to share my own passion for families staying together. And over the last few years, my husband has joined me as we speak at marriage conferences encouraging couples.

What I learned in writing and speaking was that the more I understood what God intended for sex, the better sex was. Good Girls really do have the edge, and I want you to know that edge so that your marriage can be great too.

So welcome to our journey of sexual discovery. Whether you're married, engaged, or thinking about it; experienced or virginal; abused and hurt or just naive and questioning, God has a path for you that leads to deep connection relationally, spiritually, and physically. In these pages, I hope to help you find it.

PART 1

the beauty of sex

CHAPTER 1

How Good Girls Think about Sex

You were created for sex. God made you just the way you are — with your anatomy, personality, sexuality, and desires — so that one day you could be united with that special someone. It's not an afterthought on God's part — it's deeply wired into you, into the very center of who you are. You are a sexual being.

When we're single, we may try to downplay this because we don't want to get tempted, but once you're married, embrace it, because it is awesome! God made sex to be so wonderful that for a few moments, it's as if the only people who exist in the world are you and your husband. Everything is supersensitive. Your senses are heightened. You lose control.

And God made this to be a good thing. He wants us to be overcome with our husbands, to experience that pinnacle of pleasure, and to feel truly and fully alive.

But just because sex is beautiful, natural, and God given doesn't mean it's easy. And, in fact, it's often those things that are the closest to our hearts, to our souls, to our very selves, that get the most twisted. Nowhere is this more evident than with sex. In this chapter we're going to cut through the grime and discover what God really meant sex to be.

BAD GIRL TRAP: Sex Is Entirely about Genitalia

In the movie *Fried Green Tomatoes*, Kathy Bates plays an insecure, introverted doormat. Everybody takes advantage of her, and so in defiance she joins a women's self-help group meant to boost confidence. This little mouse of a woman walks into her first meeting only to find the leader instructing everyone to take out a mirror, hike down their panties, and study their vaginas. Mortified, Bates rushes out, hyperventilating all the way.

What would you have done?

Personally, I've been there, and let me share a bit of my background since we're going to be talking so intimately in this book anyway. Today I have a great marriage, and I'm definitely a Good Girl who has fun. But I was not always that way. When I walked down the aisle, I was carrying a huge amount of baggage related

A GOOD GIRL SPEAKS: *"Sex truly belongs between a husband and a wife. Outside of that, it is empty and meaningless." (married 8 years)*

to trust. I had been left by my dad as a baby, abandoned by my stepfather as a teen, and rejected just two months before my wedding by my fiancé. The latter man eventually changed his mind and came crawling back, and I welcomed him with open arms. Unfortunately, the rest of my body didn't cooperate. As much as I loved my husband and wanted to make love, I was scared to get too vulnerable, and my body wouldn't relax. And when you can't relax, sex hurts.

One of the problems of coming from a family full of doctors, as I do, is that anything to do with the body must, of course, be seen by a physician. So after confiding to a close family member about my problems, I was marched off to a gray-haired gynecologist who explained to me that I just needed to get in touch with my vagina. He would conduct a full examination, with my husband present, inviting me to touch everything and name everything so I wouldn't be scared of anything anymore. Apparently magically saying the word *vagina* is supposed to eradicate deep-seated trust issues. And just like Kathy Bates' character, I hyperventilated and beat a hasty retreat, never to darken the door of that particular doctor again.

Amazingly, I recovered from the pain without the use of mirrors and physicians once my husband and I were able to work through our trust issues. And it verified something important to me. Too often we get sex wrong because we think it's all about body parts:

God created genitalia to fit together, and when you're married, you're allowed to connect the puzzle pieces. Sounds kind of silly that way, doesn't it? As if it doesn't have anything to do with the relationship at all but is just an "extra" that you get in marriage, sort of like "Do you want fries with that?" Now I don't mean to diminish physical problems that can make sex difficult or painful, and we'll go over some helpful strategies to solve some of those challenges later on in this book. Nevertheless, too often we do think of sex as purely a physical act instead of understanding it in its wider context.

Yes, sex involves our bodies. But it doesn't involve only — or even primarily — our bodies. It is so much more than that. And too many of us, both Good Girls and bad girls, have bought into the idea that sex is primarily a physical thing when it's not. The physical can be awfully fun (and there's lots more coming in this book about how to experience those physical fireworks). But if we see sex *only* in the physical realm, we miss out on the potential sex has. We degrade it to be far less than it was created to be.

Ironically, the bad-girl message, when it comes to our bodies, sounds quite progressive and woman-positive, which is why we believe it. It says we need to take control of our own sexual satisfaction. We need to be in touch with our own bodies, have fun with ourselves, know what we like, and celebrate our own sexuality *before* we can have any sort of sexual relationship. In fact, the relationship itself is only secondary to our own sexual selves. We need to know how to have an orgasm, know what feels good, and know what we like, all before sex can be good with someone else. To me, this turns our husbands into sex toys rather than partners.

Yet the approach makes sense. In a world that believes in premarital sex, it's assumed you'll have sex with many men. The only constant in your sex life, then, is you. To get sex right, you need to research *you*. In a Good Girl marriage, though, you know you're with this man till death do you part. You have time to learn. You don't have to know what's good to *you*; you get to learn what's good for *us*.

Maybe you're already struggling with this. Isn't this insistence that sex is only for marriage a throwback to a more prudish time when the church wanted to exert its influence by making people feel guilty? Today we know better, don't we? We know that the Christian message is freedom, not control.

Actually, I think the Christian message is grace in a fallen world. We live in a world that has distorted what God created and has turned against God. But God doesn't punish us for it; he punished Jesus in our place, giving us grace and freedom. It's not a freedom to do anything, though; it's a freedom from the power of lies, the power of sin, and the power of ugliness that has control over this world. When you experience that kind of freedom, life is richer, more beautiful, and far more abundant.

If you don't buy this and you're reading this book more for the tips on how to make sex stupendous, that's okay. But may I suggest something? Read with an open mind. Listen to the voices of the Good Girls in this book. Listen to what God says about sex. And you just may see why keeping sex to only one man, once you're married, isn't restrictive. It's actually a blessing.

Many people, however, just don't believe this. Last year my family and I traveled to a Christian children's home in Kenya, home to over a thousand abandoned or orphaned children. Our trip was primarily a medical mission, but in the evenings the pastor asked my husband and me to speak to the teens about adolescence. In one of the question-and-answer sessions, a boy stood up and asked, "Are there disadvantages on your wedding night if you are a virgin?"

After beating around the bush trying to figure out exactly what he was getting at, I finally asked bluntly, "Are you asking if sex will be bad if we don't have practice first?" The room erupted in laughter, and the boy confirmed that this was his concern. And so we told him in no uncertain terms that anyone can learn how to have sex — it is learning how to make love that is important. And the more people that you join your body with, the more difficult that becomes.

Practicing with other men doesn't help you to figure out what you like. In fact, it can harm you. And the numbers bear this out. Those who rate their sex life the highest today are those who were virgins when they were married. To prepare for this book, I conducted two surveys of a thousand women each, asking them about their wedding nights, their religion, their sexual experiences, and their sexual satisfaction today. Those who were most satisfied with their current sex lives were not those who had had lots of practice before they were married, but those who had saved all their practice for their husbands. They rated their current sex lives at 7.5, a full point higher on a 10-point scale than those who had had sex with multiple partners before they were married.

Sex is not about genitalia. It's about relationship. When God said "the two shall become one flesh," he didn't mean it only physically. When we focus on the physical, we neglect the real power sex has to bond us together in multiple ways, not only physically but mentally, emotionally, and spiritually as well.

BAD GIRL IDEA: Sex Is Shameful

If only all bad girl messages were consistent, we'd have an easier time demolishing them. But while one bad girl message says we should glorify our bodies, the other says we should feel embarrassed by them, as if sex is somehow shameful. Many Good Girls begin marriage with this feeling. Either it's because they've already shared their bodies with others or because sex really wasn't talked about at home except to say, "Don't do it!" They don't have information. It's been treated like a secret, as if it's not a legitimate subject for discussion, because no good person would raise it.

How did this misconception start? People have always been suspicious of women enjoying sex too much, because if we do, we may decide to have sex indiscriminately, stray from our marriages, or leave and disgrace our families. So as a way of keeping girls from experimenting, families often taught them to be ashamed if they liked anything or wanted anything. Families didn't tell girls the names of their body parts. They hushed little girls when they mentioned them or swatted their hands away when, as toddlers, they inadvertently touched between their legs. Instead of teaching them the truth as they matured — that sex is truly a beautiful gift they can unwrap when they're married — parents in most cultures and throughout history tended to say that it was something bad.

Yet I don't think the fear that girls would stray is the only reason that sex has been portrayed as somehow shameful. I also think it's because the vast majority of people don't have sex the way God intended. I don't mean that physi-

A GOOD GIRL SPEAKS: *"It's good for married couples to have fun together, and sex is not a 'dirty little secret'! It's a wonderful gift from God to be celebrated together." (married 23 years)*

cally they don't fit together; pretty much any two people can figure that out given enough time. I mean that people stress the physical aspects of sex beyond everything else, and that cheapens what should be an intimate bonding experience. We're left with this suspicion that perhaps sex actually isn't beautiful, because we're minimizing the aspects of sexuality that grow our souls, and we're stressing those that have the capacity to shrink them. Sex, then, becomes associated with something that is selfish, animal, and base, rather than something that is precious, uniting, and sacred.

Look, girls, there is nothing wrong with sexual feelings. You were meant to enjoy sex. Yearning for your husband to take you; feeling excited when he looks at you; even enjoying a quickie before work are all wonderful things. Not every sexual encounter has to be imbued with great significance. But the sexual relationship itself should be something special, and all too often it's not. God made sex to be wonderful physically, but he didn't make it *only* to be wonderful physically. It's so much more than that, which is what our culture too often fails to understand.

BAD GIRL IDEA: Great Sex Needs an Amazing Body

Since our culture is so obsessed with physical pleasure, it is only natural that it is also obsessed with "sexiness" — and sexiness defined in very narrow terms. When sex is about grabbing pleasure from as many people as you can, you've got to be hot to attract those partners. So we start to think that a hot body is indispensable for hot sex. No wonder so many of us suffer from low self-esteem! We can never measure up.

That's why if there was one thing I would ban from normal conversation, it's calling virtual strangers "hot." Judging people solely by their physical sex appeal is so rampant — and technology only makes it worse. One of the things I love most about Facebook is the ability to spy on the junior high kids in the youth group where I volunteer. And what continues to sadden me are the Hot or Not polls that keep popping up. The girls will post a picture of some guy they like with the caption: "He's hot!" The boys do the same thing about the girls. We talk about people's sexiness solely based on how they look. But when we divorce sex from relationship, sex isn't about connection. It really is only about the body.

But guess what, girls: you can be sexy without liposuction! *You may think that's fine to say, but Sheila, you haven't seen me naked.* You're right. I haven't. And I don't particularly want to, either. But, honey, if you're thinking that you need a certain body type to have good sex, then you've bought into some bad-girl thinking. Those studies on marital bliss showed very little relationship between one's *waistline* and one's sexual satisfaction, and a lot of relationship between one's *marriage* and one's sexual satisfaction. Get it? It's not about being 34 – 24 – 34. It's about loving someone.

A GOOD GIRL SPEAKS: *"The most arousing thing we did just after our honeymoon was to go shopping to buy a wastebasket and a broom — they signaled to me that we were in it for the long haul, that we were not just having sex but were making a life together." (married 17 years)*

If you're not a size 4, you can still be sexy — to your husband. It really doesn't matter what anyone else thinks of you. Have you ever seen a picture of Queen Victoria? Let's just say the good-looking genes William and Harry have didn't come from her side. But boy did she love her Albert, and her Albert adored her. As much as we may call the Victorian era "sexually prudish," there's no evidence to suggest that Victoria didn't like sex, and in fact, there's a lot to suggest she and Albert had a great time. After he died when she was only forty-two, she went into mourning that lasted the rest of her life. She and Albert had fit in every way. I don't think she was necessarily uptight; she simply ushered in an age when sex was to be put back into the bedroom, between married people, not flaunted in the streets. And I think she had a point.

BAD GIRL IDEA: Sex Is about the Next Great Orgasm

If an alien were to come to earth and see all of our sex stores, he would invariably think that we must all be having an amazing time having sex. I live in a small town, but we have a sex shop, two bondage stores, an adult video store, and two strip joints. When sex isn't about relationship, it becomes about how many things you can do together in bed. And what happens when your body gets used to physical pleasure for its own sake, without any relationship commitment? You need more and more of the same stimulus to keep up the pleasure. Alcoholics need more alcohol to get the same buzz a little used to give them. Drug users need more drugs. The more we use, the more desensitized we become.

When sex is all about the physical, the physical stimulation has to become more and more extreme to bring the same high. No wonder our society is experimenting with multiple positions, with multiple partners, and even with multiple things that use batteries! Sex is so shallow that people need more and more to keep them going. Without relationship, sex has no depth. And so people talk about it all the time and do weirder and weirder things, yet according to research, they're not having better sex. In fact, men are losing their libidos. Sexless marriages are on the rise. Sexual dysfunction is increasing. And orgasms are decreasing. Sex only works well if you do it the way it was designed.

My friend Tracey didn't always understand this. Growing up completely unchurched, she embraced the idea that life was all about pushing the limits and having as much fun as possible. She worked hard, but she played harder. And she was as promiscuous as you could be in university. "I was always looking for the next greatest orgasm. I'd try anything once, hoping that it would give me a new high, because everything else was getting boring." Sex was physically wonderful, but it was never enough. It left her empty. So she was always trying to find another guy, another trick, another position. Then one night she suffered a drug overdose and ended up in a Parisian hospital. She told God that if she got out of there alive, she'd try to figure out who he was. God gave her a second chance, and she honored her promise, big time. Now, twenty years later, she's a wonderful godly wife and mother. But many women out there are lost, just like Tracey was, desperately seeking that next greatest physical high.

GOOD GIRL IDEA: God Created Sex to Be Awesome — in Context

Physical highs are wonderful, but they're actually more satisfying and more likely to be achieved in the context of marriage. And that's what God wants for us: both commitment and passion. If you're going to experience awesome sex, this is something you have to get into your head: God actually created it. He didn't do it as an afterthought, thinking to himself, *Well, they have to reproduce somehow, and as icky as this is, it's the best idea I've got.* He created sex this way intentionally. He made it feel stupendous for both men and women. He gave us oxytocin, a hormone that releases during sex that makes us feel close to our husbands. He made it so that, in the most popular position, we can look into each other's eyes and kiss each other at the same time as we're connecting in other ways. It's not just about feeling good physically or reproducing; it's also about cementing a husband and wife together as one flesh.

And it works! When Maggie Gallagher and Linda Waite, authors of *The Case for Marriage*, crunched the numbers from the National Sex Survey, they discovered that the married women who were the most likely to have an orgasm (the height of sexual pleasure, when all the sexual tension is released) during sex were also those who were religiously conservative — either conservative Jews, Catholics, or Protestants.[1] We feel the best and have the best sex when we are in committed marriages that we know are for life. Conservative religious women tend to be in those types of relationships. They take marriage seriously, as do their husbands. So they feel the most cherished and the most loved. And hence they experience the most fireworks.

For women, commitment is the best aphrodisiac, far better than Botox, breast enlargements, or sex toys. That doesn't mean all married, Christian women are going to have great sex. I sure didn't for the first few years of my marriage. But they are the *most likely* to have great sex, and if you're one of the married ones who has yet to discover the key to unlocking that sexual bliss, I hope this book will help. But for now, here's the thing to stuff prominently into our brains: sex is about connection, not cleavage.

Healthy sexuality is not just about our attitudes toward our bodies then, but also, and perhaps more importantly, about our attitudes toward God and toward our husbands. Sex is really a relational thing that happens to involve our bodies far more than it is a physical thing that happens to have an impact on our relationship. And it only takes reading the first few chapters of the Bible in the King James Version to see this.

GOOD GIRL IDEA: Sex Is Meant for Relationship

I'm not normally a King James girl, but I have to admit there are some elements of Scripture that are easier to understand in the good old KJV.

And one of those can be found in Genesis 4:1: "And Adam knew Eve his wife; and she conceived." For those of you who grew up with the KJV, you probably remember snickering as a teen when that passage was read in church. "Oh yeah! Adam *knew* Eve! Riiiiight." We'd elbow each other and giggle. We all thought it was a euphemism, a way to cover up what was really happening.

A GOOD GIRL SPEAKS: *"Sex is too special to waste on anyone other than your spouse."* *(married 18 years)*

But perhaps that Hebrew word "to know" wasn't God's way of being delicate, but actually God's way of being accurate. In Psalm 139:23, David writes:

> Search me, God, and *know* my heart: test me and *know* my anxious thoughts. (emphasis added)

In that same chapter, verse 1, David says:

> You have searched me, LORD, and you *know* me. (emphasis added)

The same Hebrew root is used in all cases: *haw-dah*. David has just spent a chapter writing about how God knows us inside and out, and how God is everywhere. We can't escape from him. He knows everything we do and think, and he planned our days before we were even conceived. At the end of all this, David's response is to ask for an even closer communion with God.

What does this have to do with sex? Only that God uses the same word for Adam and Eve having sex as he does for us deeply and intimately knowing our Lord. Chuck MacKnee, associate professor of psychology at Trinity Western University, explains that sexuality and spirituality are intimately connected. "Both are based in incompleteness and searching for wholeness. In sexuality, we're looking for connection and fulfillment in another person. But this is really the same reason we search for God."[2]

Sex is ultimately a longing, a passion, a deep desire for connection. God created in each of us this longing for intimate connection with him, and he put that same longing in us for each other to mirror how he feels about us. Sexuality, then, isn't something you can have on your own. It's something that only exists properly with another person.

That doesn't mean that single people aren't sexual beings. We all are born with a sex drive. One of the reasons that single missionaries have been able to be so effective is that they have been able to channel the sexual energy they do have into a more intimate connection with God, even if that sounds weird to the rest of us. But for sexuality to be properly understood and experienced, it has to be experienced in relationship, not in isolation and not with a mirror and a bunch of aging hippie women.

> **A GOOD GIRL SPEAKS:** *"Sex is a covenant promise between God and a man and wife. I wish I had seen it as something sacred, rather than simply physical, so that I would have waited and shared that covenant only with my husband and only after our marriage vows." (married 19 years)*

GOOD GIRL IDEA: Sex Is a Way to Show Love

Billions of people have had sex. I am not sure how many have actually made love.

To have sex is simply to do the physical. To make love is to connect on many other levels as well, which is exactly what God made sex for. He made it to help us truly "know" each other, in every sense of the word. He wants us to know each other physically, to memorize each other's curves and freckles and scents and likes and dislikes. He wants us to know what our spouse yearns for and what makes our spouse uncomfortable. But he also wants us to know our spouse's heart, mind, and soul. He wants us to be joined. That can only happen in an intimate, committed relationship, which is why people can have sex with so many but can make love only to one.

Unfortunately, too many people are settling for far less than what God made sex to be — and they may not even realize they're missing out on the best. When my oldest daughter was four, we attended a playgroup every day. One day the woman in charge asked the children, "What's your favorite food?" All the preschoolers offered variants of macaroni and cheese, ice cream, or hot dogs, until one little girl, Victoria, shouted out, "Lobster!" Her father owned a gourmet restaurant, and she dined on leftover lobster frequently. She didn't know what macaroni and cheese tasted like. The other kids, though, were equally ignorant of lobster. They thought mac and cheese was scrumptious because it was the best of their experience. I suspect that many women are settling for mac and cheese and missing out on delicacies because they don't know how great sex can really be in the right context.

A GOOD GIRL SPEAKS: *"Before I got married, I was not a Christian, so sex was sex. Now I realize sex is making love to my husband. I wish I had known how good things are when it's about love and not just about sex." (married 12 years)*

Listen to what one respondent said in the survey:

> I wish I had known that it really takes trust, commitment, and more trust to have a fulfilling sexual relationship. I never reached *real* fulfillment until I had all the above plus intimacy.

In a society that talks so much about the physical aspects of sex — since that's all we have when connection is taken out of the picture — how can we understand what it is to experience love during sex? I think we have to go back to how we understand the God who made sex — and understand why he created it the way he did.

We serve a triune God — Father, Son, and Holy Spirit — and he has made us to be triune people too — body, mind, and spirit (or soul). In sex we should connect on all three of these levels. Unfortunately, too often we focus only on the body. But we can also connect in our souls — a real spiritual union, where we feel completely one, as if we are entering into another person. And then there's the mind. Connecting with the mind symbolizes the reaffirmation of the relationship, the nuts and bolts of what brings a couple together, the decision we make, day after day, to love our spouses exclusively. It's the reason that we connect — the goodwill and friendship we feel for one another. Making love is a statement of that connection, a reiteration of the reason for a couple's relationship. Every time we make love to our spouses, we declare once again that we are committed to each other.

For millennia Christians have understood the threefold nature of sex, though they may have phrased it differently. Thomas Aquinas, writing in the thirteenth century, called its purposes offspring, fidelity, and sacrament. Offspring coincide with the physical aspects of sex. Aren't children, after all, the ultimate "two shall become one flesh"? While sex may feel amazing physically, God also designed it to be the doorway into parenthood, so that the physical could never be the only motivation. Because sex can bring children, two people need a commitment first to protect any children who come.

This leads us to the second purpose: fidelity — the relational aspect, where we reaffirm our commitment each time we make love. Finally, there's the one that Aquinas calls "sacrament": that spiritual union where the couple becomes one flesh in *every* way. It is a supernatural, rather than a natural, experience. And that's what Aquinas says: "In every way sacrament is the principal among the three goods of marriage, because it pertains to marriage in so far as it is a sacrament of grace, while the other two pertain to it in so far as it were a service to nature; now a perfection of grace is more worthy than a perfection of nature."[3]

That's awfully heavy philosophizing, I know, but here's what it boils down to: the physical and relational aspects of marriage are the parts we accomplish ourselves. Take the physical aspect, for instance. Through it we become one flesh physically, have a marvelous time physically, and even produce children, the embodiment of the "two become one flesh" promise. And fidelity, or the relational aspect of sex, is something we deliberately commit to.

Yet there is a spiritual joining that takes place in sex that goes beyond this — and here's where the sacramental element comes in. Paul writes in 1 Corinthians 6:16:

> Do you not know that he who unites himself with a prostitute is one with her in body? For it is said, "The two will become one flesh."

What does this really mean? Obviously "the two will become one flesh" means far more than just the physical act of sex, because I'm pretty sure that the Corinthian church would have been clued in that during sex the bodies are physically united. No, what is implied is that a spiritual union takes place, whether we acknowledge it or not. God himself unites the two together; it's not something we do alone; it's something God does. When we participate in the making of that union, sex becomes something very precious.

Perhaps you're not much of a philosopher or theologian and you want something easier to understand, so let me give you some statistics and stories from modern-day Good Girls that illustrate this same point. In one survey I conducted for this book, I asked women to rate their sex life now on a scale of 1 to 10, with 10 being amazing and 1 being lousy. Then I asked them how often they reached orgasm during intercourse. Of those who stated they "always" reached orgasm, 29 percent rated their sex life as between 6 and 8. They didn't give it a 9 or a 10. And 3 percent actually rated it as pretty lousy. Physically they're doing great, but they still don't think of sex as perfect, because the physical is not all there is.

Or let's look at it from the other perspective. Of those who never reach orgasm during sex, 17 percent still rated their sex life as a 9 or a 10. They may not have reached that physical goal, but they're still having fun, and they feel deeply and satisfyingly connected. It's like Tim Gardner wrote in his book *Sacred Sex*: "The Big O is not orgasm; it's oneness."[4] There's more to sex than the physical. It all goes together like a three-stranded cord.

That's what this book is about. You're a Good Girl, so you have the inside scoop on how to have a great sex life. You know it can be powerful physi-cally, but what really makes sex meaningful and out of this world is not only physical fireworks, but a true union in every way. So we're going to look practically at how to make things go right in each of these three areas and then troubleshoot when common roadblocks pop up.

A GOOD GIRL SPEAKS: *"I wish I had known that sex was some-thing important and of value. No one ever told me what a pre-cious gift it was and why it was so special." (married 7 years)*

But first, let's look at how God designed the genders. Males and females have different needs and motivations. And it's these differ-ences that can be so much fun!

CHAPTER 2

How Good Girls Understand Good Boys

S how up naked and bring food.

That's the key to a man's heart — and other body parts. At least according to the men at the marriage conferences where my husband and I speak. Whenever we use that line, the men hoot and holler, while the women giggle right along.

Men look. Men see. And men want. As females, it's easy to look at guys who would like nothing better than to have their wives greet them at the door in Saran Wrap and wonder what's wrong with them.[1] Why are they so pathetic? Is that *really* all men think about?

Well, yes. And no. We've just spent a chapter talking about how God designed sex so that it's about far more than just physical fireworks. But he also made us so that we approach sex differently — and it's these differences that ultimately bring us together, that cement other motivations and purposes for sex. Let's take a look.

GOOD GIRL TRUTH: We're Not Better; We're Different

When girls read that God created sex for relationship, we want to cheer right along! He wants us to love each other. Awww. Isn't that sweet? We get it! We're the gender that is more relationally focused, so this resonates with us. Close intimacy is marvelous, romantic, and beautiful! What bliss.

Then we turn to the men, who started getting erections in seventh grade whenever some girl wore a tight sweater, and we begin to suspect that males are somehow the lesser species. We were created a little closer to the angels, and men were created a little closer to the lizards. We flourish on deep, important things, like emotional connection, while they focus on breasts. And we just have to humor them.

That's not a very Good Girl way of thinking. Sex was not created just for men, and men are not wrong for wanting it. We Good Girls just need to understand the reason that men desire sex so much and to see this drive as part of God's bigger picture. It's not something to disdain men for. They are not morally inferior while we are morally superior. We're simply different. And it's the differences, after all, that are usually the most fun!

Let's take a look first at how to understand men's desire and motivation for sex, and then we'll turn to our own.

GOOD GIRL TRUTH: Men Need Sex in a Different Way than We Do

You're probably aware of the "wet dream" phenomenon that hits boys just after puberty, much to their own dismay and their mothers' chagrin. If men's bodies don't get sexual release every few days, their bodies will do it for them during the night. The testicles produce a buildup of semen, and when the pressure gets to be too much, out it comes, usually accompanied by some rather graphic sexual dreams. We have these dreams too, by the way; it's just that they're easier to keep secret because laundry isn't involved.

A GOOD GIRL SPEAKS: *"Sex, for my husband, is a need just like breathing." (married 9 years)*

When men are married, then, their bodies are revved to go. They look at us, and they get turned on. They aren't deterred by the fact that we're carrying a few extra pounds around the middle or that we're tired or that they've had a busy day. They see us, they want us, and so they figure, *Let's do it!*

Men's bodies desire sex in a far more basic way than women's bodies do. For instance, imagine how a couple would view such a night: You're engaged in some rather fun erotic play and the phone rings. It's your sister announcing she's getting married, ecstatic to share all the details. You're thrilled for her, and you chat up a storm, thoughts of what you were doing with hubby long gone. You'll be fine if nothing else happens that night between you and your husband. Women aren't like balloons, bursting when there's too much pressure. We're more like teeter-totters. We go up and down and have a great time doing it, but we don't suffer if we never reach climax. In fact, we may even look back on that night that ended with the phone call and be quite content with it because we were having a good time — even if we didn't reach orgasm. He, on the other hand, is going to be distinctly uncomfortable until something eventually happens to relieve the pressure. The poor guy's actually hurting.

> **A GOOD GIRL SPEAKS:** *"Sex is important to a man, not only because he's a guy, but because it means he feels loved and supported. When I was first married, I thought it was just surface fun." (married 16 years)*

For those of you who aren't married yet, it's important to understand this: If you're involved in some pretty heavy petting, you'll likely be okay even if it goes no further. You can have fun flirting without going too far and still be able to smile at feeling so close to him. He, on the other hand, will be in pretty rough shape. It's wrong to get a guy who is not your husband worked up like that, even if you are engaged. It isn't your fault, of course, if he "looks at you with lust," or however you want to phrase it. But if you are revving his engines because you like the feeling of power or because you like kissing or because you like the sexual thrill you get without needing to go further, you're endangering him, and it needs to stop.

You also need to realize that assuming you'll always be able to stop is pretty stupid. We always *can* stop, but it's not always easy, and there may just be a time when your feelings get the better of you. We're motivated by love and affection, and you'll feel that in spades as your wedding day looms. So stay clear of these situations! Talk to him, make rules, and stick to them. No kisses longer than ten seconds. No hands around front or below the waist. No lying down together. Whatever you have to do. Use your courtship to figure out how to have nonsexual fun together. You're going to need that afterward, anyway, because you can't have sex twenty-four hours a day. You need something else to do to forge your friendship. Develop hobbies together. Be active together. It's much easier on him and kinder to both of you.

Men's sex drives are more body-focused, and women's are more relationship-focused. God, in his wisdom, made us this way, partly so that when we women wake up in the middle of the night, we're more likely to tend to the baby who's crying than to turn to the man beside us. It keeps the species healthy.

But it also leads to an interesting dichotomy between us: men make love to feel loved. Women need to feel loved to make love. What a complete recipe for disaster!

Don't let looks deceive you, though. Let's follow this logically. Women's deepest drive is for intimate connection on all levels. Men need that too, but they tend to experience it after they make love, not before they make love. Sex is their doorway into intimacy; intimacy is our doorway into sex. Remember oxytocin, that hormone that we talked about?

A GOOD GIRL SPEAKS: *"It's the wanting to make your spouse happy that makes sex fabulous; and it's more in my head and heart first, and then it goes into my body." (married 23 years)*

Men produce it too, in the rush after they have an orgasm. It's why men become crybabies after sex. They tell us over and over again how much they love us. They want to snuggle. They want to hold us. In other words, they become like women! And sometimes women make love simply to get that out of their men. That's not necessarily a bad thing, either. That's the way God made us.

And I think he did it with a bit of a smile on his face, because he gave us these deep drives for each other that are met in different ways. For women to get our deepest needs for relationship met, we need to focus on our spouses' needs for sex. For men to get their deepest needs for sex met, they need to focus on our need for relationship. It's a give and take. Women learn to think of men, and men learn to think of us. Doesn't that sound like the relational bonding that sex was partially created for?

If women had the exact same motivation as men, we'd all be jumping into bed at the drop of a hat with little impetus to really know each other or give to each other. If men were made like women, we might never have children. It's the combination that works. Of course, the combination is also the source of much conflict and frustration, but instead of getting mad at your husband, remember that he's this way for a reason.

Shortly after we were married, my husband, who never gets sick, developed a rash all over and a fever of 102. After letting him sleep for a bit, I tiptoed to the bedroom and opened the door to check on him. "Is there anything I can do for you?" I asked sympathetically.

Immediately his bloodshot eyes started to glisten as he replied, smirking, "Well, since you mentioned it …" In my newlywed state, I assumed that he was sick, in more ways than one. But he wasn't sick. He was just a guy. A good guy. And that's the way he was made.

GOOD GIRL TRUTH: Sex Is in Our Heads

While men are focused on the body and become aroused easily and stay aroused easily, women are far more focused on the relationship. We want to feel close. That doesn't mean that we don't have sexual feelings; it's just that those feelings pop up not necessarily when we see a naked guy as much as they do when we feel loved and safe and romanced. That's what makes us want to jump him!

Because of that, sex is far more in our heads than it is between our legs. And that's why headaches actually do hinder a woman's sex drive! If we can't concentrate on what's going on, we're not going to become aroused.

Often I'll be having a fun time with Keith and everything will be going well, when out of the blue this thought enters my head: *Is there milk in the fridge for cereal in the morning?* I didn't mean to think about cereal.

A GOOD GIRL SPEAKS: *"Women need to work harder at clearing the mind of all the daily junk that clogs our brains and prevents us from truly 'being there.' Men don't seem to have that clutter, they can 'be there' in a microsecond!" (married 9 years)*

The thought just wandered in there. But now that it's in my head, it's hard to banish it. *Well, if there's no milk, what else can we have for breakfast? And when am I going to have a chance to buy some? Can*

I go before lunch? I wonder what else I should pick up. And my poor husband, who thought he was doing so well, knows that he has lost me. And it's all because of a grocery item.

There's a positive side and a negative side to sex being in our heads. The negative is that we are easily distracted, and we have to work hard on keeping our mind focused on what we want our bodies to respond to. But the positive is that we do have some control. I have heard it said that men are like microwaves and women are like slow cookers, and I don't think it's only because men are done fast. It's supposed to be because men heat up quickly while women take more time. But I think calling women slow cookers misrepresents our fair gender, because it implies that we will, eventually, heat up. And there's actually no guarantee. It all depends on our heads.

One night he could be doing exactly the same thing to you he did the night before that had you in raptures, but this time you're lying there wishing he'd finish quickly so you can get to sleep. Or perhaps you're seething because of a fight you had earlier. Women won't become aroused unless we flick the switch on the slow cooker ourselves. We have to become engaged in the process.

That's how females work. We become aroused because we allow ourselves to be. It makes us much more vulnerable during sex, because we need to willingly open ourselves up to enjoy it. We need to let him in, not just physically, but emotionally as well. We need to let our guard down. To make love to someone is to completely bare one's soul, and this is especially true for us women. And that's also what makes it so powerful. When we are able to be vulnerable, when we feel pursued and cherished, we can have the most amazing and fulfilling experience.

Now that we understand our sex drives better, let's look at our different motivations for sex.

GOOD GIRL CHALLENGE: Understand His Need to Give You Pleasure

As much as men may desire sex, in order to feel fulfilled they don't just need an orgasm; they need to feel wanted. A Good Girl doesn't just "let" her man make love to her. She doesn't "lie there and think of England," as Lady Hillingdon once advised her nineteenth-century young protégées.[2] A Good Girl jumps in with both feet. The key to a man's heart isn't to placate him; it's to actually engage in the process. A man's self-esteem when it comes to sex is largely based on whether he can make her feel so good her toes curl. It isn't just about whether he experiences pleasure; it's whether he can give *her* pleasure.

A GOOD GIRL SPEAKS: *"It does not matter to him that I don't have a perfect '10' body. It just matters that I am (eagerly) willing." (married 15 years)*

If you haven't yet walked down that aisle, and you are still only imagining sex, then chances are most of your imaginings have to do with how good it's going to feel. Keep thinking that way! Sex should be something to look forward to, and God certainly created women with the capacity to have an amazing time physically while we make love. We're capable of multiple orgasms. We often experience much deeper orgasms than men do, at least according to researchers who have tried to measure such a thing. God even created women with body parts whose only purpose is to bring sexual pleasure. We've got a clitoris (that little knobby part of flesh just in front of the vagina), and we've got a G-spot, a small oval-shaped bit of knobby skin found somewhere between an inch and a half and three inches up the vaginal wall. (Some researchers debate its existence; others swear by it. I say consider it a dare and have fun trying to figure it out!)

There's no question, then, that women can have fun making love and can find it a deeply satisfying physical experience besides also being deeply satisfying from an emotional and spiritual standpoint. But none of this is automatic.

Most men, aside from those suffering from erectile dysfunction (impotence, or the inability to get or maintain an erection), are pretty much guaranteed to have an orgasm during sex. In fact, that's usually the way a sexual encounter ends, since after a man orgasms, he tends to lose his erection, or at least finds it rather diminished, and he's much more sensitive in that area, making further intercourse difficult. Women, on the other hand, are not guaranteed much of anything. Our arousal level has very little to do with whether sex can actually take place (as long as we are willing regardless). Men, then, often take pride in their ability as lovers to be able to bring pleasure to their wives, since this pleasure is in no way guaranteed. It depends on the care, attention, and skill of the husband (as well as the mental engagement of the wife).

A GOOD GIRL SPEAKS: *"It gets better over time, because it's not just physical lust but oneness on so many levels. I didn't understand the closeness men find from sex and how important it is that we meet that need, and not just physically." (married 10 years)*

And men also know that since a woman can physically make love without being at all turned on (though it may be more uncomfortable that way), the only way to tell whether she wants to or not is whether she is actually aroused. Most men want their wives to feel pleasure, and they want to feel capable of giving that pleasure. That way they know that we value sex the way they do — that we truly do want to connect in the same way that they want to connect, and we're not just placating them. It's just another difference between us, rather than a sickness or weakness on their part!

GOOD GIRL IDEA: Recognize That We're Not Men

Now that we understand men's motivation for sex, let's figure out our own. First and foremost, Good Girls know that in order to be a Good Girl, you actually have to be a *girl*, not a boy.

Let me explain. Next time you're in the grocery store, check out the covers of *Maxim* and *Cosmo*. *Maxim* is meant for men. *Cosmopolitan* is meant for women. But if you were to cover up the title of the magazine, could you tell, just from the picture, which magazine was meant for women and which magazine was meant for men? Both feature very similar cover pictures and poses: scantily clad women who look like they want to jump any man who happens to walk by.

When my youngest daughter was four, standing in line at the grocery store with me, she stared at the *Cosmo* cover and asked loudly, "Mommy, why is that woman trying to show her boobies?" Summer had just ended, and we had spent that year trying to explain to Katie why it was important not to strip in public every time she felt a little sweaty. It was not an easy task. But we had accomplished it, and now here was a grown woman undermining all our hard work!

And so I'll ask you: why is that woman trying to show her boobies? After all, it's a magazine for women, not for men. So why depict a half-naked woman on the prowl on the cover? Why would women buy that?

Since men are aroused by sight, it makes sense to try to attract them with scantily clad women. What arouses a woman, though, is the feeling of being wanted. Stasi and John Eldredge, authors of *Captivating*, explain this well: "Every woman wants to be romanced; every woman wants to play an irreplaceable role in a heroic adventure, not just to be useful but to be irreplaceable; and every woman longs to have a beauty that's all her own to unveil, both an external beauty and an internal beauty as well. To be the beauty and to offer beauty."[3] We want to be pursued, to be chased, to be found, to be the Beauty. Ideally this was supposed to be in relationship, but even the world understands that women want to be desired. What attracts women to that *Cosmo* cover, then, is not the thought of that woman sexually, but the thought of *being* that woman, being the one everyone wants.

A GOOD GIRL SPEAKS: *"I thought my happiness with sex was secondary to his and that it was my job to please him. I didn't realize until after we had been married awhile (and actually started talking about it) that he enjoyed making me have a good experience." (married 14 years)*

Of course, that's a twisted view of sex, because that kind of desire divorces sex from marriage, its proper context. But most distortions of what God intended aren't polar opposites; instead, they incorporate little bits to make the lie seem attractive, plausible, even good.

Yet increasingly the cultural portrayal of women's sexuality is becoming even more distorted. Take the cougar stereotype, for example. Sexually overstimulated older women on the hunt for younger men who can fulfill them physically now grace our magazines and televisions. It's not about being the Beauty, the object of the chase; it's about being the hunter herself. It used to be only men who looked for sex and sex alone; now women do too. And they're doing this in the guise of sexual liberation! Imagine: we told men that women are just as good as they are and we can do anything a man can do, and we did this by jumping into bed with men without asking for commitment so that we could be just like them. Yeah, that's the ticket. For centuries unscrupulous men have been trying to discover the secret to getting women to go to bed with them with no strings attached, and today women have handed it to them on a silver platter, all in the name of sexual equality. Sure doesn't sound very liberated to me.

That's because the sexual liberation movement, I believe, is not based on women's rights or women's advancement as much as it is based on erasing God from our culture. We have to remove any vestiges of morality so that we can all stop feeling guilty about everything and start doing what we want to do! And the way our culture does this is to convince women that we want something that we fundamentally do not want.

A 2006 study of 1,280 young women conducted by MTV, of all organizations, found that 92 percent definitely wanted to get married one day. Young girls still dream of commitment. Yet they're not acting in a way to find that goal. They're hooking up instead. We have bought into this culture that teaches women that to be liberated they have to act like men, interested only in the physical and not the relational. It's not true.

GOOD GIRL IDEA: Our Sex Drives Are Based on Our Need to Be Cherished

To understand your own sexuality is also to understand this deep desire to be cherished and needed that is at the heart of our sexuality. When God created Eve, the very first thing that happened was that Adam was blown away by her, saying, "This is now bone of my bones and flesh of my flesh" (Gen. 2:23). She was created to attract him, to fulfill him, to have him yearn for her. And we share her DNA.

That's why pornography for women has never taken off in the same way as men's porn has. We're just not aroused by sight in the same way men are. *Playgirl* never had the following that *Playboy* does, and it eventually folded. Most porn featuring naked men is consumed by gay men, not by straight women.

That doesn't mean that women don't use porn, though. Unfortunately, we do, and 30 percent of all porn addicts are now female. But women don't tend to stare at men's bodies. We tend to stare at the same stuff men stare at: women's bodies. It's not because most women have latent lesbian fantasies; it's because women are attracted to the idea of being wanted far more than we are by simply watching naked men. Women don't ogle. They dream.

I'm generalizing here, and if you're one of those women for whom the male form has always been a temptation, there's nothing wrong with that. God did make us to desire the other gender, and as long as you keep your fulfillment and fantasy to marriage, you're fine. In general, though, women tend to be more relationship centered than body centered. When surveys ask men and women to name the sexiest scenes in movies, for instance, women tend to pick very different things. Men pick the "down and dirty" graphic scenes. Women pick the romantic ones.

I actually find graphic sexual scenes more funny than erotic. They're just so bizarre, and since my husband and I always fast-forward through them anyway, they seem even more bizarre. But that doesn't mean I don't find movies erotic. It's just that I find them erotic very differently from the way most men do.

What are my favorite scenes? Do you remember when Darcy finally proposes in the Keira Knightley version of *Pride and Prejudice*? There's not even a kiss, but it's the look on his face that's appealing. He's so in love with Elizabeth he can't stop himself. It's the same feeling I get with the old *Pride and Prejudice* (the only true one, starring Colin Firth), when Darcy's at a fencing club, hoping vigorous exercise will expunge Elizabeth from his mind. "I will conquer this!" he vows. Or that scene where he dives into the pond to banish her, once and for all — and, of course, fails.

And then, of course, there's the scene in *The Notebook* when Noah and Allie are standing on the dock in the rain and Noah yells, "It wasn't over for me, either. It still isn't!" and then grabs Allie and kisses her. I enjoy that scene much better than the more graphic stuff that follows. It's not what they're doing that's sexy; it's not even the guy that's sexy. It's how much he loves her, and how consumed he is by her, and how he needs her. That's what's sexy. Women yearn to be desired like that.

To be a sexually confident woman, you do not have to walk around flaunting your cleavage. You do not have to attract the attention of everyone who walks by. You certainly do not have to stare at men's crotches. You simply need to be a Good Girl, understanding God's design for sexuality, and committed to a man who will cherish you and treat you well. That's the key to unlocking your sexuality, and you can't find it in a sex shop.

Women today are being told that to be fulfilled they have to give up on being a woman and have to act like a man instead. God tells us the opposite. He says to you, "I made you a woman. I made you to be captivating. I made you to be loved. I made you to nurture and to love in return. And I made you to have a deep desire to be intimately connected to your husband." In that relationship, you can learn what it is to be female — to be chased, cared for, and loved. And that, my dear Good Girls, is so much more beautiful than anything the world can promise us.

The Good Girl's Role in the Sex Department

That's how we fit together: our spouses are attracted to how we look, and their bodies want us. We're attracted to being loved and chased, and when we feel that way, our bodies follow too.

You know what makes you tick, and now you know what makes your husband tick. So let's try to put both these things together and come up with a biblical way of looking at your responsibility when it comes to sex.

Lots of marriage books, and especially those in certain Christian circles, emphasize the wife's responsibility for the husband's sexual satisfaction. To a certain extent I agree with this. Men do have biological drives that we don't have in the same way, and they do often experience love through sex far more than they do through a hug. So we need to jump in and have fun!

Nevertheless, I have read some very popular Christian books that make me rather uncomfortable. Simply having sex whenever he wants it however he wants it in order to satisfy him so he doesn't stray — as if his straying is somehow your fault — isn't really a biblical way of looking at sex. You are not a receptacle. In 1 Corinthians 7:3–4, Paul writes:

> The husband should fulfill his marital duty to his wife, and likewise the wife to her husband. The wife does not have authority over her own body but yields it to her husband. In the same way, the husband does not have authority over his own body but yields it to his wife.

When you are married, you *both* need to give and take. You need to go out of your way to satisfy him, but he also should go out of his way to cherish you and treat you gently.

There is a thread in a lot of this literature that sex is somehow all about him, and so we need to adjust and make it fun for him. Do what he wants. Be his every fantasy! Yes, we do need to think about him. Yes, we do need to be sensitive to the fact that he probably needs sex more than we do. Yes, we do need to initiate. But when we start talking about how we need to satisfy his sex drive, we're making the same mistake with sex that the world makes. We're pigeonholing sex so that it's all about the physical and not about the spiritual or emotional connection that it's supposed to encompass as well.

If you're just into "meeting his physical needs," then you start to think of it in that way: sex is all about satisfying him, as if he's some sort of an animal. Sex doesn't become something that brings the two of you together; it becomes something that almost dehumanizes both of you. And that is not what God intended.

Unfortunately, part of the Christian church buys this. They think that because the woman was created to be man's "help meet," we have to help men in this area. We have to relieve his sexual tension! But if we go into marriage with that attitude, we miss the potential that sex has to be something that binds us together beautifully. And we can do some serious damage to our own sexuality.

Sex is something beautiful that is meant for the two of you together. So instead of thinking of it as something that you have to do to satisfy him, think of it as a journey of exploration that you take *together*, where you get to know each other's bodies, explore each other, and look into each other's eyes. It's not just about his release; it's about the bond that needs to come between the two of you. That bond is not going to happen if sex becomes only about satisfying him.

Women, we need to challenge ourselves to make our husbands' sex lives the best that we can. But sex is best not when we do it as often as possible solely for him; it's when we embrace everything that sex should be, and that includes a deep emotional and spiritual connection. Work on forging that bond, on pursuing romance, on being that beauty, and sex will be great. Think of sex as a chore in which you have to act all excited or your husband won't feel loved, and you do great damage to your own sexuality. You feel cheap, used, and resentful. Don't fall into that trap.

Think of your distinct approaches to sex as an exciting difference between you, a difference that will create some amazing sparks when you embrace it and work on it together. But realize that sex is supposed to be something completely mutual and agreed upon, not just acquiesced to. We're going to learn how to make this a reality in your marriage now, whether you're just starting out or whether you've been married for a while. Let's start with the nuts and bolts of how we fit together physically, and then we'll move on to how to make sex amazing in all the other ways that it was intended to connect us as husband and wife. Are you ready?

PART 2

physical discovery: fireworks

CHAPTER 3

Lighting
the Fireworks

When my daughter Katie was eight, she asked me that dreaded question, "Where do babies come from?" I took a deep breath and explained the basics.

She crossed her arms and sighed. "I see," she said. Then she peered at me through squinted eyes. "How long does he have to leave it in for?"

The conversation went downhill from there.

The next morning at breakfast she threw her arms around me and said, "Thank you so much for doing that terrible thing with Daddy, Mommy, just so that I could be born." Obviously something was lost in translation. And I had to try to retranslate it for her.

In this chapter, I want to make sure that nothing is lost in translation with you. If you're engaged, you likely want to know how sex is going to work. But even if you're already married, and you've already had plenty of sex, don't skip this chapter. It's always good to refresh ourselves on how our bodies are supposed to work.

First, though, let's get a few things straight. I'm going to tell you here how the physical side of marriage works at

A GOOD GIRL SPEAKS: *"There's no 'right way' to do it. It's about feeling comfortable with your partner and doing what makes the two of you feel good together."* *(married 17 years)*

its best. That doesn't mean you're necessarily going to reach that right away — and that's okay. Marriage is a journey, and it's likely going to take you a while to get your body working like clockwork. So relax, and as you read, think of what I tell you as exciting things you're going to learn to get more comfortable with as time goes on. When you're starting out, it's okay to be totally naive. It's okay to laugh about it. And it's okay to be a little bit awkward.

Sex and Procreation Basics

Here's what I couldn't fully explain to eight-year-old Katie when she wondered about the timing of his "putting it in." Sex is not just "insert tab A into slot B," as if you're assembling a bookcase. He becomes aroused and his penis gets "hard" (erect) and protrudes from his body, so that it's rigid enough to enter your vagina. That's the A goes into B part. But that's only the beginning. He'll then begin to thrust back and forth in and out of the vagina until he reaches climax — or orgasm — when he also ejaculates (releases semen). There's a lot of movement going on, at least on his part (and, if you want to have fun, likely on your part too).

Pretty much every time intercourse occurs, a man will have an orgasm. And that orgasm means that he's releasing semen (the milky white fluid that contains the sperm) inside you. Those sperm are now going to take a journey, swimming up the vagina, into the uterus, and eventually into the fallopian tubes, looking for an egg. Every cycle, about 10 – 14 days before your period, you'll release an egg — and occasionally several eggs — from your ovaries. That egg will travel down the fallopian tubes into the uterus. If one sperm happens to come across this egg during its migration, then — bingo! — you're pregnant. But pregnancy is really only possible for about five days each cycle. The egg only lasts about a day, but the sperm can stay swimming for up to five days (they're rather persistent). So while most of the time pregnancy isn't possible, it still is a vital component of the sexual relationship.

A GOOD GIRL SPEAKS: *"I didn't need to be afraid. We'd been so careful not to sin sexually that I was afraid of it all — that there would be pain, that I wouldn't like it, that I'd be a disappointment to him. I didn't need to worry at all. I love sex now, and we enjoy each other thoroughly — and my body is not anything like a Hollywood actress's." (married 13 years)*

Before we jump into how to make sex wonderful in a whole variety of ways, then, let's deal with the practical aspect of family planning.

Natural Family Planning (NFP)

Many Christians, both Protestants and Catholics, feel that procreation (having babies) is an inseparable part of making love. Remove the possibility of pregnancy, and according to this philosophy, you're saying that sex is all about pleasure; it's not something sacred where God is in control. Natural family planning takes care of these reservations because pregnancy is always *possible*, though if you do it correctly it's not necessarily *probable*.

> **a good girl dare**
>
> If you don't have children yet, spend a whole Saturday morning in bed together. Make love several different times in different ways — and talk, cuddle, and pray too!

Those following NFP keep track of their fertile days and then abstain from sex during that time. And how do you keep track? You can chart your temperature every day, because the temperature changes right around ovulation. Another option is to chart the amount and consistency of cervical fluid.

Pros

One of the benefits of natural family planning is that you're going to be much more in tune with your body. You pay more attention to your body's cues, and thus you can more easily figure out when you're going to be moody, when you're going to be frisky, and when you're going to need chocolate to get over that hump.

Cons

My husband, a pediatrician, often tells this joke: "Do you know what you call people who use natural family planning? Parents." There's some truth to that. You have to be very diligent at both charting and at abstaining to prevent pregnancy. And who wants to abstain on her wedding night if her body decides not to cooperate with her dates? This method also requires you to abstain from sex right in the middle of your cycle when your libido is likely to be the highest.

Condoms

The thin latex barriers called condoms have been the birth control staple for generations. Unrolled onto the erect penis and worn during intercourse, they catch the semen so that pregnancy doesn't occur. They also protect against most STDs, so if an STD from a past relationship will continue to be a factor in your marriage, this would be the method of choice.

Pros

Condoms make sex far less messy! There's no leakage after sex. They're also quite cheap, at about fifty cents each. One Good Girl reports overcoming her initial reluctance: "In my mind, condoms were what single men carried in their back pockets for one-night stands so they didn't get diseases. Thirteen years and four children later, my thinking is a little different. We've used condoms off and on this whole time and only became pregnant when I wanted to be."

And here's another pro that one Good Girl reports: "Condoms decrease sensation for my husband, which can help prolong intercourse — and that can be a good thing for me!"

Cons

A barrier by any other name is still a barrier. As one Good Girl reports, "It really truly feels like it takes away from close intimacy. We felt cheated on closeness." It's also harder to be spontaneous, because you have to pause what you're doing and root around in the drawer for one of those little square packages.

Fertility Awareness Method (FAM)

The charting from the Natural Family Planning method combined with condom use gives you a natural, noninvasive way to protect against pregnancy with no side effects. You simply chart your cycle, and then, on your fertile days, turn to condoms or other barrier methods, like a diaphragm (see below). Since you can't get pregnant on most days of the month anyway, this means that you can avoid barriers most of the time and avoid medication altogether.

Now I know that some readers will disagree with any form of birth control during those fertile days, even condoms, and I completely respect the faith that these women have to let God choose the size and timing of their families. I also respect the desire to keep sex as something sacred.

Nevertheless, I personally believe that God made us with the ability to choose whether or not to get pregnant. After all, we humans aren't fertile most of the time. That means that we can't get pregnant at random; we're really only capable of it a few days a month. And God made our bodies so that they would give signs during those few days. To me that signals that God decided to give us some choice over whether or not to get pregnant. And FAM seems like a good balance for those who don't want to use anything hormonal or permanent, but still desire to choose the timing and size of their family.[1]

Pros

As with Natural Family Planning, you become very acquainted with your body. When you do want to become pregnant, you don't have a waiting period for any medication to leave your system. And you're so aware of your body's cycles that pregnancy is often easier to achieve. For most of the month you don't need to use any method at all. And, if used correctly, it is as effective as the Pill in preventing pregnancy (above 95 percent).

Cons

You must diligently track your cycle! If you have irregular periods, it can be trickier, but most people using FAM do not have perfect cycles.

The "Pill" and other Hormonal Methods

Now let's turn to pharmaceutical options of birth control. Probably the most popular method of contraception, the Pill has a 95 percent success rate at preventing pregnancy if used correctly. Taken daily, the Pill's mixture of hormones "tricks" your body into thinking you're pregnant so that you won't ovulate and thus can't get pregnant.[2] For seven days a month, the hormones aren't present, so you have what looks like a period, though the flow is often lighter.

If you don't want the bother of daily pills, you can also ask your doctor for hormonal injections every few months that eliminate your period, or you can use the hormonal ring, which is inserted in your vagina and left there for several weeks. A hormonal patch that excretes hormones into your body can also be placed on the skin. In these cases, too, your period will be lighter.

Pros

Hormone therapies are very effective at preventing pregnancy, and they also minimize acne, PMS, and cramps. One of my friends, now forty-two, says this: "The Pill made me gain weight and get emotional, but it was perfect for the early days of marriage. No other method really worked, because my cycles weren't regular."

Cons

First, it isn't clear if these hormonal methods always prevent ovulation, or if they can sometimes allow ovulation but then prevent implantation. Here's why this matters: preventing ovulation means conception never occurs. Preventing implantation means that the sperm may have met the egg and thus conception occurred, but the uterus won't allow a fertilized egg to be implanted, instead flushing the embryo out with the next period. Because of this, hormonal methods have been accused of being abortifacients. You should definitely investigate this possibility before you take any hormone birth control. Go on the company's websites and see what they say about how they work.[3] Talk to your doctor.

That's not the only con either. There's also the simple cost factor since the average pill costs about $1.50, and they must be taken daily, whether you have sex or not. The Pill's hormones also work against our own natural cycles which cause a libido surge in the middle of the month. One study of 1,086 German female medical students found that those on the Pill were far more likely to suffer from low libido or other sexual problems.[4] Also not so happily, hormone therapies have been linked to weight gain and moodiness, which are never a good combination. Even worse, they've been linked to blood clots and strokes in some women, and potentially breast cancer.

One Good Girl reported her feelings about the Pill like this: "After going off the Pill, I realized the chemically induced roller coaster of emotions I was on monthly. I would *never for any reason go on it again*." Others just loved it. So my final thoughts: really investigate hormonal therapies before you let the doctor write that prescription.

Other Methods

While these are the most popular methods of birth control, others are also very effective. Diaphragms are another barrier method that prevent the sperm from ever reaching the egg. You do, however, have to be completely comfortable inserting it far up your vagina so it covers your cervix. It can be removed every morning, washed, and then reinserted so that sex can still be spontaneous.

IUDs, or intrauterine devices, are inserted by a doctor at the cervix, the opening to the uterus. IUDs come in two main types: hormonal and copper, both of which can stay in place for extended periods of time. Manufacturers claim that they make the cervix inhospitable to sperm so that the sperm can't meet the egg. However, IUD manufacturers also claim that one reason they work is that they're preventing implantation. Check out the manufacturers' websites yourself before you try them.

Finally, permanent forms of birth control, like vasectomies or tubal ligations (and some new variants that are not as invasive) are also options. They involve either tying off or closing off the fallopian tubes in women, or tying off the tubes that release the sperm into the semen for men. Before doing anything permanent, pray a lot. Make sure you won't want to have any more children, even if something were to happen to your husband.

Ultimately, how do you make the decision of which method to use? Talk to your fiancé or husband about it. Pray about it. Talk to your doctor. But I'll give this wise Good Girl the last word: "No birth control is perfect for sexual enjoyment, preventing pregnancy, or interacting with a woman's body. The key is to find the one that works the best for you."

Now that we have the practical considerations out of the way, let's turn to how sex works!

Let's Talk Arousal

For guys, arousal is fairly obvious. When a guy becomes sexually excited (which can occur quite frequently and quite easily), blood rushes to his penis, and it becomes hard and erect, standing at about a 45-degree angle from his body, or at about 2:00 if you're looking at him while he's turned to your right. That's the perfect angle for making love, which is why he's made that way. He can enter you while lying right on top of you, which makes it more intimate, since you can kiss and look at each other at the same time. And he's hard like that pretty much instantaneously. He springs into action and he's ready to go!

A GOOD GIRL SPEAKS: *"Men are very sensitive about [their sexual skills!] Keep your words gentle to him if you want more or something different. For me, realizing that I don't have to have an orgasm every time is okay. Just be present and willing." (married 15 years)*

Women don't work quite that way, though some physiological similarities certainly exist. Blood rushes to your genitals too, and your clitoris, the little knob of flesh above your vagina toward your pelvis and between the big folds of your skin, will become engorged (or "erect") just like he does. You will usually experience this as a desperate wanting to be touched there and feeling yourself get "wet."

Why wet? Our bodies are designed so that when we're aroused, our vaginas produce fluid, which makes us slippery so that it's much easier for the penis to enter and move around. When you're not wet, you can experience too much friction of the bad kind. To feel pleasure, then, you should be aroused before you start any kind of penetration, but this tends to take much longer for women than it does for men.

Let's turn now to what feels good for both of us, so we can put it all together.

What Makes His Toes Curl

Guys are visually stimulated, and they tend to be ready to go right out of the starting gate. But just because men are ready to go doesn't mean that they wouldn't enjoy a little effort on your part to make them feel even better. Besides, it's awfully fun to explore your beloved's body, and it can make you feel very sexually powerful when you see the effect you have on him!

So what parts of his body feel the best?

Let's start with the obvious first. Your husband's main erogenous zones are his penis and his scrotum (the sack that holds his testicles, hanging down behind his penis).

So let's talk about the penis. If you haven't seen an erect one before, it isn't like a tube, where it's the same thickness all the way up. The penis has a head where it's a little bit thicker at the top. In uncircumcised males, this head is covered with the foreskin, which can be pulled back a little bit. In both circumcised and uncircumcised men, the most sensitive parts of the penis are the head itself and the rim, or ridge, right below the head. There's also a slightly enlarged area called the frenulum, right below the rim where the foreskin is attached (if the man is uncircumcised) on the underside of the penis (or the side that faces you when he's erect). Most men also find that deliciously sensitive. When you do touch him, just ask him where it feels best. And let him show you how to touch him. You'll catch on.

The scrotum is also very sensitive, and many men like their testicles to be stroked or squeezed. But keep in mind how much guys hurt if they're kicked there. Don't be too rough! Ask him to guide you and show you what kind of pressure to use.

Just like women, men also find it very arousing to have their nipples stroked or licked. And your husband probably has other body parts, like his ears or elbows or toes, where he would love to receive attention in order to drag out the encounter. His whole body is yours once you're married, so have fun exploring. And how should you explore?

Kissing

You've likely already kissed his mouth before you were married, but have you kissed passionately? Explore his mouth, suck on his lip or tongue, and try different things. There is no right and wrong.

Kissing doesn't have to be limited to mouths either. Kiss his neck and his chest. Kiss his nipples. And you can even kiss his penis, if you're comfortable with it. Don't worry about pee either. Once a guy is erect, he is physically unable to urinate. Also, his penis is covered in the same skin as the rest of his body, and if he washed, kissing his penis is really no different than kissing any other part of his body. It's also a big bonus that there's no hair on the actual penis, unlike his chest and legs. And when you use more than just your hands, you really get to understand how his penis feels and responds!

Nibbling

Kissing is gentle. Nibbling is playful and a big turn-on for many men. But be careful *where* you nibble. The penis and the scrotum are very sensitive, and it's best to keep teeth away from those areas. Stick to nibbling earlobes, shoulders, and his chest, where he can really enjoy the combination of teasing and a little bit of pain.

Touching

Don't hesitate to touch him all over. His body is yours now. Use your fingertips to memorize his contours. Run your fingers from his toes up to his head. And pay special attention to his penis and learning what it feels like and how it reacts. He'll appreciate the effort!

Squeezing

If you've ever been really aroused without actually having sex — say, after waking up from a graphic dream — you've probably experienced the sensation of your clitoris being so aroused it actually hurts. It wants desperately to be touched. That's what a guy's penis feels like too. And the thing that often feels best is to squeeze, and squeeze hard. Let him show you.

One thing that often surprises new couples is how differently men and women like to be touched. Women need touch to be more delicate; men need it more deliberate. Chances are, then, that he'll be too rough when touching you, and you'll be too gentle when touching him, because you won't recognize how each other's bodies work. If you touch his penis the way you want him to touch your clitoris, it will feel more like teasing to him. So don't be afraid to squeeze! Ask him to let you know how hard you should go.

These aren't steps you have to memorize to do right. You don't need to bring a primer to bed on your first few encounters. I put all this here just to help you realize there are many ways to explore his body, and you should feel free to do so, as soon as you're comfortable. And ask him to show you! He will be thrilled with the request.

What Makes Your Toes Curl

Just as guys have very specific areas that produce major sparks when you give them some attention, so your body has parts that cry out for attention too. But not everyone has the same sensitivity in the same areas. Here's a road map, though, of where most women are sensitive, and if your husband explores all of these areas, you'll probably find some are winners.

Ears and Neck

Many women find their ears one of the most sensitive spots on their bodies. Encourage your hubby to explore — to kiss, to nibble, to blow gently. And necks invite passionate kisses.

Hands and Feet

Fingers and toes tend to like being sucked — but a bath or shower beforehand may make you more amenable to it! When you're newly married, many women feel a little bit shy and think they're smelly, so wash beforehand and you don't need to have these qualms.

Legs and Arms

Women love massage. The more he rubs and strokes the back of your knees or your arms, the more other areas of your body will call out for attention. Our bodies crave touch all over, and when you're naked and your husband touches you in places other than the typical erogenous zones, the teasing can be delicious. By not touching you between your legs right away, for instance, you'll become even more aware of how much that part of your body actually yearns to be touched. So pass him some massage oil and give him permission to tease you. It's a great lead-up to the more "exciting" areas!

Breasts

Now let's turn to some of those more "traditional" erogenous zones. When it comes to breasts, don't worry that being diminutive in the bra department means your breasts won't appreciate the attention. Size bears no relation to sensitivity, something for which I am eternally grateful.

Remember how I mentioned that men often like to be stroked and squeezed with pressure, while women like it more gentle? This is especially true around the nipple area. A guy's approach can often be too rough. Show him the right pressure (you don't even have to use words if you're shy, just take his hand). When you become aroused, your nipples will become erect and hard, similar to the way they do when you're cold. When you're really excited, you can often handle (and even yearn for) more direct pressure. So while you may prefer that he starts out gently, you may not mind something more later. This applies to his mouth too. A gentle lick may work at first, but later you may want something more. Find a way to signal to him, even if it's just murmuring when he's doing something delicious!

Clitoris

The most important erogenous zone in us girls is the clitoris, the knob of flesh between the two outer lips (labia majora), right in front of the opening for the vagina. Almost button-like, it protrudes a bit from your body. It's the most sensitive part of you, containing 8,000 nerve endings. It actually has twice as many nerve endings as the penis, despite being so much smaller. It's a little bundle of intense pleasure.

Because it's so sensitive, though, it's easy to touch in the wrong way. Your husband may be too rough initially, because he doesn't know how to touch it (and perhaps you don't either). Again, the key is communication. If it feels good, tell him. If it's too much or too rough or not exactly the right spot, reposition his hand. Men often have a hard time figuring out just where the clitoris is, and you can act as his tour guide.

Vagina

Though the clitoris is the most sensitive area on a woman's body, guys often assume it's the vagina, since that's where the "main event" happens. The vagina is one of those areas that women either love to have touched and probed or hate to have touched and probed. Some women enjoy it when their husbands insert fingers into the vagina, and some find it a little too much. If you start out feeling awkward with it, that doesn't mean you'll feel that way throughout your marriage. As you get more used to sex, you might actually find that you want to start trying it.

For maximum brownie points in the arousal department, though, guys should probably not plunge straight for your vagina. They should start by nibbling ears or sucking on fingers or kissing the palm of your hand. Even if you do like to have your vagina touched and explored, you'd probably rather be aroused and wet first.

When and if you want him to explore inside you, some women swear by the "G-spot," a knob of bean-shaped flesh between one and three inches inside the vagina on the front wall (the wall closest to your stomach, not your back). Rubbing there with the penis or the fingers can be the easiest way for some women to experience orgasm. But if you can't find the G-spot, don't fret. Just have fun hunting!

Foreplay

Now you know where and how most people enjoy being touched, so don't go for that "main event" too quickly! Spend time exploring, figuring out what both of you like. It's relaxing, and helps make intercourse, when you do start, more exciting. Even after you know each others' bodies, you should still spend most of your time in foreplay, because women tend to need it in order to get really steamy. And it's hard to become aroused if you're also nervous and scared.

Remember how we learned that for women our sexual response is largely in our heads? When we emotionally want sex and are emo-

A GOOD GIRL SPEAKS: *"The habits you start early on tend to stick, and if you get lazy about sex, [you can have] a hard time getting past lazy again." (married 12 years)*

tionally ready, we tend to physically respond. When we're really nervous, we often don't.

Not only that, but we tend to take much longer to reach orgasm than the guy does, especially at the start of the marriage. If he can touch you and take his time and help you to relax and drive you crazy beforehand, then you'll likely find you enjoy sex a whole lot more.

But to be really arousing, foreplay should resemble a tour of an exotic island rather than a treasure dig at a specific place. Too many men think that foreplay just involves rubbing the clitoris, but it should be more than that. If he touches and kisses and nibbles you all over, and you do the same for him, you'll be more aroused and feel more intimate. I've heard women declare, "I don't like foreplay," but I often wonder if that's because their husbands are rushing it or not exploring quite enough. If you're totally dry because you're nervous or because you're preoccupied and it's going to take some time to get you in the mood, then having him rub your clitoris back

A GOOD GIRL SPEAKS: *"My husband and I had sex before marriage and had a child as a result. We married shortly after she was born. Before our marriage our sexual activity was through the roof. After marriage I struggled with wanting to even be touched by him. My sex drive had diminished while his increased.*

"It wasn't until ten years into our marriage that I knew that I wasn't being the wife that God called me to be. It was at that point that I made the decision to really love my husband sexually.

"He jokes and says that the only proof that we ever had sex is that we have six children. So sad, but basically true. People thought that we were always having sex, but we weren't.

"So, for me, it was a decision to love him. My sex drive came back with a roar." (married 18 years)

and forth can be annoying. Encourage him to pay attention to your whole body. And it's easier for him to want to do this if you also pay attention to his whole body. Reciprocate!

Now I don't want to give you a step-by-step guide to what to do in foreplay, girls. I've already laid out how most men and women prefer to be touched, and I think that's enough. Explore and make up your own routine. You'll be able to figure it out, and figuring it out is half the fun. What I would suggest, though, is that you gear yourself up to talk to him about it early in your marriage, even on your wedding night. Don't start your marriage without sending clear signals about what you like, because you'll find it hard to ask him to change later. The first time you're naked together, with only those wedding bands on, start communicating. And words aren't even necessary! Just guide his hand, and if he's doing something a little bit wrong, show him how to do it right. Make reassuring sounds if he hits a hot spot. You may not even know what you want him to do, but as you become aroused, you'll find that certain areas of your body are yearning to be touched. Guide him to those areas.

Incidentally, this is perhaps even more important for couples who have already had sex before they were married. Just because you have had sex doesn't mean that you did it well or that you enjoyed it. If it hasn't been overly satisfying, it's even more important to act right at the beginning of your marriage to make it better. You have a new start; take advantage of it. And if you've made love in the past with other guys and something felt good, don't assume that this is what's going to feel good with your husband. Try to launch into marriage with a blank slate and learn what feels good when he does it. Let it be something that you experience together with no preconceived notions. You just may find that you like something with him that you never thought you'd like with anybody!

> **a good girl dare**
>
> Spray perfume on your breasts or behind your knees. Use different scents and ask him to find them.

Understanding the Big *O*

We've talked about arousal and foreplay. Now let's talk about climax (another word for orgasm).

The Male Orgasm

A male orgasm is pretty easy to understand because it's rather obvious. When a man reaches orgasm, his pelvic floor muscles will contract about twelve to fourteen times, quickly in succession, and he'll ejaculate (eject) semen. He won't necessarily feel all of those contractions, but he will feel exhilarated. After that orgasm, he'll likely be unable to make love again for about forty-five minutes to an hour (some men remain erect even after orgasm and can continue to make love until she reaches orgasm, but that's not terribly common, and any friction can also be quite sensitive for him). He'll release about one to two teaspoons of semen, depending on how long it has been building up. That doesn't sound like very much, but you'll want to have a towel handy for afterward unless you're using a condom.

What about a female orgasm? Quite frankly, it's a lot more complex, as most things about women are. So let's start with some basic facts.

How a Female Orgasm Feels

When you reach orgasm, you'll likely know, because you'll feel an intense buildup followed by an incredible physical rush that will wash over you in waves. You'll feel your vaginal muscles squeeze involuntarily and rhythmically (they do this because your contracting muscles end up squeezing him when he's inside you, which in turn causes him to reach orgasm), and your head will tend to thrash around. Your legs will go stiff, and your pelvis will automatically tilt upward (to allow the guy maximum penetration at that time).

In one children's book that explained sex, which my mother gave me when I was six years old, it explained that an orgasm is like a sneeze, which builds and builds until your body finally lets it out. I never liked that analogy much, because I hate sneezes. But there is a bit of a similarity: your body is building tension — sexual tension in this case — and is going to release it.

Freud was one of the first to postulate that women had two different kinds of orgasms: clitoral and vaginal. He believed the clitoral kind was reached due to a woman's clitoris being stimulated, whereas a vaginal orgasm was reached during intercourse and was due to one's vagina being stimulated. Freud also believed that a clitoral orgasm was somehow inferior, or more immature, to a vaginal one. More modern research has shown that he was both right and wrong, though mostly wrong.

Let's start with what he got right. Women do have two kinds of orgasms (and those who swear by the G-spot would likely add a third). These orgasms feel different, but at their heart, they both rely on clitoral stimulation (that's what Freud didn't understand). Even a vaginal orgasm is caused because one's clitoris is stimulated upon penetration. So let's go over the importance of the clitoris to female arousal.

Here's something amazing to understand: the clitoris has absolutely no purpose in the body except arousal. Men don't have any bits of anatomy that are meant only to make them feel good. But God made women with this little knob of flesh that's only purpose is to make us fly when we're with our husbands. God wants you to have a good time! Sex is not something to feel ashamed about enjoying; he made it that way. He wants you to desire it. He wants you to love it! Cool, isn't it?

How to Reach the Big O

While many couples yearn for that magical "simultaneous orgasm" when both of you come (climax) at the same time, this usually takes some practice. So if you don't reach orgasm through intercourse as soon as you're married, do not fret about it. You have plenty of time to figure this out, so it truly doesn't matter. However, if you want to increase the likelihood of reaching orgasm, here are some pointers.

Clitoral stimulation is what brings a woman to orgasm even during intercourse. So you have to make sure that you're achieving an angle while you make love that is stimulating that part of you.

One simple thing to do is to tilt your pelvis up when you're in the missionary position (you on bottom, him on top). When your hips are tilted up at a 45 degree angle and he's entering you at the same angle, his pelvic bone is going to hit your clitoris every time he thrusts.

Some women place a pillow under their rump to elevate that particular part of her body, but research shows that that action doesn't work as well, because the act of physically tilting your pelvis yourself actually puts some pressure on the clitoris already (seriously, just try it; tilt your pelvis forward by tensing the muscles in your bum, and you'll feel your clitoris getting squeezed). Merely sticking a pillow under you doesn't engage the muscles. Do both in combination, though, and you'll likely have a winner!

Other women find it easier to make sure the clitoris gets enough pressure by making love while she is on top. Move your body up and down around his penis, and each time you come down, aim so that your clitoris falls into contact with his pelvis. You may have to fool around with the angle, but some women swear by this position.

When orgasm does occur during intercourse, it feels different from a clitoral orgasm. It's less focused on the one part of your body and more focused on the whole genital area. It's usually much deeper. A clitoral orgasm is often more intense, and you're frequently very sensitive afterward, far more so than with a vaginal one. But perhaps intense isn't the right word. Think of the difference between a knife cutting you and an ankle sprain. The ankle sprain probably hurts more, but the knife cutting you is more intense in that one place. If you try to relax during the orgasm and don't worry about it, you'll likely find that orgasm can last a long time. With practice you can even feel secondary and tertiary waves afterward. But orgasm is the one thing you will never reach if you're worried about it.

So let me say it again: you do not have to reach orgasm through intercourse on your wedding night, or even on your honeymoon. Many women take a few years of marriage to accomplish this feat. It might be nice during that time to reach orgasm some other way (such as through him stimulating your clitoris), but if you're too tense, don't rush it. Do what seems fun to you! If you can't laugh through it or pant through it, it's probably not the time. Wait and just learn to relax being naked together and touching each other.

He's likely to want to figure out how to bring you to orgasm, though, and when you think you're ready to try, why not?

Expanding Your Repertoire

When you first get married, it's as if you've unwrapped the biggest toy that you're ever going to get, and most guys are likely to be very interested in wanting to experiment as much as possible with that toy. You likely will too, although women are usually more nervous than guys are. After all, we're the vulnerable ones here. We're the ones who are actually inviting someone else into our body. We're the ones who experience some pain. And we're the ones who aren't guaranteed an orgasm. But here are some variations that you can throw in once you're comfortable — and some thoughts on how to make the typical not-quite-so-typical.

Different Positions

The man-on-top, woman-on-bottom position (otherwise known as the missionary position) is popular because it's the easiest. You can also look each other right in the eyes, which is very intimate.

A few tips to make this one as comfortable as possible: tilt your pelvis. Don't use a pillow under your head, because that can raise the top of your body and distort the angle where you need it to be just right! Make sure that he has something to anchor his feet on, since it's hard to thrust (move back and forth) without some kind of lever-

A GOOD GIRL SPEAKS: *"I've enjoyed learning little by little and becoming more comfortable experimenting with new things over time.... I knew only the bare minimum when we got married, but I don't think I needed to know too much at first — I wasn't comfortable enough to do more yet." (married 9 years)*

age. If he can anchor his feet, it's easier for him to take some of the weight off of you too. If there's a big weight discrepancy between the two of you, sex may be easier for you if he puts a lot of weight onto his forearms while the two of you are making love so that you don't feel like you're being suffocated. Just try it, and if you can't breathe, laugh about it, shove him up, and get the position the way you want it. Do this early in your marriage, because you want to set the stage for finding out what feels good. You don't want to be uncomfortable for a year without saying anything and only then tell him that he's been doing it wrong all along.

Another alternative is the woman-on-top, man-on-bottom thing. This one usually involves him lying down and you straddling him while sitting up. This position is intimate because you can still look in his eyes, and he often likes it because he gets a good view of you bouncing around (he can also feel your breasts more easily). If he's a lot heavier than you, this can also be more comfortable. When you're just starting to make love, being on top can be less stressful for you, because you can take control. You're the one who decides how deep to go, so if you feel tender or you're still getting used to penetration, you can experiment a bit and make sure you're doing what feels good. Again, because you're the one on top, you can also arrange for the clitoris to come into contact with his pelvic bone more easily and can sometimes control your own pleasure a little bit more. In fact, this was the only comfortable position for one new Good Girl bride:

> I wish I had known the position that "worked" was me on top. We tried the "missionary" position but couldn't get penetration because that was too uncomfortable for me. We actually fell asleep before successfully having sex and then woke up sometime later and were able to figure it out better. I know my husband was disappointed at first when he thought it wouldn't work, but then later … he definitely wasn't!

The third most popular position is the "rear entry" position, where the woman typically kneels on all fours, and he kneels behind her and penetrates from behind. (I'm not talking about anal sex here; he's still entering the vagina.) Most men are rather eager to try this one because they feel really powerful, and it is awfully intense for them. Some people shy away from it, though, because it doesn't seem as intimate, since you can't maintain eye contact. It's really your call (and more on that in chapter 8).

However, this position can be very uncomfortable when you are new to sex, because the angle is quite different and it tends to feel quite a bit tighter. If you experience pain the first time you make love, then trying this right away is not a good idea. It's really better to save the more adventurous stuff for later in your marriage when you've learned how to relax a bit more.

Nevertheless, if you want to give it a shot, the benefits for you are that he can also put a hand, or a finger, on your clitoris while you make love, and thus stimulate you that way while you're having intercourse. Guide him in this, or he's likely to be too rough. Some women also find that this position is the best one for stimulating the G-spot, that oval of flesh between one and a half and three inches up and on the front wall of the vagina, which is extremely sensitive, and which, when stimulated directly, often results in a very intense orgasm.

Of course, our bodies fit together in any number of ways, and once sex has stopped hurting for you, experiment all you want. But you don't need a long list of positions as much as you need an imagination. If you find a new way his penis can fit inside you, go with it. Sometimes varying what you do with your legs can make a position feel very different too. Wrapping your legs around his torso in the missionary position, for instance, lets him go deeper. Moving your legs up to above his shoulders takes some flexibility, but lets him feel like he's going even further. So try intercourse sitting or standing or with your legs up or down, and it will feel different each time. By varying whether you're sitting in a chair or lying on a bed, you'll also vary the angle at which he's entering you, even if he's the one on the bottom both times. But don't pressure yourself to do anything that you're not ready for. You have a lifetime to get this right, and if it doesn't click on the first try, laugh about it. It's trial and error for at least the first few years with most couples, anyway. But that trial-and-error period will be shortened if you become comfortable telling him what feels good.

Relax

You have a great deal of freedom now, but that freedom does not have to be exercised all at once. The important thing is not what you do but how you feel about it, because *how you feel about it* will determine your enjoyment level way more than *what you do*. Sex for women is all in our heads; we need our heads to be in the game for it to feel good. If you feel too scared, too guilty, or too nervous, it's not going to work. It's better to go slowly and try only one or two things for a time than to try to jump in, thinking you have to do everything. You don't want to give your body the message that "none of this feels good, and it's all for him," because that's not true. But it does take many women a long time to be able to feel free sexually.

A GOOD GIRL SPEAKS: *"I wish we had taken more time to experiment and explore more of our bodies. We are just getting into that now, and we have three kids and have been married for seven years."*

In fact, that's one of the things that kept coming up in my wedding night survey, over and over: *I wish I had figured out how to relax*. When you aren't relaxed, sex isn't going to feel exciting and you're going to have a hard time telling him what you want. Talk about this beforehand (if you can without conjuring up too much temptation), and promise each other to take it slowly and focus on your comfort levels.

Listen, girls, I did my wedding night and honeymoon so wrong. If I could go back and do it again, I would probably save about four years of misery in my marriage. I tried to do everything all at once, even though it hurt and even though I was scared, because I didn't want to "fail." If I had taken a few days just to relax, things would have been so much better.

When you're first married and getting used to sex, you will likely enjoy it much more if you focus less on the success of your sexual encounters and more on the journey of discovery that you are taking together. Don't see everything as success or failure — see it as increasing the levels of intimacy as you know each other better in every way. You have decades to get this right, so don't try to accomplish everything at once if you're nervous, tired, or shy. Instead, rejoice in this new adventure that is put before you and jump in at your comfort level.

Now, if your wedding is still looming, the next chapter is just for you. We'll keep talking about how sex will work, especially that first time when you're together as husband and wife. And don't ignore that chapter even if you're not new to the whole sex thing! If your ceremony is still in the future, read on for suggestions on how to make the start of your new life together truly beautiful.

If you're already married, though, you can skip ahead to chapter five, where we'll start looking at specific challenges when it comes to the physical aspects of sex.

CHAPTER 4

Beginning the Journey to Very Good

A few weeks before my wedding, I bought a bestselling Christian sex book. I read it cover to cover while sitting in the bathtub. (That's where I get most of my reading done. It's just a little dangerous when I'm reading library books.) Instead of helping me feel confident about my wedding night, it left me a nervous wreck. And a little angry besides.

First, it was all about the mechanics of sex. The book's focus was on making sure that you, the woman, had an orgasm on your very first sexual encounter. It went through everything you were supposed to do and everything he was supposed to do in explicit detail, complete with a time schedule. After reading and raging at the book, I drowned it. I stuffed it under the water and held it there until it died, and then I unceremoniously dumped it in the garbage.

Let me try to explain why I felt so homicidal toward a book. I didn't like feeling as if my every action was prescribed. I didn't want sex to feel choreographed. I didn't want to feel like there was a right way to do things. But perhaps most importantly, I didn't want the night to be so stressful that it could be measured based on whether I had "succeeded." What if I simply wanted to get comfortable with my husband and have fun exploring rather than trying to force my body to do something?

Given that that particular book sold hundreds of thousands of copies, I'm sure it has helped many women enjoy their wedding nights. But there is a trend in Christian thinking that goes something like this: *the wedding night is the big night you've been waiting for your whole life, so you had better do absolutely everything right or you will ruin it.*

A lot of pressure, isn't it?

Perhaps I'm being a party pooper. Perhaps that book is right, and we all should be aiming for physical bliss. So I decided to test my own hypothesis. I took a survey of married Christian women, some of whom had waited for the wedding to be sexually active and some of whom had made love before, and I asked them to rate the sex on their wedding night.

I discovered that despite selling so many copies, the book's message hadn't succeeded in making wedding nights more explosive. Of the women in my survey who had been virgins when they were married, only 16 percent reached orgasm on their wedding night through intercourse. Another 14 percent reached it another way (we'll talk about that later), but 70 percent didn't experience an orgasm at all. In fact, even among those who weren't virgins, in no category did over 50 percent of women reach orgasm through intercourse on the night they were married. It simply isn't that common.

A GOOD GIRL SPEAKS: *"At a conference, the speaker addressed a bunch of engaged women and shared her wedding night story. I had a preconceived notion of what a 'godly' wedding night might look like. I wish I had thrown that out the window and done what came naturally. My expectations were based on someone else's experience, and it was a letdown. I felt like a failure much of our honeymoon too!" (married 6 years)*

Here's the way I see it: fireworks are great. Everyone wants fireworks. But the point of the wedding night is that it's a *wedding* night. It's about the marriage. The bliss is that you're now together in every way. So you can now explore, have fun, and discover all on your own time. For some people, that's going to mean fireworks right off the bat. For others it may take longer. But it doesn't matter, because now you're finally married, and you have decades to get it right!

Remember those 84 percent of virgins who did not have an orgasm through intercourse on their wedding night? Today 57 percent of those women usually or always do, and another 20 percent sometimes do. They got better with time.

Pete and Shirley Unrau, a couple now in their seventies, have been speaking at Family Life marriage conferences in Canada for fifteen years. My husband and I have had the privilege to tag teach with them, and they are a riot. At one particular confer-ence, Pete was commenting that sex had gotten so much better since their honey-moon, when Shirley piped up: "That's not saying much, is it?" Everybody giggled. They'll be the first to tell you that they didn't know what they were doing back then. But they've had decades to practice, and now, in their senior years, they continue to enjoy mutual pleasure and excitement.

> **a good girl dare**
>
> Before you make love for the first time as a married couple, pray. Ask God to bless the physical part of your marriage.

Paul and Eleanor Henderson, another couple we've spoken with, have a similar story. Paul is a Canadian legend, since he's the one who shot the game-winning goal in the Soviet-Canada hockey series back in 1973. And here's his comment about sex: "It's like what my coach always told me: 'Henny, if you want to be good, you've got to practice, practice, *practice!*'" He and Eleanor did. And now they're good.

We can look at that paltry 16 percent figure and conclude, "Wow, we need to educate people more about how to have sex so that more women can have orgasms on their wedding night." Or we can say, "Maybe for most people sex is a fun learning curve, not an instan-taneous achievement. And that's okay." Personally, I like the second option.

So if I could give one piece of advice to those of you who aren't married yet, it would be this: relax about the wedding night. The more you relax, the more fun it will be. Think of it as a voyage of discovery that is only just beginning on that particular night. You have lots of time to get your physical relationship working well! So make the wonder of the wedding night about get-ting to know your husband in a new and exciting way and not about

A GOOD GIRL SPEAKS: *"I wish we hadn't gotten stressed out about how it 'should' be and just tried to make it fun. (I also wish I had taken that advice for the actual wedding!)" (married 15 years)*

reaching some sort of physical milestone. Otherwise it becomes so, well, *serious*. And who wants to be serious on their wedding night?

C. S. Lewis, in his book *The Four Loves*, wrote, "Banish play and laughter from the bed of love and you may let in a false goddess."[1] Sex is funny. Our body parts are funny. It's a little messy, a little quirky, and often awkward. But it's fun. And if we make an orgasm something that we have to achieve or else, we lose the fun.

A GOOD GIRL SPEAKS: *"Take the time to relax, enjoy each other, and have fun. Don't focus too much on the act itself." (married 35 years)*

So, in the spirit of not being so serious, let's take a lighthearted but realistic look at what the wedding night is likely to be. Some of you are newbies at this whole making love thing. You've never done it before, and you're gearing up for your first encounter. Others of you have already made love to your fiancé, and you're wondering if you can reclaim that "Good Girl" you want to be and still make the wedding night meaningful. Whichever group you're in, let's look together at the wedding night from all kinds of angles and see how we can best bring out the Good Girl aspects of it! First, let's turn to the things we need to think about at least a few months before we walk down the aisle — birth control and medical checkups.

Plan Birth Control (or Lack of It)

If you're planning on getting married, you also need to start planning whether you want to be parents right away. Give some thought to birth control early — months before the wedding, if possible — because many methods need a bit of a lag time beforehand to work out. In the last chapter, we looked at different birth control methods — including choosing none at all — and this is a crucial decision that you should talk to your fiancé about now.

Book a Checkup

Whether you're walking down the aisle as a virgin or you've had plenty of experience beforehand, a trip to the doctor before the wedding can help you get off to a more reassuring start to your married life.

I'll talk to the sexual novices first. A doctor's visit will likely involve some pretty pointed questions about sex — "Are you *sure* you've never had sex before?" — and questions about your fiancé's sexual history. Don't take it personally if the doctor doesn't believe you're a virgin. Doctors are trained to ask probing questions and to be suspicious if things seem out of the ordinary. And waiting for marriage is definitely out of the ordinary. Nevertheless, it's beneficial to take some time and talk to your physician about what you will be doing — or not doing — about contraception.

A GOOD GIRL SPEAKS: *"We should have cherished it a bit more instead of just getting it done because you're supposed to!" (married 4 years)*

Conversing with the doctor about sex is one thing. Putting your feet up in stirrups is another altogether. Doctors are in the business of assuming things could be wrong, so he or she will likely want to do an internal exam to make sure you're healthy. That exam consists of you lying spread-eagle on an examining table, with your feet in stirrups, while the physician inserts a speculum inside you, which looks a little bit like a hair straightener. Once the speculum is all the way in, the doctor will open it so that he or she can swab your cervix (the opening to your uterus). Then he or she will remove the speculum, exchange it for a couple of fingers, and feel around to ensure that everything is in the right place and the right size and shape.

I'm not a doctor so I can't give you medical advice, but here's what I will say. Talk to your doctor about this before you just acquiesce. The doctor is looking primarily for cervical cancer, and over 90% of cervical cancers are caused by the sexually transmitted disease, human papillomavirus (HPV). If you're a virgin, you don't carry HPV, so your risk of cervical cancer is miniscule. And if you've been having regular periods, with normal amounts of cramping, the chances of something being physically wrong that requires immediate treatment is also very slim, though you may want the reassurance that your reproductive organs are good to go before you wed.

Speaking as a woman who, twenty years into marriage, still has to hum and "go to my happy place" to get through an internal exam, I wouldn't recommend it for a virgin unless your doctor says it's essential or unless you want reassurance that you're normal and healthy. Ask your physician what, specifically, he or she is looking for and what the chances are that you have a problem. Perhaps your physician will agree that there isn't an immediate need for an internal exam. If, however, you decide to go ahead for your own peace of mind or to satisfy your doctor, ask the doctor to go slowly, to make sure you are comfortable, and, if possible, to use an adolescent speculum.

On the other hand, if you've been sexually active before, be fair to everyone and have the full exam — and the battery of tests for sexually transmitted diseases. You don't want to pass along something nasty. Physicians are also very accustomed to helping people deal with STDs that have long-term effects. If you're worried you may have something, don't stick your head in the sand. See your doctor so that you start out your marriage in complete honesty. If you do have something, like herpes, for instance, you can still be sexually active. Your physician can help you learn to tell when herpes is dormant and what to do if it's not.

If the tests do come back positive for any STD, you'll likely experience a period of grieving and shame. Talk to your fiancé about it and be completely open with him. He loves you. He wants to marry you. The chances of that changing are very slim, but if you keep this from him, you're starting your marriage on rocky ground.

And if your fiancé isn't a virgin, ask him to have all the tests done too, so you can be reassured that when you start having sex, you won't catch anything. Reassure him that no matter what the outcome, you will still love him and still want to marry him. After all, if you can't say that, you likely shouldn't be walking down the aisle in the first place!

Now that we've dealt with the medical side of marriage, let's focus on how to plan for the actual wedding night.

Think Exhaustion

The most common regret women completing my survey reported about their wedding night was plain and simple exhaustion. If you're up at six in the morning the day of your wedding to dress, head to the hairdresser, apply your makeup, pose for pictures, actually get married, take more pictures, host the reception, and then dance until midnight, how alert and energetic do you think you're going to be once you get back to that hotel room?

Listen to these Good Girl warnings:

"I wish I'd left the party earlier so I'd have more energy."

"As awful as this sounds, I was so exhausted on my wedding night, I didn't even want to have sex."

If you want maximum energy at night, schedule an early ceremony. If you have to fly for your honeymoon and the airport is a distance away, take a day together in a hotel before you leave. Don't force yourself to drive for a few hours after your wedding or schedule yourself to get up at five in the morning to catch your plane. Think relaxation. You want to be able to lounge in bed with your hubby. So don't make unrealistic plans that sound fun in theory but are actually going to be exhausting!

On the other hand, maybe that dance until 2:00 a.m. and the big party is important to you. Maybe you really do want to take off for Jamaica at dawn the next morning. If these things matter, that's fine. But be realistic about your expectations, and consider postponing that first sexual encounter until you can be rested and relaxed.

A GOOD GIRL SPEAKS: *"I don't think sex was a priority on our wedding night. We were having plenty of it on our honeymoon! We had so much fun celebrating on our wedding night with all of our friends and family that we both collapsed at the end of the night in each other's arms. To me, that was more special than leaving early or staying up late just because we were supposed to." (married 5 years)*

One other bit of advice from our Good Girls: lay off alcohol at the reception. For many newlyweds, and especially the younger ones, alcohol hasn't been a big part of their lives. This wedding is one of the first really "grown-up" things they've done. And perhaps there's wine on every table or even an open bar. Now is not the time to see what having three glasses of wine feels like. Stay away from the alcohol, and encourage your husband to do so as well. A full 10 percent of our survey respondents didn't make love that first night because their husbands passed out or because they were too tipsy after drinking for the first time. Definitely not a highlight for a wedding night.

Think Memorable

Many women who completed my survey also reported putting a lot of thought into the wedding but very little into the honeymoon. They felt selfish or wasteful spending too much money on a vacation, so they poured it all into the ceremony. But what's more important? The day you say your vows or the few days afterward, the first few days of getting acquainted as a newly married couple? They're both key, aren't they? Prioritize both.

A GOOD GIRL SPEAKS: *"We took a several-hour nap first, after the party, then woke up around midnight for some intimacy. I love that we cuddled and stuff first, before getting into the hanky-panky. Plus, we were just exhausted!" (married 7 years)*

Personally, I would not pay for a limo to the hotel or a horse-drawn carriage or an expensive rental car. What I would pay for is a nice hotel room. Many women in my survey expressed appreciation for their Jacuzzi tubs! And when you plan your honeymoon, plan one with something to do. As strange as it may sound, you aren't going to be able to do nothing but have sex for a week. You're going to want to be able to walk, play golf, swim, sightsee, or something else you enjoy. So book your vacation accordingly.

Think Bed Size

When you're booking your hotel, also keep in mind what kind of bed you want. If you have spent your entire life sleeping by yourself, it can be hard to learn to sleep next to someone else. I sleep all curled up with my husband now, but at the beginning of our marriage, I couldn't sleep if he was touching me. It wasn't that I didn't like him; I just wasn't

used to it. Reserve the king-sized bed so this isn't a problem. If you do want to snuggle, you can always just scoot over.

Think Period

It's your worst nightmare. Your wedding day arrives, and so does your period. You have to wear a white dress all day, and your plans for the night are ruined.

If you have enough lag time leading up to your wedding, a little planning can make this less likely. Keep track of your cycles as soon as you can. You'll notice that there is at least a little bit of regularity, hopefully, so that you can make educated guesses, about six to eight months out, about when it's likely you'll be having your period. And then try to schedule your wedding smack in the middle, so that even if you're off in calculations by a week or so, it won't matter.

If, after all your best planning, your period comes anyway, cry about it for a few minutes and then try to let it go. In the broader scheme of things, it isn't going to matter that much. You have decades to be married. Decide instead to make your honeymoon into a time where you can just get to know each other and have fun outside the bedroom.

And *in* the bedroom, he can focus on other parts of your body rather than your vagina, and if you're comfortable with it, you can ask him to show you how to bring him to orgasm another way (since he will probably be rather eager to do *something*). Don't consider it a failure; just have fun doing what you can, and know the rest will come in its time.

Now let's turn to some specific issues where sexual experience makes a difference. First I have something to say to those who will be having sex for the first time, and then I'll address the rest of you Good Girls who also want to have an amazing wedding night and honeymoon.

Just for Virgins

Last year Keith and I were speaking at a marriage conference in Atlantic Canada, where we conducted a session with the six engaged couples who had joined the hundreds of married ones. Keith talked to the men; I talked to the women. The men were mostly interested in learning how to wait until the wedding night, because they were finding it incredibly difficult. The women were far more interested in the technical stuff: "Does it hurt?"

A GOOD GIRL SPEAKS: *"I enjoyed learning about sex with my husband. I knew the basics, and that was enough." (married 27 years)*

"If I can't use a tampon, does that mean I can't have sex?" "What's the hymen?" So let's go over all of these things in detail.

Does It Hurt?

That book that I drowned said that first-time sex won't hurt if you do everything right. I'm not sure that's true. Here are a few comments from our Good Girls to set the record straight:

"The first time doesn't hurt."

"It is soooooo painful."

Guess that didn't clear the issue up very much, did it? I suppose we should conclude that the correct answer is, "It depends."

Most women do experience at least a slight sting when the hymen, the layer of skin that partially covers the opening of the vagina, tears. When it breaks, you appear much more "open." If you're aroused, it's not that it doesn't hurt; it's just that you often don't care! So asking him to spend some time on foreplay (stroking and petting and kissing) to get you aroused will likely help diminish the pain factor greatly. You can also encourage him to use his fingers to stretch you open a bit, if you're comfortable with that. But remember that the pain isn't like the way your anus feels when you're constipated or anything like that. It's really more abrupt, and then it's over.

A GOOD GIRL SPEAKS: *"You may think it is really bad that we didn't have sex on our wedding night. We were both virgins and had not gone very far physically. So our wedding night was getting to know each other physically and just starting a process!" (married 13 years)*

Before I was married, a close friend who had been wed for a year told me that she was quite surprised at how sex in the "missionary position," with him on top, stopped hurting pretty quickly, but over the next few days, whenever they tried new positions, the pain came back again. It makes sense. Your body isn't used to it, and stretching things in ways they haven't been stretched before, especially if you're still a little raw from the hymen tearing, can be sore. But the pain will go away, and if something hurts too much, you don't have to do it now!

If you find that the pain is more intense, then you're likely having muscle pain rather than hymen pain. That's usually because you're having a hard time relaxing, and when you're tense, the muscles at the top one and a half inches of your vagina (closest to the opening) can tense involuntarily. Here's what to do: ask your husband to stop moving once he's inside you (if you can manage this at all). Tense as hard as you can around his penis, and then relax deliberately. That can cause that "involuntary" muscle spasm to stop. Do that for a few minutes, and usually the problem goes away.

Here's what one woman said about this:

> My husband was a virgin as well and was very patient with me despite being excited. When I couldn't relax enough to allow for penetration, he suggested waiting until the next day and

cuddling. The next day we were both rested from our large wedding, and we were able to have intercourse. It was great!

I think that's a great attitude and great advice! Remember, if you get tense about being tense, it's only going to make you more tense. If you can both manage to wait, give it a little bit of time to see if you just need to relax. After all, you've been through the most stressful and busiest period of your life. You may just need space to breathe again! Talk to your husband about this, and keep trying other things to get your body to respond. We'll talk more in chapter five about what to do if you're still having this problem after some time.

Another question I get asked quite frequently is, "Will I bleed?" Some women do, and some women don't. In general the hymen tear is rather small. Just make sure you have a towel nearby to protect the sheets, and you'll be fine. If you don't bleed, it doesn't mean you didn't do it right. Some women tear their hymens earlier in life without realizing it. It also doesn't mean that you weren't a virgin. It just means that you're blessed with less pain!

Think Big

Men may worry about whether their penises are large enough, but the first time a woman sees an erect penis, she's usually pretty surprised at its size. To a virgin, it looks big. After you've squeezed a few babies out, it may not seem so huge, but when all you have to compare it to is a regular tampon, it's big. But don't worry; it fits. Really. Your vagina is designed to stretch and actually feels good when it is stretched. So don't worry too much about the size. You'll get used to it and come to like it!

a good girl dare

Study his body. It's yours now! Memorize how it feels, smells, and even tastes.

Think Messy

It wasn't as "neat and tidy" as is portrayed on TV or movies. The guy can wash off; the girl "leaks."

After you have sex (without a condom) you will be "leaking" (a combination of his and your fluids), and you'll have to get up and go to the bathroom! Not so romantic, but necessary, because if you don't, you will start to "puddle." I wish someone had told me this!

When your husband reaches orgasm, and especially if semen has been building up for a while, he's releasing a lot of "stuff" inside you (unless he's using a condom). Combine that with the natural fluids that women produce when we're sexually excited, and quite a puddle can form that is no fun to sleep on later that night. Stick a towel or some tissue by the bed to wipe up afterward or to put underneath you when you make love.

On television couples always snuggle after making love. They don't ever get up and do something so mundane as going to the bathroom. But your husband will likely need to, and it's a good idea for you to do so as well. Urinating afterward reduces the chances of urinary tract infections. And that's something important to keep at the back of your mind, because a burst of sexual activity can all too easily lead to a UTI or a yeast infection. And UTIs don't just hurt; they also leave you with this horrible feeling like you have to urinate constantly. And yeast infections itch. Not fun.

Not to give Too Much Information here, but the few times I've had a UTI have been after anniversary weekends when my husband and I escaped by ourselves and rarely left the bedroom. Then we landed back home and all of a sudden I felt like I just downed three Big Gulps on my way to visit Niagara Falls. As I've mentioned before, my husband is a pediatrician, and he works in our local Emergency Room. When a doctor you personally know asks, "So have you done anything different or out of the ordinary lately?" it can be slightly awkward.

But you can avoid this! UTIs are caused by germs entering the urethra. Women tend to get UTIs more easily than men, and having sex can make it easier for germs to get where you don't want them. Yeast infections, on the other hand, are caused by an overgrowth of yeast in the vulva and vagina, which can be triggered by eating too much sugar, not drying off the genitalia properly, a bacterial imbalance, or other hormonal changes. Yeast infections can be treated with prescription drugs or over-the-counter creams and antifungals, while urinary tract infections are usually treated with antibiotics.

The tricky part is that if you get a UTI and take antibiotics to get rid of it, the antibiotics kill off all the good bacteria in your body. The lack of good bacteria can lead to a yeast infection, which leads to more treatments. It can be a vicious cycle!

But never fear! As long as you take a few simple precautions, you will likely avoid these two issues. Both you and your husband should urinate after each sexual encounter, because, as weird as it sounds, pee is sterile. It cleans everything out. Also, make sure your husband washes his genital area every day so no germs are transferred (though he doesn't have to rush to the shower before sex each time).

There's no need to become paranoid about these issues, though. Our vaginas are self-cleaning. You don't need to buy feminine wash products, because they can often throw off your healthy bacteria balance and lead to more problems. So go to the bathroom a lot, take probiotics, and for extra caution, do what I do now and bring along some cranberry juice and yogurt.

Think Shower

Speaking of staying clean, showering before you make love — if you're not too eager to jump into bed — can make the whole experience more pleasant. After all, if you're arriving at your honeymoon suite after a three-hour dance, chances are you're both pretty sweaty. Showering can make kissing and touching his body a more attractive proposition.

Now that you've dealt with the messy unknowns, what should you bring for your wedding night?

Think Lingerie

You'll want something pretty to wear on your wedding night. I've heard it said that lingerie is the most expensive item of clothing once the amount of time we wear it is factored in, since we tend to only have it on for a few seconds before it's ripped off of us. But it's the effect that counts! Besides, you'll likely feel far more confident in something — even if it's barely anything — than you will naked. So bring something cute.

A GOOD GIRL SPEAKS: *"I wish I had been less self-conscious and able to enjoy being naked together rather than worrying that my husband would notice my imperfections." (married 13 years)*

But don't *just* think lingerie. Here's the brutal facts: lingerie doesn't cover very much, and most hotel thermostats are set at 68 degrees. That's awfully cold if you're not wearing anything. So be sure to pack some regular pajamas too. Just make them satin, not flannel ones that button up to the collarbone!

But just because it's comforting to put something on (and warmer too!), don't be scared of being naked. Your husband is going to want to see your whole body — all of it. That can be scary if you're a virgin, because chances are few people have seen you naked before. Even if you're not a virgin, if most of your sexual encounters have been rather quick, you may never have been fully gazed at before.

He'll likely want to gaze. And that's good.

Even if you're a little nervous, try to drink it in. Realize how much he loves your body. It's like you're one big playground for him, and he will adore your body, no matter what it looks like. It's his now. If you can make yourself calm down, relax, and revel in how much he enjoys you, you'll start to feel far more sexually confident. Most of us are very insecure about our bodies. Instead of focusing on your feelings, see how he feels. Look at how much he loves you. See what an effect you're having on him. That's all you, honey. He finds you attractive. He finds you beautiful. Start believing it about yourself too.

A GOOD GIRL SPEAKS: *"What would I have done differently? Nothing, except maybe flushed my husband's contact lenses down the sink!" (married 19 years)*

When I was in grad school, a fellow student confided in me and several friends that his wife, after five years of marriage, still changed in the closet every day. He had never actually seen her naked with the lights on. Now the guy shouldn't have told us that; that was private information. But I always felt sorry for both of them. Many women are going to be very nervous and shy when they get married, but keep telling yourself: "I am beautiful. My husband thinks I'm beautiful." And hopefully you'll be able to fully appreciate your body too.

A GOOD GIRL SPEAKS: *"We should have taken more time to 'get to know' each other's bodies and desires!" (married 5 years)*

Think Lubricant

This Good Girl sums up the issue of using lubricants:

> I wish I had known that he wouldn't need *any* foreplay before sex and that I definitely would and how to deal with those differences.

Her solution?

"I wish I had brought lube!"

Sex is much easier if you're well lubricated (or, in other words, if your vagina is slippery). It makes it easier for your husband's penis to enter and makes it far more comfortable for you when he thrusts. When women are aroused, our bodies naturally produce fluids to keep us "wet." But when we're nervous, lubrication isn't something that is easy to achieve. Your husband may also be in quite a hurry, given his level of pent-up energy, so he may not spend as much time on touching and petting and kissing that you require in order to get aroused. So bring some lubricant with you, which is put on his penis to make him slide inside you more easily. You may not need it, but it's good to have it just in case (it also

A GOOD GIRL SPEAKS: *"I was thankful that someone had prepared us with this advice: (1) Get some lubricant. (2) You have the rest of your life. Don't ruin a good night with forcing the physical when you are tired." (married 13 years)*

makes quickies easier, and later in your honeymoon, if you're sore from a lot of "action," it can be a godsend)! K-Y Jelly is the best-known lubricant, but it can be a little messy. Astroglide works well and is less like petroleum jelly.

If you're like my respondent, disappointed that your husband rushed the encounter and didn't spend as much time on foreplay, take heart: once he has made love once, he's far more likely to take more time the second time to make it nice for you too. If he's a newbie at this, it will take awhile for things to start working well. In my survey, 30 percent of couples made love more than once that first night — and it was probably better each time!

Think Purity

The biggest surprise I had from my survey was how few of the respondents were virgins on their wedding night. The survey group was overwhelmingly Christian, and the Christians were taken from a pool of those who had been to retreats I was speaking at, those who read "Christian mom blogs," those who homeschool, and those who are actively involved in women's ministry. In other words, these are the groups that you would expect to be virgins when they wed. But only 37 percent of this group had been virgins on their wedding day. Another 24 percent had been sexually active with their fiancés, 32 percent had been sexually active with their fiancés and others, and 8 percent had been sexually active with others but not with their fiancés.

A GOOD GIRL SPEAKS: *"I don't regret a thing. It was as perfect as two virgins could produce!" (married 3 years)*

An open-ended question on the survey asked, "If you could do anything differently on your wedding night, what would it be?" Of those who were not virgins, 34 percent volunteered that they wished very much that they had waited. And that was without me even prompting. Had I asked the question outright — Do you regret previous sexual activity? — I'm sure the response would have been even higher. Listen to their voices:

"I wish we had waited for our wedding night."

"I wish I had saved myself for my husband."

"Although my husband and I only had sex twice before we got married, I wish we had waited until our wedding night for the first time."

"I wish I had been a virgin. I wish I had been less nervous and more relaxed. I wish I had felt more able to communicate about what I felt. I wish I didn't feel like 'What's the point? It isn't even real; we've already had sex.'"

"I wish that someone would have told me that every partner you have before marriage joins you in your marriage bed."

"I didn't know that God doesn't prohibit fornication to keep us from having fun, but to protect us. I wish I had known that having sex before marriage would create 'baggage' that would interfere with my intimacy with my husband (nothing physical, just emotional)."

"I wish I had not had sex with my husband before we got married. Even though he has been the only one, I have struggled with guilt over our entire marriage."

I've heard hundreds of these regrets. It's actually quite heartbreaking to read through them all. And here's what's even worse: many of these women reported making love for the first time just a few weeks before the wedding!

Perhaps you've been flirting with sex, letting things go further than they should. Take these women's comments to heart. No woman who had been a virgin on her wedding night reported, "I wish I had had more experience so I'd be better at it." Not a one. But over and over again women said, "I wish I had waited."

A GOOD GIRL SPEAKS: *"Wait for sex until after the ceremony. Even though my husband was the only one I had ever slept with, it was emotionally very different after the wedding." (married 12 years)*

And it wasn't only having sex they regretted. Here's one woman who wished she had been *more* of a virgin:

"Although we hadn't had intercourse, I wish we hadn't done so much sexually before we got married."

And here's another Good Girl:

"Though technically we were virgins because we hadn't had intercourse, we had done everything but. I wish we'd been committed to purity and spent more time talking/getting to know each other, because the sexual part took over and, I believe, robbed us of getting to know the 'whole person.' I ended up spending too much time with my now hubby, and relationships with girlfriends drifted. For that I'm sad."

Statistics also show the benefits of waiting. When asked to rate their current sex life on a scale of 1 to 10, with 1 being lousy and 10 being fireworks, only 18 percent of women who were virgins before they were married rated their sex life today as between 1 and 5 — as neutral or worse. In contrast, 27 percent who had had multiple partners rated it that way, and 24 percent who had slept with others, but not their husbands, rated it that way. Women who were virgins at their marriage were also more likely to rate their sex life higher today than were those who were more experienced. Only 12 percent of those who had been virgins rate their sex life as worse today than it was on their wedding night, compared with 26 percent of those who had had sex with their now-husbands before they were married and 27 percent who had had multiple partners. And it's not just because virgins tended to rate their sex life on their wedding night as bad! It's also because those who had more experience are more likely to rate their sex life *today* as being bad.

A GOOD GIRL SPEAKS: *"It likely sounds harsh, but if I could do anything differently, I would have married a Christian, and it would have been our first time. Perhaps it would have been terrible, but I plan to tell my daughter that it may be terrible, but it will get better!" (married 26 years)*

You will not regret waiting, but you likely will regret it if you don't. So make a commitment today, with your fiancé, to wait. You will start marriage on a much better footing!

Now I want to speak to those who already have some sexual experience before I address specific ideas to make sex meaningful, fun, and special on your honeymoon.

For Good Girls Who Are Already Sexually Active with Their Fiancés

I was speaking at a marriage conference recently when a young couple shyly approached me. They had a question. They agreed with everything we had said about sex in marriage, but they had a problem. They were already living together, and they weren't married. Their wedding was in two months. And they were in disagreement about what they should do now. She thought they should stop having sex until the wedding, and he figured, what's the difference? We've already done it. The horse has already left the barn.

I told them that God always honors those who choose to live by his standards — even if they've violated those standards in the past. Besides, they only have one honeymoon and one wedding night. If they keep having sex, then that night is just like any other night. They have the rest of their lives together, so surely they could sacrifice two months.

That's what Michael McManus, founder of Marriage Savers, encourages couples to do. He told *National Review Online* of a cohabiting couple whom he advised to separate until the wedding, and after much angst they agreed. "The couple had no sex for four months. They went on a honeymoon to the Caribbean, flew back to Miami to change planes, and called us from the airport.... Then they told us, 'Thank you for giving us a fantastic honeymoon!'"[2]

A GOOD GIRL SPEAKS: *"My husband and I became Christians about five years after we were married, and we were both sexually active before we met each other. I'd had one partner before him, and he'd had a few before me. Now our prayer for our children (we have three) is for them to wait until the commitment has been made and to enjoy each other for the first time on their wedding night, and for the rest of their lives, knowing there are no connections physically to anyone else in the world." (married 18 years)*

According to McManus, divorce is 71 percent higher for those who are not virgins when they marry compared to those who are. But even deciding to stop having sex now, before you're married, can reduce your risk of divorce and substantially help your relationship. When you do, you force yourself to find other things that bring you together. You work on your friendship. You talk. You have to build your relationship around something other than sex — which is key, since sex alone will not hold a marriage together.

Listen to this Good Girl:

> Even though we were sexually intimate before our marriage, we abstained during several months before the marriage. We wanted to make sure that that was not the main thing bringing us together ... and it was a wonderful night.

God knew what he was doing when he said, "Sex only in marriage." You can reclaim his blessings for yourself today. Talk to your fiancé about deciding to wait from today forward. And if he isn't willing to change, then I would ask whether he really does put God first. It's a matter of obedience to God and respect toward you. For your own good and the good of your marriage, I'd encourage you to stop what you're doing and wait!

For Good Girls Who Want to Reclaim the "First Time"

Can your wedding night and honeymoon be special if you've already "done it"? Absolutely! But it probably requires you to have some important talks with God about your sex life. Once you've confessed that you messed up, God doesn't see you as tainted, and you don't need to see yourself that way, either. Pray that God will help you have a new, fresh start with your husband. For the first time, your union will be blessed in every way.

It's not just about forgiveness or purity, though. It is also about realizing how different married sex can be from premarital sex. If you have had other sexual partners, you may assume that you already know what you're doing, or he may assume that he knows what he's doing. That's not necessarily so. We all react differently when it comes to sex. Not every woman enjoys her breasts being touched, for instance. Some women can't handle direct clitoral stimulation. Nobody should ever think they are a "good lover" based on past experiences before marriage, because everybody is different.

Even if you have already made love to your husband before marriage, don't assume that it will go the same way once you are married. The dynamics are completely different. Before marriage, sex is something forbidden, and that lends to its allure. Many couples who have amazing sex before marriage find that after marriage it becomes blah. A combination of factors conspires to rob us of pleasure: guilt, loss of the forbidden, and regret.

That doesn't mean that sex is a lost cause, though. Sixty-one percent of my survey respondents who reported deep regret for not waiting until they got married also report that today their sex lives are at least an 8 out of 10. They've recovered. That recovery, though, takes a willingness to see this as a new phase in your relationship. Don't make assumptions. Pretend that you've never had sex before, and try to get to know each other in a whole new way, because it *will* be new. You are now one flesh, not two. When you do make love after you're married, it's the first time you'll make love as an expression of commitment. For the first time you can really be free. Rejoice in that!

FOR ALL GOOD GIRLS: Think beyond the Wedding Night

We've gone over all the practical aspects of what to expect on the actual wedding night, but I feel a little bit like Paul at the end of 1 Corinthians 12. In that chapter, he outlined all the purposes and gifts in the church and how they're all vital. In chapter 14, he took up the same subject and went over decorum during worship. But in the middle of all these practical things, he took a bit of a detour, announcing, "And yet I will show you the most excellent way."

A GOOD GIRL SPEAKS: *"I wish I had taken more time to focus on making love and not just on having sex." (married 6 years)*

And then he wrote that beautiful chapter on love.

And now, girls, I would like to show you a more excellent way too.

And just like Paul's more excellent way, this one has everything to do with love as well.

Now that you are married, your husband is a new person and you are a new person. You are truly one flesh. No matter what your sexual experience, or lack thereof, this is the first time you're exploring his body when it's not just his body — it's also yours! Make it meaningful. Consider praying before you make love to dedicate the sexual part of your relationship to God.

But let's get practical. How do you bring the emotional and relational elements into something that is so physically anticipated? It sounds very mysterious, but I think it simply means paying attention to those areas of your relationship. Bring your friendship into it! Laugh together. Learn to be comfortable naked. Have a bath together. Play Scrabble or Monopoly naked together. Touch each other. And remember that if things don't work perfectly now, it's okay, because you're learning, and learning is good.

And how about feeling that spiritual connection? Kiss and memorize each other with your fingers, your eyes, your lips. You don't need to hurry. Use your different senses to memorize his body — and

A GOOD GIRL SPEAKS: *"Our wedding night wasn't that great, but we were both virgins, and our love life has greatly improved over the years. We have learned together, and that has been wonderful."* *(married 12 years)*

encourage him to use his. Trace your fingers along his body with your eyes closed, so that you can concentrate on what it feels like. Do the same with your eyes open. Revel in the newfound discovery. And when you do make love, look into his eyes when he enters you. Remember to say, "I love you."

If you spend time and care in the lead-up to actually making love, the physical side will also probably be wonderful too, because you've taken more time to get aroused, and you've taken time to reaffirm your relationship (which is, after all, the key to a woman's sex drive).

Many women do feel very nervous on their wedding night, and one thing that contributes to that nervousness is this idea that sex is something that happens "to" women — *he* is going to do something to *you*. No wonder sex can seem threatening! You may be one of those women who has no qualms about it at all, but if you do feel nervous, try to reframe the experience in your own mind.

This is something beautiful where you can truly share yourself — all of yourself — with someone who will love you forever. Instead of seeing sex as something that he does to you, then, think of it as something you do together. And the easiest way to deal with that is to take the lead in touching him and in getting to know his body. If you're more active, you'll be a participant, not just a recipient. Then you're much more in control.

Finally, if and when you decide to actually have intercourse, remember that he may be awfully quick. Don't be disappointed. Men tend to need less stimulation than women do to reach orgasm, but as you get used to things together, he will likely be able to make his erection last a little longer. He can also practice bringing you to orgasm another way, if you're comfortable with that. Be open to what you want at the time. You don't need a complete game plan now, before the fact, because you don't know how you'll feel in the moment.

A GOOD GIRL SPEAKS: *"We finally gave up on sex and just snuggled. I wish we would have just snuggled to start with and eased into the sexual relationship more." (married 14 years)*

Not everybody consummates their marriage on their wedding night, either. Whether it's because of exhaustion, tension, or your period, it may not happen for you. In our survey, about 15 percent of women didn't end up having sex on their wedding night. But that had absolutely no bearing on whether they enjoy sex today! So don't build the whole thing up in your mind too much. The more relax-and-see-what-happens attitude you both can have, the better it will be.

Does all of this mean you shouldn't care about reaching orgasm? No, of course not! God created our bodies to have the capacity to respond amazingly, and it's a beautiful thing. But we're more likely to experience that pinnacle when we also are cementing our friendship when we make love — by laughing and talking and feeling all those warm fuzzies. We're also more likely to reach it when we're feeling spiritually connected. All these things go together. Maybe you will be one of the few who reaches orgasm on her wedding night through intercourse. But whether or not you do, you can still feel that oneness. You can hug and rejoice and explore. You can experience that first taste of beautiful intimacy when you can be naked together, which is wonderful in and of itself. That is the real celebration.

Besides, if you have a "bad" wedding night, when you're not particularly relaxed and you don't orgasm, this has absolutely no bearing on the quality of your sex life later on. *Absolutely none.*

Don't believe me? Here are the numbers. Of the women who were virgins on their wedding night yet who orgasmed anyway, 65 percent rated their sex life today as great, 30 percent rated it as okay, and 5 percent rated it as awful. Among those who didn't orgasm at all? Sixty-four percent rated their sex life today as great, 28 percent rated it as okay, and 8 percent rated it as awful,[3] *virtually the same results.* Some women are really nervous on their honeymoon, and some are not. Some are willing to try lots of stuff right away, and some just can't. But it doesn't matter which group you're in; give yourself a few years of marriage and you'll end up in roughly the same place. So don't stress about it; be true to yourself, and you'll find that things will work out just as they're supposed to!

> **a good girl dare**
>
> Tell him what you like. Take a deep breath and let him know what feels good — even if you're still a little shy.

That's the basic outline of how sex works, and pretty much all you'll need to know for your wedding night. But after the honeymoon, when you've had time to explore a bit and you want sex to get even better, it will be time to learn more about the three aspects of sex that make it so great: the physical, the spiritual, and the relational. So now that you're prepared for the wedding night, let's look at how to prepare for your married journey together, by starting with the physical challenges some couples encounter.

CHAPTER 5

From Fizzle
to Sizzle for Her

I've already confessed that I love the movie *The Notebook* — though unfortunately it does romanticize sex before marriage. If I could have my wish, I would ask God to take Keith and me together, wrapped in each others' arms, the way Noah and Allie left this earth.

But movies like *The Notebook* can also send us into spasms of self-loathing, because sex doesn't work for us the way it worked for them. Everything went perfectly for that couple from the first time they made love, even though she was inexperienced. We wonder, *Why can't it work for me? What's wrong with me?*

Probably nothing. *The Notebook*, after all, is just a movie, and movies rarely bear much resemblance to real life. (How many of us wake up in the morning and kiss our husbands deeply with no thought of morning breath?) Nevertheless, before we marry, we tend to assume that sex will be just like that famous *Notebook* scene. We will fall into bed, collapse into each other's arms in ecstasy, and each time thereafter will be a glorious encounter.

Life doesn't work like that. Most couples experience physical issues with sex at some point in their marriages. Now maybe you're in a blessed marriage where everything began working like clockwork right off the bat. This chapter may not be necessary for you. But if you are having difficulties, here are some strategies to deal with the more common physical issues couples encounter. We'll start with the ones we women can be prone to.

A GOOD GIRL SPEAKS: *"It's not like the movies. It requires my active participation and concentration."* (married 10 years)

I Can't Reach Orgasm

You're not alone! More than half of women have difficulty reaching orgasm, according to a study of 587 women published in the *Journal of the British Association of Urological Surgeons*, with those under thirty reporting the biggest challenge.[1] Fifty-four percent of these women reported having problems, compared with 43 percent of women in the 31 – 45 age range.

So what to do? For women, orgasming is not an automatic response the way it is for most men. We need to feel relaxed, comfortable, loved, and cherished before we can even become aroused. And then, once we're aroused, we need to get even more relaxed before we can climax. It's quite tricky! Movies may paint it as the most natural thing in the world, but just because it's natural doesn't mean it's second nature. You may still have to work at it. And it's that working at it that can make it even harder to achieve. Get all nervous about attaining orgasm, and you're less likely to get there.

At its most basic, an orgasm involves a woman losing control and completely surrendering. You can't do that if you're still holding back — and worrying about whether you're going to get there is a big part of holding back. So you have to learn to relax. That's much easier to do if you take the attitude, *This will happen eventually. So let's try for it, but let's not get all worked up about it. Let's just enjoy ourselves and see what happens!* That being said, there's nothing wrong with trying to reach for the sky. And if you've done everything I've said in the previous chapter, then here are a few more tips.

It's usually easier to reach climax from your husband stimulat-

A GOOD GIRL SPEAKS: *"A woman needs to take responsibility for her own orgasm. You can't just lay there and expect it to happen. You need to tell your husband what you need and do the things that will help your body respond.... Sex is a learning process between two people. It is not like the garbage in the magazines that says objectively you can be a good lover. A good lover is someone who listens to and responds to the one they love. It is such a lie that there are 'special moves' you can do that will 'drive your man wild.' It's all about what turns your spouse on and feels good to your husband, not what five hundred other guys like."* *(married 17 years)*

ing your clitoris either manually or orally (with his fingers or his mouth) than it is through intercourse. That doesn't mean that you'll never experience an orgasm when he's inside you; it simply means that it sometimes takes time to perfect the technique. But the more you learn to experience an orgasm another way, the easier it can be to have an orgasm through intercourse. You'll then know what feels good, and you'll be far more aware of the changes your body is going through and your various arousal levels.

Take a week or so and teach him how to bring you to climax without intercourse. Get rid of the pressure on yourself to orgasm through sex, and work at reaching it in easier ways — through him touching your erogenous zones, whether they're your breasts, your mouth and ears, or between your legs. And pay special attention to how aroused you're feeling, on a scale of 1 – 10.

Intermittently during this play have him stop and ask you to rate your arousal level. Now notice how you're breathing, how wet you are, and how much you want him to keep going. Start to recognize the difference, for instance, between a 7 and a 4. Then notice the difference between a 9 and a 7. Think of 9 as the stage where it wouldn't take much to put you over the edge — that point where, if he were to stop, you'd burst into tears and desperately beg him to keep going. Just a little touch and you'll be there.

Once you've had a few sessions of this fun and you're very familiar with what a 9 is, have him touch you until you reach 9 and then start intercourse. You'll likely reach orgasm very quickly. Once this is easy for you, try to do the same thing at arousal level 8, and then at 7. The more attention you pay to your body's cues, the easier it will actually be for you to let go, because you're focusing on your body and what feels good rather than focusing in your mind on what you're supposed to be doing.

Perhaps you've tried something like this and you just can't get aroused. You're likely either too tense, or you have an abnormally low libido (see below under "I Never Seem to Want It"). If the problem is tension, starting your night together with a bath, a massage, or something that helps you relax, rather than just trying to "get to it" can help. Spend some time talking. When you're new at this, you need to feel safe and cherished first.

Sometimes, though, our tension goes deeper than that. An orgasm is the ultimate in letting go: you can't climax if you're overanalyzing everything. You have to be able to let your body be swept away with what it's feeling. That can be very difficult for some women, because it means letting go of control. Many of us like things orderly, clean, and predictable. That's one reason we're not always so fond of our bodies, because they can be smelly and messy and awkward. Sex, then, can seem vaguely distasteful at best, if not downright wrong. Letting go, being vulnerable, and being messy can all seem very threatening.

> **a good girl dare**
>
> Have trouble feeling in the mood at night? Jump in the shower with him in the morning!

As much as we may think that being orderly is being godly though, God is the one who designed sex to be messy! He doesn't want us to feel in control, because we're not supposed to be in control in anything. He is. And so perhaps it's only natural that in the most intimate moments we're not supposed to be totally clean and tame and sterile. Throw your head back and go with it. If that's a little intimidating, take some deep breaths and spend a lot of time just getting comfortable with each other's bodies until you can begin to value them just as they were made. So don't be afraid to tell your husband if you're struggling and you need to slow down while you make love. The more time he gives you, the better it will turn out for both of you.

I Don't Get Very Wet

Lack of lubrication is a problem that is relatively easy to solve. Lubrication is essential if sex is going to feel good for women, because dry skin rubbing against dry skin is just not that nice. Think of the difference between having a massage when you have oil all over your back and having a massage with rough hands and no oil. No comparison.

But we only produce lubrication if our hormones are in the right balance (menopause, for instance, just about kills lubrication in many women). Women also have normal fluctuations throughout the month when it's easier to get "wet." Right around ovulation tends to be a wetter time, while right after your period tends to be a relatively dry time when you might have to spend more time warming up to become lubricated. Devote enough time before you actually start intercourse to getting yourself relaxed and turned on! Take a bath together. Ask him to massage your back (just don't fall asleep!). Draw it out so that you're relaxed, and tell him why that's so important. Show him what you want. Guide his hand. No matter what the time of the month, if you're not relaxed, lubrication isn't likely to happen.

If all of that fails, though, there is an easy solution, and it costs about eight dollars. Just head on down to the pharmacy, and go to the area where they sell condoms. Somewhere around there you'll find products called "personal lubricants," like Astroglide. Once you use it, you'll likely find that it's much easier to get aroused.

If none of that works, check out the advice below under "I Never Seem to Want It."

It Hurts!

About 14 percent of women suffer from pain during intercourse, with 2 percent having full-blown vaginismus, the fancy word for pain caused when the vaginal muscles contract involuntarily. For those few who are tormented by this condition, it's horrible indeed. Many of these women can't insert tampons or handle pelvic exams at the doctor's office, either. One survey respondent, age twenty-nine and married for eight years, said, "My vaginismus put an end to sex years ago." Today she and her husband make love less than once a month.

Before you start panicking, let me assure you that most of those 14 percent of women who experience pain when they make love don't actually have vaginismus. It's simply that they're a little nervous and therefore a little bit more tense than they usually would be. And some women do feel more than just a little sting when the hymen tears. If the couple has sex a number of times over the next few days before that tear has healed, the pain can be aggravated. It will, however, subside with time.

The medical condition of vaginismus, on the other hand, is caused when the muscles at the one and a half inches closest to the opening of the vagina tense up. If you've used a tampon, you've probably encountered these muscles without realizing it, because once you get the tampon past that first inch and a half, it glides in much more easily.

A GOOD GIRL SPEAKS: *"Sex really does not feel good to me at all, so I am hesitant to have sex and rarely ever initiate it. I think that my husband has a problem trusting me because of this issue. I think he feels I'm not being completely honest when I say it hurts." (married 14 years)*

These muscles tense involuntarily; you're not doing it on purpose. Reassure yourself and your husband that if you're having this problem, it certainly is not deliberate. In fact, it's rather difficult to get those muscles to untense. But you can!

The best route to a cure is to identify the underlying reason for this condition. For some it's caused by a childhood trauma, like sexual abuse. For others, it's a relationship issue: you just don't feel safe and are unable to relax. If you take things slowly and work on why you don't feel safe and talk to counselors or mentors if any past abuse issues are a factor, you'll likely find that the pain will subside as your heart is healed.

Unfortunately, for many the causes just aren't clear. Even worse, there isn't very much a physician can do. In extreme cases, some women have had surgery to loosen the muscles or injections to make them more pliable, but this has a long recovery period, is very invasive, and is probably the last thing you want if you're already in pain "down there." Usually these treatments only become options for women who have experienced such extreme pain that they haven't been able to make love for years.

Hopefully you're not in those dire straits. What you can try to do is to train yourself to control those muscles and thus learn to relax them. Here's how: When you're peeing, try to stop the flow of urine. Feel those muscles? They're the pelvic floor muscles, the same ones that tense up when you have pain during sex. When you pee, try to tense and relax, tense and relax, three or four times until your body learns how to relax itself.[2]

Then, when you start to make love, have him enter you just a little way until it starts to hurt, and try the same thing: tense first, and then relax. You may have to spend a few minutes doing this (try to treat it like a game, and for him it will probably feel pleasurable, anyway, because you're squeezing him), and eventually you'll likely find that it doesn't hurt as much.

Other treatments include progressively larger "vaginal dilators." This sounds horribly clinical, but it's just another way of saying "putting increasingly larger things in there," building up to something that is about the thickness of an erect penis. Gynecologists and family doctors who specialize in this field often provide small silicone devices of various sizes to use, but if you really don't want to go to a doctor, you can be creative. Just make sure it's safe and that you use safe cleaner afterward to avoid infection. You can use this as part of your foreplay too, and see if you can handle narrow things, building up to thicker things.

When Debbie was married, she was afraid she'd have issues because she had never been able to use tampons, and she had been sexually abused as a child. Sure enough, she found sex very difficult. Her husband, Max, was extremely patient with her for the first four months, taking time to play around with her and get them both more relaxed. Then, when they finally did try intercourse again, she found that the pain had gone away because she felt so accepted and loved.

If sex hurts, tell your husband that story. Sure, it's hard to be patient. But his being patient will often be what helps you to be able to relax and release your real sexuality. For most women, vaginismus is a head thing. Our muscles tense up because we're scared, threatened, or worried, but it's completely involuntary. You can't make yourself stop. If you put pressure on yourself and feel badly about it, the pain will likely last a lot longer. The only thing you can do physically is train your body to relax. Emotionally you can learn to feel more comfortable in your relationship.

One more thought: communicate to your husband that you dream of a great sex life too. If he knows that this is still your goal — even if you don't know how you're going to get there — it's going to be much easier for him to be patient than if he thinks you're resigned to staying this way for the rest of your life.[3]

I Never Seem to Want To

In one of the surveys I conducted leading up to this book, 29 percent of women reported that they believed they had a lower sex drive than most women (though how they would judge this is difficult to say!). *Low*, though, is a relative term. Many women report having a low sex drive when really it's just that it's lower than their husband's. He wants sex every day — or several times a day — and she's content with a few times a week, or even once a week. That's not a low sex drive; that's just a discrepancy between sex drives. She's actually perfectly normal.

A GOOD GIRL SPEAKS: *"For the first ten years of our marriage, he had a high sex drive. Now that I've hit thirty, it seems we've switched places! So we're just relearning what a new normal is for us."*

And how is normal defined? According to research conducted at the University of Chicago, only 33 percent of women actually think about sex on their own initiative two or more times a week.[4] Truly low libidos are associated more with difficulties becoming aroused than they are with not thinking about sex very frequently. If you're doing everything right but just don't find your body responding *and* you rarely think about sex, even in your dreams, then you very well may have an abnormally low libido.

Ask to be tested for testosterone levels, since it's testosterone in both women and men that contributes to libido. Unfortunately for women, though, treatment has rather unpleasant side effects, including an increase in body hair, changes in voice, and mood swings. Nevertheless, for many women, testosterone cream, applied to the genitals, has worked wonders.

Before you turn to hormone therapy, with all of its side effects, though, perhaps a better route is to look at other factors to see if they could be contributing to lowering your libido. Some medical issues, like diabetes and thyroid disease, can lower libido too, so do talk to your doctor first to rule out serious health issues. Following are some other physical factors to be aware of.

Depression

Depression is definitely a libido killer, and to make matters worse, the medication used to combat most mood disorders is even more of a libido killer. Before you take antidepressants, talk to your doctor about whether this is the right course for you (for many women it is, but for some a temporary course may be sufficient). Thankfully, some antidepressants aren't associated with low libido, so if you do need them, ask if it's possible to take one that doesn't have that side effect.

Contraception

Hormonal birth control methods, like the Pill, have also been known to lower libido, so if you're using something hormonal and you find that your sex drive has disappeared, talk to your doctor about trying something else. Women often feel an increase in sexual desire smack in the middle of the cycle — when we are also the most fertile — because that is when testosterone levels increase. The Pill and other hormonal methods, like the ring or the injection, get rid of these peaks by eliminating ovulation and the hormonal burst that goes with it.[5]

A GOOD GUY SPEAKS: *Earlier in our marriage my wife's sex drive was a lot lower due to her being on the Pill. It was very frustrating to always be the one initiating and to often be told she was too tired. At times I felt resentment but just tried to suck it up and realize that she was still a wonderful person to be with. Now that she is in her early forties and no longer on the Pill, her sex drive is much higher and she enjoys sex a lot more. If only it could have been like this in our twenties! (married 18 years)*

Inactivity

Libido is largely a "use it or lose it" phenomenon. Those who have sex frequently are far more likely to think about sex and to become aroused faster than those who don't have sex very often. Single people who practice chastity, for instance, can often go for quite long periods without really thinking about sex, because their bodies become accustomed to doing without.

On the other hand, train your body to think about it and become responsive, and your libido may increase. That's what this twenty-seven-year-old Good Girl found:

> I feel that his drive is abnormally high and mine is abnormally low. (He agrees mine is low but thinks his is normal — what he would compare it to, I don't know!) He would like to be having sex daily; I'd be content with once a week.... We've settled into three-ish times per week usually, though that varies. I have learned through experience that if I just do it more — even if I'm not in the mood, if I will make the time — then I end up enjoying it, and it increases my own desire. So I have made efforts over the last couple of years to simply do it more often, and it has definitely helped my drive.

One way to help your body respond better is to actually make love more often. In fact, the more you make love, the more your body produces lubrication, which makes sex more enjoyable. Again, if you're simply not able to become aroused, a talk with your doctor is warranted. But if you just "never feel like it," try to jump in anyway! That's often the best way for those feelings to return.

I'm Pregnant!

By now you've probably gotten the message that sex for women depends on our brains. We have to be able to concentrate to enjoy it. And it's very hard to concentrate if you feel like you're going to throw up — which is one of the reasons that pregnancy can wreak havoc with your sex life. If nausea doesn't flatten you, it could be the extreme fatigue in the first few months or the kicking in the later months or the discomfort of being so huge. And if you become pregnant soon after you marry — or if you marry already being pregnant — then your marriage will be more challenging right from the beginning.

Here's some good news, though: many women find that pregnancy hormones actually increase their sex drives. That second trimester, between months four and six, can often be a sexually exciting time! One of my friends who has numerous children reports that she often has to wake her husband up at 5:30 a.m. in those middle months because she's just so turned on. Pregnancy does not have to be all bad news for your sex life.

Nevertheless, it does pose a challenge, especially since chances are your husband, as excited as he is about the baby, is also afraid of losing your attention. This doesn't mean he's a selfish pig; it simply means that you are important to him, and he's worried that a baby is going to supplant him. And you don't want that to happen, either.

But what do you do if you're busy puking and dreaming of nothing but sleep and food you can actually keep down? It may be that your sex life will take a dive in those first few months, but try to compensate by doing lots of touching and massaging or taking baths together, which can help you feel physically better.

What about if you do want to try sex? It won't hurt the baby. Honest. If you're having bleeding and the doctor tells you to refrain, that's one thing, but in the vast majority of healthy pregnancies, sex doesn't hurt the child at all. Later in your pregnancy, you may find that positions other than the standard "missionary" one are more comfortable, though. Many women enjoy being on top, since lying on one's back becomes impossible. "Spooning," with you both lying on your sides, him behind you, can also work. Then he can also reach around and stimulate your clitoris at the same time — even if it's a bit of trial and error of pregnancy gymnastics to make the position work in the first place!

The added benefit of sex is that it can bring on labor — so if you feel like a beached whale at your due date and Junior doesn't seem eager to emerge, why not try it? It just may benefit all three of you!

He Doesn't Turn My Crank

Last year I was teaching at a retreat where I was also asked to do a breakout session on increasing our libidos. During the question-and-answer session, one bold woman put up her hand and asked, rather emphatically, "What do you do if your husband is just gross?" Since their wedding, her husband had gained over a hundred pounds. She didn't exactly look at him and think, *Oooh, baby, come and take me.*

Besides the rather obvious problem of not being attracted to one's spouse, there's also the simple physical issue of him being rather heavy. Breathing, after all, is one of most people's favorite things to do, and feeling as if one is suffocating is hardly conducive to arousal.

Let's deal first with the attraction issue. As we've already looked at, sex is more than just the physical. It's the union between the spiritual, emotional, and physical aspects of our lives. Our society tends to glorify the physical over everything else, and so the intimacy that we can feel just from being close to someone we love is underrated. If the physical part of your marriage isn't exhilarating, maybe the companionship is. So focus on being emotionally intimate. Take walks together. Do things together. Laugh together. Play together. The more you spend time in each other's company cherishing each other, the more you will want to express that physically.

And then just stress the companionship when making love. Look into his eyes. Remind yourself of what you love about him. What you find sweet about him. What makes him a great husband. Repeat these things over and over to yourself so that you're concentrating on his assets rather than his paunch. After all, wouldn't you rather have him, even with the extra weight, than not have him at all?

When you do make love, focus on positions that are easier for you. Try being on top, or have him sit back in a chair while you straddle him. That way you can still breathe comfortably, and his girth doesn't obstruct the action quite as much!

Now let's get back to the issue of what he looks like. You're the woman! Chances are you control what food comes into the house. Start cooking healthy meals, and get rid of high-fat foods and empty carbs. And while you're at it, move the television to a place where it's not central in the house. Head out for a walk every evening after dinner. Take up cross-country skiing or bowling or ballroom dancing. Find something you can have fun doing together that gets you off the couch. You likely influence the household's activities more than he does, so use that influence to your advantage. Men who are married live, on average, about eight years longer than single men because their wives take care of them. Start taking care of your husband!

A few years ago I was noticing that both my husband and I were inching up on the scale again. I had gained about ten pounds in one year, and while I wasn't gaining anymore, I didn't want those ten pounds, either. He had gained twenty, and I was finding him a little heavy. So we made a bet. I had to lose ten pounds, and he had to lose twenty. And whoever achieved their goal first got whatever they wanted for two weeks straight, every day. That's right. Whatever they wanted. I was looking forward to a forty-five-minute massage every night, and he was leaning toward something far more basic.

> **a good girl dare**
>
> Reserve one common activity — like making the bed, doing the dishes, or folding laundry — where you commit to thinking about sex while you do it. That gets your libido jump-started at regular times throughout the day!

He won. And I followed through. He was a very happy man, but I won as well because he had lost that weight! And I came within two pounds of my own goal, so it was a good motivator.

I Don't Feel Sexy

When we women don't feel sexy, it's hard to make love, because for us so much of sex is feeling desired. How can we feel desired if we don't think we're worthy of it? We know our every extra inch, every pimple, every roll of fat, every stray hair, and we're not happy about it. Our instinct is to keep it covered up — and go for the chocolate.

And sometimes our husbands make it worse! I have been out to lunch with couples and heard the husband question his wife's menu choices. It made me want to throttle him! Here's how one Good Girl describes her struggles:

> My husband is not as attracted to me sexually because of my size, which is a size 12. His preference is about a size 4. I know he loves me, is so good to me … but he makes it clear he would be more [attracted to me] if I was smaller. I'm happy with myself even though I know he isn't. Even so, I am trying to lose weight. I want to please my husband and still like myself. My husband is so wonderful to me. If he was more attracted to me, I can't imagine what it would be like, yet he tells me this is how he feels. I sometimes feel very undesirable because I am aware of his feelings. He doesn't want to hurt me, but he is honest with me.

If your husband is making disparaging comments about your body, even if they're "honest," tell him how that makes you feel. And add this: most people who lose weight are able to do so because they feel confident about themselves and who they are, not because they feel ashamed and defeated. Which does he want you to feel? If disparaging comments about your weight become commonplace, and if he starts criticizing your food choices in public, seek out a mentor to confide in. This type of behavior can border on abusive, and it's likely a good idea to find some wise counsel and a new perspective on your interactions.

How can you start feeling more confident? Maybe it's time to think differently about our bodies. We need to use our bodies or lose them; use them not just because we want to look good, but mostly

---

A GOOD GIRL SPEAKS: *"After I had my first baby, I weighed twenty pounds more, and … my body had changed for the worse. My husband would 'caution' me on what I was eating (even though I was breast-feeding). He also would make comments about 'fat' people. Because I felt embarrassed about my body and no longer felt sexually attractive, I no longer wanted to be seen naked or initiate sex. When my husband questioned me on this, I told him I felt under constant judgment by him and that I knew that my body disgusted him. From that day forward, he stopped being critical of what I was eating and started showing me how much he enjoyed my body. After twenty years together, sex only gets better every year."*

because we want to *feel* good. I've started an exercise program lately, and I'm really enjoying it. If I begin my day in an active way, I tend to want to end it that way too. I feel proud of my body throughout the day. I stretch it. I push the limits. I make my heart rate go up. When we feel less like schlumps, we're more inclined to be excited about our bodies!

So if you want to turn up your sex drive, discover what your body can do, even outside the bedroom. Push your limits. Don't be so ashamed of your body that you hide it in oversized clothes (more on that later). The more we love our bodies, the more we're going to want to use them in other ways.

Last Thoughts: Embracing Sex When You Feel Awful

I recently received an email from a woman, married ten years, who was in a very difficult spot. She suffered from chronic pain, which made sex very difficult; she preferred not to have sex at all. Her husband didn't think he could live like that. Interestingly, the next week I received another email from another middle-aged woman in turmoil. Her husband had announced that he was going to start having affairs. They hadn't had sex in five years since her hysterectomy, which had stolen her libido. She hadn't felt like it, so she had told him their sex life was over. He now wanted to stay married for their social life and their children, but he was going to look for sex elsewhere.

At times in your relationship, whether it's due to pregnancy, hormones, or health concerns, sex may become painful or difficult. That leads to the unfortunate dynamic where your husband wants to get pleasure from something that causes you pain. You're at loggerheads: he wants something that you feel that you can't give him, so you don't feel loved; and you don't feel like you can give him what he feels he needs, so he doesn't feel loved. Both of you require the other to give something that seems too large to give. What needs to happen is not that someone gives in and just ignores their own needs; for true oneness, a mind-set shift is necessary.

Since women's sex drives are largely in our heads, in order for us to become aroused, our heads have to be engaged. But we are extremely distractible. If a stray thought comes into our heads, we can lose any amount of arousal we feel. Thus, "Not tonight, honey, because I have a headache" is very real for most women. When we're feeling the intrusion of pain, it is supremely hard to get in the mood.

A GOOD GIRL SPEAKS: *"Through a very good Christian mentor who had a great marriage, I learned very early that a man's need for sex must not be minimized. It was as important to him as anything on my list was to me. It did not make him shallow to want sex so badly; it made him male. As his wife, I needed to understand that and make it a priority." (married 12 years)*

Nevertheless, sex is often the best treatment. Researchers have found that one of the best cures for migraines is sex. The sudden release and euphoria often stop the pain. Frequent sex even seems to prevent migraines. So even though it's counterintuitive, sex often helps with headaches. The same is true for muscle pain. Sex allows muscles to relax, giving a tremendous physical boost. And it helps us sleep so much better!

I know it's hard to see sex as a cure when you're in pain, but pray that God starts prompting you to view it as something that can actually help with pain, not something that contributes to it. When sex becomes all about something you do for your husband, it's a chore, and it's only going to add to your pain and exhaustion. When sex becomes something you can share that can help you relax and feel less pain, you have a stake in it too.

That's a pretty big leap, and I'm not trying to minimize how large the gulf may be. But for most conditions, sex, in and of itself, won't make anything worse. On the other hand, it has the potential to actually make you feel better and certainly sleep more deeply!

The key is to get to the point where you can actually physically enjoy sex even when your body itself is in great discomfort and very tense. It may be that you need to spend a lot of time relaxing first, in a hot bath with your spouse or with a massage. You may need to work at finding a position that feels comfortable for you. You may even need to work at achieving orgasm for you some other way than intercourse (even if he achieves orgasm through intercourse), since it's orgasm that's most likely to help you relax.

Explain to your husband that you really do love him and cherish him, and you want your marriage to be great, but you're really down and exhausted by this pain. You want to see if you can start connecting physically and sexually so that you feel better together, but also so that your body finds new ways to relax and get some sleep. That means that sex has to be something, for you, that is gentle, drawn out, and low pressure. But it also means that, for him, it's something that should be regular. He'll have to become awesome at foreplay, especially massage. But the good part is that you get to connect a lot more and feel a lot more intimate.

I know that's not easy. I know it feels like he's being selfish. But there is no way to fix this problem without sex being part of the solution. The woman who swore off sex after her hysterectomy destroyed her marriage. Somehow you have to change the dynamic so you're not at loggerheads. But you won't succeed unless you make that mind shift that sex can be about you and for you; it's not just something you do for him that you need to "get through."

Sex was not created just for men. It was created for us to enjoy, and learning to experience sexual pleasure is part of living life abundantly. Sure, sometimes we're going to feel physically awful, but wouldn't it be wonderful to get to the point where sex is seen as something that makes you feel better — something that you long to do to feel energized, relaxed, and just plain amazing? That's what it can be! If that doesn't seem possible right now, just believe it, pray about it, and commit it to God. It is his intention for you, and in his grace he can help you discover the sexual woman inside you.

a good girl dare

Spend some real money on a proper bra fitting and a high-quality bra. Find one that makes you look amazing—and feel really sexy.

CHAPTER 6

From Fizzle
to Sizzle for Him

When our daughters were six and four, we treated them to a day at the zoo. They loved the orangutans, penguins, and polar bears. But when we hit the Japanese macaque exhibit, Keith and I froze in our tracks. All around us, parents were shielding kids' eyes from these large monkeys. For there, for all to see, was one very large male macaque humping every female in sight. He'd launch onto one, thrust a few times, and then grab another for good measure.

"Look, Mommy!" Rebecca exclaimed. "He's playing horsey! The monkey is playing horsey!" She talked about that randy monkey all through the zoo that day, and as we were exiting, she announced to the smiling attendant, "We saw monkeys playing horsey!" The woman shot a knowing glance our way.

Many men would secretly love to be able to copy that monkey — though we hope they'd settle for only one partner rather than four. Having sex all day without any problems is definitely alpha male behavior. But while men may share goals with these monkeys, they don't share much else. In the animal kingdom, males with mates don't have problems with sex. Virility is pretty much guaranteed, because if he can't do the deed, the female will move on to a younger, more virile animal that then gets all the sex. So most male animals only mate when they're young, tough, and able to perform. Those young animals don't have to worry about things like romance, relationship issues, or rejection. Their females are always ready. And if things somehow don't work, they get ousted. End of story.

While male sexual dysfunction gets weeded out in the rest of the animal kingdom, it finds rather effective breeding grounds in modern marriages. Health problems, relationship issues, and stress can all hinder a man's ability to perform sexually. And when things start to go wrong in the bedroom, men often panic even worse than women do, because their self-esteem is so closely related to their sexual prowess. Panic, though, almost always makes things worse. So when things aren't working, here are some specific strategies to relax and rebuild your physical lives.

Erectile Dysfunction (Impotence)

Men's biggest fear in the bedroom is that they're going to start the deed but not be able to finish, that they will lose their erection during the main event. Most men experience this at least once in the first decade of marriage, and the incidence of it increases with age.

A GOOD GIRL SPEAKS: *"We both have health issues and medications that affect [our sex life], and we are very supportive of each other. We find other ways to be close."*

According to the National Institute of Health, chronic erectile dysfunction (ED) affects 4 percent of men in their 50s, 17 percent of men in their 60s, and 47 percent of men over 75. Transient, or temporary, ED affects about 50 percent of men between 40 and 70.[1] About 70 percent of chronic ED has physical roots, while the rest has psychological and emotional roots. Let's tackle the physical roots first.

Erections are caused by blood flowing to the penis, so an erection depends on good circulation. That's why erectile dysfunction can be one of the first signs of coronary artery disease, even in men with few other risk factors. In fact, those with erectile dysfunction double their risk of heart attacks.[2] Men may hate going to the doctor, but if ED is a chronic problem, it's definitely worth having a doctor take a look.

Anything that hinders circulation or decreases one's heart rate can also easily lead to erectile dysfunction, including smoking and alcohol use, so encourage your husband to cut back if he wants to have more sex. Diabetes and hypothyroidism are also strongly linked to ED. If your husband has chronic ED, talk to a doctor, since it could be an early warning sign of all kinds of medical conditions. And even if it's not, those little blue pills can help a lot!

One woman, whose husband is in his sixties, wrote this:

> He is having prostate problems, and although he can still function, he is embarrassed, feels he isn't as much a man. In the past this might have been a big problem, but it's actually not bad now; we're actually growing closer in other ways because of it. Getting to be closer friends, etc.... That's pretty cool.

This woman has a great attitude and a wonderful way to look at the problem. When your husband's body stops working like clockwork, remember that there is more to your relationship than sex.

Even if your husband doesn't suffer from ED, as men age it often takes more direct stimulation to produce an erection and to keep one, let alone to reach orgasm. For many men, this is actually a major benefit — they find they can make sex last longer than when they were twenty-three and desperate. It's also part of the reason why older men are labeled better lovers — they're able to last a lot longer.

But when true ED strikes, without obvious physical roots, it can certainly take its toll on a relationship. If a physical cause can't be identified, the problem is usually a psychological or emotional one. Whether the culprit is challenges at work or worries about the relationship, the cause of ED is often directly related to a man's insecurity about his masculinity. *Am I able to provide for the family? Does she really respect me? Does she still want to be here?* It also often strikes around issues of fatherhood: many men develop ED during periods of infertility, and many others develop it after a child arrives — they're afraid of the added responsibility that babies bring. Others experience it during periods of unemployment.

In all of these cases, ED shouldn't really be a cause for concern,

---

a good girl dare

Does he spend time on his computer and you on yours? Set up a video connection between the two of you (if you have a secure Internet connection that's password encrypted). Pop up on his screen to entice him to bed in a more graphic way.

because it will likely end as soon as the man feels better about himself. Take the focus off sex and put it on your relationship. And above all, don't contribute to the "impotence domino effect" that occurs when one night doesn't go very well and he freaks out about it and questions his masculinity so much that it keeps recurring. When it does happen, laugh it off and tell him, "I know it will work tomorrow, so let's just do something else fun," and then watch a movie together. Don't dwell on it. Don't even talk about it too much. Certainly don't baby him! Just treat him exactly as you normally would, and then try again a day or two later.

If the problem keeps recurring for several months and your husband has seen a doctor to rule out physical causes and you've worked on your friendship, your husband may benefit from talking to a counselor or an older mentor to deal with whatever insecurities he feels.

Premature Ejaculation

Premature ejaculation is when a man ejaculates before the woman can enjoy sex. Personally, I hate the term: it's labeling the man with a problem because *the woman's* response time is later. It's really a couple's problem, where he reaches orgasm before she is anywhere near. By the term currently used, though, a guy who reaches orgasm after twelve minutes, if his wife takes closer to twenty, is suffering from this condition too!

Doctors used to try to define premature ejaculation as a specific time frame — for example, men reaching orgasm before two minutes — but that has been thrown out since we now know that most men can reach orgasm that quickly if they try. Now it's being defined as when a lack of ejaculatory control interferes with the sexual enjoyment of one or both partners.

It's quite likely that most men, when first married, aren't going to be able to drag intercourse out beyond a few minutes before they climax, especially if they are sexually inexperienced. Sex is something new that's highly exciting. They haven't yet learned to control their body's reflexes. So don't start worrying about premature ejaculation until you've given your poor guy time to get used to sex!

Once you've been sexually active for a while together, though, he can start to develop some strategies to delay orgasm. Some men simply think of something very unarousing — like baseball stats, football games, or multiplication tables. That technique may not sound romantic, but it helps a lot of guys last longer! Others try the "start and stop" method, where he gets aroused but then stops intercourse and concentrates on stimulating and petting you, in order to draw out the encounter.

If sex continues to be over too quickly for you to enjoy it, don't start actual intercourse until you're already highly aroused. Spend a ton of time relaxing together and in foreplay, so that by the time he enters you, you're almost ready to go.

He's Never in the Mood!

On my blog, I write predominantly about marriage and sex, and because of that, women who face problems in the bedroom often email me. And the most common complaint? "My husband doesn't want to have sex." A typical email says something like, "I am so sick of hearing women complain about how their husbands want it all the time. I just want my husband to want it *some* of the time!"

One forty-two-year-old woman, married for eighteen years, explains the rejection she feels this way:

> Because my husband does not want me sexually, I have a hard time believing him when he tells me how much he loves me. We have a friendship, a life together, but without sex and affection it feels like we are roommates more than anything else. I often feel very alone in this, because so many women talk about how their husbands want sex more than they do. I'll just say that not being wanted feels awful.

Another twenty-three-year-old woman, married just a few months, echoed her thoughts:

> I expected my husband's drive to be stronger than mine, so

when mine turned out to be stronger, I felt extremely unwanted. It has impacted the beginning of our marriage in a terrible way.

If you're experiencing something similar, you are not alone. Many women who endure their husbands' low sex drives, though, are often greeted with jeers from their friends — "I wish my husband would give me a break sometimes!" That doesn't help. You feel like a freak. Why does everyone else's husband want sex, and yours doesn't?

But you're not a freak. In one of the surveys that I took for this book, 23 percent of the female respondents stated that they had the higher sex drive.[3] The *Journal of the American Medical Association* published a 1999 study finding that 31 percent of males suffered from decreased libido,[4] so it's hardly a rare problem. Here are some of the causes.

Low Testosterone

About five million American men suffer from low testosterone, the hormone responsible for sexual arousal. If your husband seems to have a low libido, try to convince him to have it checked out. A simple blood test can verify whether he does indeed have low hormone levels. Assuming nothing else is wrong (often there's an underlying disease causing low testosterone, which would have to be treated), low testosterone on its own can be corrected with hormone replacement therapy.[5]

A GOOD GIRL SPEAKS: *"In the past, my hubby had little to no sex drive. His doctor tested him for testosterone, and he was way low. Put him on meds, and wowza! He wants me as much as I want him." (married 28 years)*

Weight Problems

In some cases, male low libido is simply a physical issue. And the "biggest" culprit? Fat. Fat cells produce estrogen, which works against testosterone — the libido builder — in men. The more estrogen, the less desire. Robert Rister, author and chemist who has written at length on how to cure low libido naturally, says, "Nothing does more to restore male sex drive than achieving normal weight."[6] It boosts men's self-esteem because they feel physically better about themselves, and it cuts down on estrogen. And here's another tip: stay away from beer. Hops, the main ingredient in beer, acts very similarly to the way estrogen does in your body. In the Middle Ages, monks used to make their teenage novices drink beer to quell sexual desire, reports Rister. Beer has even been linked to erectile dysfunction. Flee from hops, and the beer gut will go away too!

A GOOD GIRL SPEAKS: *"My husband was diagnosed with diabetes not long after we got married, so I have struggled with having a higher sex drive. He just does not get in the mood. He enjoys it, and everything works right — it's just getting him going that's the problem. Since he does not have much of a sex drive, he is not very intimate, and that frustrates me more than the lack of sex drive. He does not think to kiss or hold hands. There's no affection." (married 14 years)*

Pornography

Another huge libido stealer for men is pornography. The more men are into pornography, the less they are into sex in real life. Porn trains the brain to be aroused by an image and not a relationship. If your husband is into pornography, get help. Talk to a pastor. Talk to a mentor. Visit *www.pureintimacy.org*. Porn is not harmless, and it's not just fun. In the next chapter, we'll look at how to plot a recovery plan for your marriage.

Addiction

Addiction to porn will lower his libido, but so will addiction to just about anything. If he spends hours every night with video games or watching TV, he's not likely to want to make love very often, either. Addiction to alcohol or any kind of drug can also lower one's sex drive.

When addiction affects a couple's sexual relationship, it does need to be dealt with, but remember that a genuine addiction is not easy to break. The problem is not so much that your husband is rejecting you sexually as it is that, because he is so consumed with something else, he is unable to feel aroused or excited. That consuming feeling is very difficult for him to fight against. Sure, the addiction is wrong, but you'll be better able to help him through his struggles if you realize that chemically and emotionally his lack of interest in sex is not necessarily a rejection of you; it is simply a physiological response to something else. Look for addiction recovery groups in your area to get advice on steps you can take to help him.

Workaholism

Sometimes the addiction isn't focused on something negative — such as alcohol or video games or porn — but on something seemingly positive, such as work. And work provides an awfully strong temptation, because men tend to thrive when they feel competent. In fact, they thrive *where* they feel competent. And if your husband doesn't feel competent or involved at home, it is quite likely that he will look for other places to invest most of his energy. For many men, that place is work. They derive such satisfaction from building a business, earning money or prestige, or just working hard and accomplishing something that all of their passion, drive, and energy are devoted to work, not to you.

Of course, some men retreat into work when there is nothing at all wrong at home. Many boys grow up feeling as if they need to prove their own worth, and the way that men traditionally do that is through work, not through doing dishes or changing diapers or pulling out the new toilet-paper roll. But when men are so focused on work that they ignore the home, their libidos can easily suffer.

Do wives have any ability to reclaim workaholic husbands? Here's one thought: why not use his own strategies to bring him back home? A workaholic type of man tends to appreciate goal-setting exercises, spreadsheets, and mission statements. Ask him to sit down and set some goals for the family. Where does he want to see the family in ten years? What kind of people does he want his kids to be? What is important to him that he wants to make sure is passed on? And then make a plan to accomplish those things. As he starts thinking over the long term for the family, he may buy into the idea that he needs to devote some energy to home too.

If, on the other hand, you berate him and nag him for not being home, you'll likely send him running even harder for work, where he's praised and admired. Create a home where you laugh and where you demonstrate respect and love. Carve out time to value him and have fun with him so that home life becomes a haven and a source of strength for him too.

Lack of Friendship

Often when there is a problem in the marriage, it shows up in the bedroom. But because the *symptom* is in the bedroom, we often think the *solution* is too. So we concentrate on strategies that have to do with sex — buying lingerie, playing risqué games, using toys, watching porn, trying new things.

In reality, the solution is often found *outside* the bedroom. Sex embodies our spiritual, emotional, and relational selves. If your husband has a low sex drive that isn't due to health problems or addictions, then the best route to a solution is to work on your friendship. Spend more time together. Take a walk after dinner. Find a hobby you can enjoy together. Do something that he likes even if you don't (e.g., watching hockey games) simply so you can be together.

But what if you're a sports widow or a video game widow? Perhaps you're still just engaged, but you're wondering why your fiancé often finds the latest version of Call of Duty more attractive than spending the afternoon on a walk with you. Many females feel as if we're competing with electronics — and usually losing.

What do you do to recapture him? Standing naked in front of the TV doesn't work; many of my Facebook fans have reported with frustration that their husbands choose baseball over breasts. So what's a girl to do?

Don't get lazy. Many couples live separate lives because they slowly drift into them. One night he comes home, and he's tired so he slumps in front of the television instead of talking to her. She heads to the computer to check Facebook. And soon these separate lives become the norm. When kids arrive, it only gets worse. If you want to spice things up, don't look at the bedroom. Look at the gym.

Or the ice rink. Or the restaurant. Do stuff together. Eat dinner at an actual table where you can talk. Often this helps you feel connected, and then, even if the sex doesn't always follow, at least you feel more kindly toward each other.

Lack of Respect

Girls, watch how you talk to your husband. Undermining our men is remarkably easy. I know many Christian women who belittle their husbands in public without realizing it. When you open your mouth to say something about your husband to others, make sure that comment is something uplifting. And when you're alone, express gratitude much more than you express criticism. But our respect for our husbands needs to go even further than that.

John Eldredge, in his groundbreaking book *Wild at Heart*, argues that every man needs three stories to his life: an adventure to live, a beauty to rescue, and a battle to fight. Too many men don't live out any of these. At work they do what their bosses tell them, unable to take much initiative. They aren't fighting for anything or leading anything. Then they come home, where frequently their wives have set the tone, and they get very little say there, either. They don't get to rescue their wives from problems; we won't even listen to their opinions.

This dynamic often becomes evident almost as soon as children arrive. We women assume we're the better parent, and so we inadvertently shove our husbands away. It's our sphere, not theirs. Then, as the children grow, what if we raise them in a way that our husbands dislike? They may further retreat, especially if the children are not fun to be around. Many men simply want order in their lives, and children aren't orderly. If we wives push our husbands away from the kids and take on the whole job ourselves, and then we fail to discipline, kids can easily become out of control. Husbands aren't usually very enthusiastic about sharing this chaos.

Ask yourself this: is your home one in which your husband would want to participate? I'm not blaming you if he's retreating; after all, he could just as easily have taken initiative to discipline the kids or spend more time with them too. But if you have set the tone for the house and made it clear that you're not interested in his opinions or his techniques, then perhaps it's no wonder he doesn't want to be around.

When my children were six and four, I was very active with them. We ventured out to the library twice a week, to playgroup once a week, to women's Bible study, to friends' homes. We had other children in our home. We made crafts. We baked. Our home was fun, but it was also always a complete mess.

One day Keith sat me down and told me he was sick of coming home to a disaster in the living room. He could handle the basement being a mess; he could even handle their rooms or the bathroom being a mess. But he just wanted to open the door and see an inviting house.

I did not take that very well. I think the words *maid* and *Neanderthal* escaped my lips. But looking back, I can see how I was telling him, "I know what's best for the kids; I'm home all day, so you need to bow to what I say." My husband was not the kind who would retreat, for which I am eternally grateful. But I can see why many in his situation would. He was being told that his opinion didn't count for anything, and that while he wanted a place in this world that reflected him, I was more interested in what I envisioned for the family.

Ladies, if something is important to your husband, it should matter to you. Some men retreat simply because they get the impression they aren't wanted, and so they try to carve out a place in the world where they can escape. Before blaming him for running away emotionally and sexually, ask yourself if you have done anything to push him out. And if you have, maybe it's time to ask his opinion and start honoring it again.

Lack of Confidence

Other men have trouble with libido because they're scared of sex itself. One thirty-two-year-old woman who reports having sex less than once a month explains that the problem is her husband's upbringing: "We're still trying to work through the damage done by his parents' fundamentalist teachings of sex, thus making him feel like sex is a bad thing."

Still others suffer from fear: fear they're not good in bed, fear that they're inadequate compared to your past lovers, or fear that they may experience erectile dysfunction. For these emotionally based fears, the best defense is building your friendship and the trust in your relationship so that he knows you accept him completely.

When a Reason Can't Be Found

Unfortunately, though, many women will walk through life in a marriage with a husband who really doesn't seem to desire her, through no fault of her own. After all, in a given population, it's only natural that some men will fall on either end of the spectrum — some are going to desire sex more than usual, and some less. Your husband's sex drive may be atypical, but that doesn't mean that it's *pathologically* atypical. Or, to put it in layman's terms, it may not be normal, but that doesn't mean there's necessarily something really wrong.

That's hardly comfort, though, when you're lying in bed wanting to make love and he's already snoring. This is a tough thing to live with — perhaps even tougher than when the situation is reversed, because it is women who are supposed to be desired and chased. Listen to this twenty-nine-year-old woman, married for four years, explain how frustrated she is:

A GOOD GIRL SPEAKS: *"My husband's lack of interest stems from his chronic pain issues. He takes various medications every day and often feels depressed by his ongoing pain. In all honesty, I probably would too if the situation were reversed. However, despite the fact that I know this on a logical level, as a woman with vacillating emotions, I tend to blame his lack of interest on me — meaning there must be something wrong with me. It was the same when he was using pornography. I felt like I wasn't good enough to satisfy him, so he literally had to look elsewhere."* (married 12 years)

> The thing that we've fought about the most in our marriage is our sex life. I feel like I've fallen into some strange parallel universe where I have to beg my husband to have sex with me! I'm

attractive, keep myself looking nice, and I'm not overweight ... and I've tried everything. In most marriage books, I can usually relate more to the sections about frustrated husbands wanting more sex from their wives. The only problem is, there's no advice for me to turn to! Either everyone assumes that he's using pornography (he's not) or that he's cheating (he's definitely not), or that *I'm* doing something wrong as a wife, and trust me, I've tried *everything*.

It's been difficult for us, and I've started to hate approaching him for sex, because I know that I have a high likelihood of being turned down. Everything else in our relationship is great — our friendship, our compatibility, our love for each other — but we just don't "click" when it comes to how often we each need sex. He's like a sex camel — he could go for *weeks*. I need it/want it about three to four times a week.

All the books make me feel like some sort of sex addict or like I'm not really a feminine woman because I want sex and I have actual physical desire for it — not *just* for the hand holding and to be made to feel loved, but because women, like men, sometimes *need sex*. I just don't know what to do anymore, and I feel helpless about the future of our sexual relationship.

Are you married to a sex camel too? This woman is hurting, and she brings up something very important: we women do have sex drives. Many women don't experience that longing or need for sex because they have sex fairly regularly with their husbands. They never have a chance for desire to build. But when desire does build and there's no outlet, it's not only physically difficult, it's emotionally difficult too. *How come he doesn't want me?*

If your situation is similar to this woman's, you're certain no porn is involved, and you've ruled out the other causes, then you need to come to terms with the fact that this may be the natural state of your marriage. Talk to your husband about how you feel. If he's a Christian, make sure you attend a Bible-believing church that emphasizes the responsibilities that both spouses have to each other, so that he recognizes he has a duty toward you. But none of this will likely give you the frequency of sex you desire.

Unfortunately, such situations leave women with some serious temptations. You have sexual needs that aren't being fulfilled, and let's face it: many men out there would be glad to help. You may not be looking, but don't kid yourself that you're not vulnerable. Drawing boundaries around yourself is even more necessary to help your marriage. Don't be alone with coworkers unless absolutely necessary. Watch how you talk to other men. Be careful about becoming too emotionally involved with someone who is not your husband, because it could lead to something else — even if you're not specifically looking for that.

The other temptation isn't an affair per se, but it's finding sexual release outside of marriage nonetheless. We often think of pornography as a male problem, but 25 percent of the respondents in my survey also admitted having pornography issues. Turning to pornography and masturbation can seem like the "kind" thing to do when your husband looks on sex as a chore. You relieve the pressure that your husband feels to make love, you relieve your own sexual tension, and then nobody feels bad!

It doesn't work that way. The real issue is that you aren't connecting with your spouse. Creating a secret sexual side of your life doesn't help that connection; it hinders it. It gives you less incentive to work on the relationship, and it continues to frame your husband

A GOOD GIRL SPEAKS: *"I wanted to have sex all the time when we were first married and initiated it all the time and loved it. I thought I was the problem and just was a 'nympho.' I started to talk about it with some of my girlfriends, and I seemed to be the only one who wanted it as much as a guy. I have tried to find resources to help me with this, and I have talked with my husband about him being tested for low testosterone to see if that is the issue, but he doesn't want to. I have backed off considerably and have changed my attitude to what I think as a woman it should be. I don't want sex as much anymore, because I have been let down so often. We have four children now too, and so I think that might have something to do with it. All the resources about sex talk about how the guy thinks about it every ten minutes and has a hard time not looking at girls without thinking about sex, but that is not our issue. He just doesn't seem to want it that much."* (married 8 years)

in a bad light. You'll end up leading even more separate lives, and you'll corrupt sex itself, taking it from the sacred realm into the purely physical one.

If you can identify with all we've been talking about, you're in a marriage where you face some real challenges without quick solutions. You're going to have to learn how to live and find peace within the confines of your marriage — even if your husband never changes. This may sound like a tall order. He isn't fulfilling his end of the marriage, and you're lonely and frustrated, and you feel rejected.

Nevertheless, guarantees in marriage don't exist. When a spouse has health problems, we aren't as quick to become resentful and angry. But when the problem revolves around libido, we tend to feel more frustration and anger than if the problem was something he obviously had no control over.

Many of us live in difficult marriages, but this does not mean that our lives are rotten. We will just have to adjust our expectations for our marriages. It is often in these most difficult situations that God cements couples together in a new way or else draws hurting spouses closer to him.

Just today, as I was writing this, I was reading my friend Terry's blog as she discussed the pesky, little disagreements we often have with our spouses. In the middle of explaining how she often blows things out of proportion, she wrote this: "The Lord never, and I mean never, tells me what's wrong with the other person when I have a disagreement."[7] When she goes to God with her anger or her frustration or her resentment at her husband, God always shows her gently (and sometimes not so gently) where her attitude is off and what she can do to get more peace, joy, and rest. And I believe that's what God can do for you too.

It is not that God does not sympathize with you. It is not that God does not want your husband to change or that he thinks your husband is perfect. It is that in his relationship with you, God is first and foremost concerned about *your* heart. He wants you to work on yourself, not on your husband. As you start pouring out your heart to God, he'll point you to where you can go for peace. He'll help you get through the nights when you're lonely, frustrated, or afraid for the future of your relationship. And as you go deeper with God, you will likely find the door open to become far more intimate with your husband, even if it's not in the way you would primarily like.

Marriage is not an easy road, but it is also not one that God asks you to walk alone. Some of us have harder things to bear in marriage than others, but God is big enough to woo you, to help you feel loved, and to let you know that you are precious, lovely, and desirable to him. So take your resentment toward your husband and turn that energy into prayer. You just may find that God will take you on a new journey that is lovely, though it's not what you originally planned.

PART 3

spiritual discovery: bliss

CHAPTER 7

Learning to Make Love, Not Just Have Sex

On September 4, 1996, the phone rang at 1:30 in the morning. I was out of bed like a rocket, because I knew what was likely coming. Earlier that evening we had said good night to our baby boy, who was lying in the pediatric intensive care unit. Four days had elapsed since his open heart surgery, and that day had not been a good one. But by the time we left that night, he seemed to have turned the tide and the danger seemed to have passed.

As soon as the phone rang, I knew that our relief would be short-lived. The nurse on the other end of the line told me we had better come fast.

An hour later, that same nurse brought out the body of my son and laid him in my arms.

We left the hospital at 3:30 a.m. and trudged the few blocks home. We climbed back into bed and didn't know what to do. We couldn't plan the funeral yet; it was the middle of the night. We couldn't go back to sleep. We were in shock. And so we just held each other and began to kiss each other until the kissing turned into something more.

It was not that I was physically aroused; I was just grieving so much that I needed to be close to the only other individual on this earth who shared my pain. I needed to be a part of him.

I hope you never have the need to make love in a moment of overwhelming grief, but at the same time, it was a precious experience for me because I could feel how sex was something so much deeper than physical pleasure. It was the joining of everything we were; the compulsive need to be completely united. A marriage is not com-plete if the couple makes love only for physical release; they also need the extraordinary spiritual closeness that sex was designed for.

Sex Is More Than Physical

In this book we're looking at three aspects of great sex: learning how everything works physically, experiencing the deep connection that comes through making love, and creating a great friendship that fuels passion. It's that deep connection that we're going to turn to now. But that deep connection is often the hardest because it's the most fragile. It depends on being able both to express and feel love through sex. And that expressing and feeling can be awfully tricky. Let's turn first to the barriers that some women have to experienc-ing that connection during sex and then see the common outcome — and common solution — to these problems.

Problem #1: Focus on the Physical

In today's culture, experiencing a deep emotional connection while making love can be a challenge because our brains have gone hay-wire when it comes to sex. And the culprit isn't hard to find. Too often, just as we're starting to experience sexual feelings, the first sexual "encounter" we have is with a pornographic image. Maybe it's from a movie or from something we've seen on the Internet, but whatever the source, we find ourselves thinking of sex through that prism. Here's what one twenty-eight-year-old woman admitted:

> With my sex drive, I've often felt used, because sex tends to interfere with all the other aspects of the relationship. We spend so much time physically intimate that we don't get emotionally or spiritually intimate.

This woman reports that she and her husband make love almost every day. But here's what's really interesting: both of them have used pornography in the past, so for both, sex has become about the physical rather than anything else.

When couples focus only on the physical, they often sense that they're missing something. Thirty-six percent of women in my survey who had orgasms every time they had sex still couldn't rate their sex life as great, largely because it was too shallow. But our culture doesn't give couples the tools to deal with this unsettling feeling when it comes to sex. You roll around in bed, it feels great, but then what? When you know that you were looking out only for your own pleasure — or even only to give the other person pleasure, which at least is more selfless — you may feel as if sex is wrong.

Problem #2: Dealing with Sexual Pasts

If it's not the pornographic bent of sex that you struggle with, perhaps you're burdened by feelings of guilt because you gave yourself away too easily when you were young. Or perhaps you're burdened by quasi-guilt because of the things that were done to you. Many rape and incest survivors report feeling guilty, and even though they logically know they weren't responsible, the feeling won't go away.

And then there are those who had sexual experiences before marriage that were physically very satisfying. When you make love now, you too often find yourself comparing your husband unfavorably to a past partner. You try to get your hubby to do the things the other guy did so well, and it doesn't work. Too often, memories of past sexual experiences stop you from feeling connected now.

Problem #3: Fantasizing about Erotic Images

A few years ago I wrote a series of blog posts to help women whose husbands were addicted to pornography. Then the emails started to arrive. "What about *me?*" all too many women asked. "How do *I* stop looking at the stuff?" Pornography is no longer just a male battle. In one

A GOOD GIRL SPEAKS: *"[Fantasy] used to be a big issue for us, because I was always craving sex and my husband wasn't. That's when I started looking into pornography to fill that void I felt I was missing. We talked things out, got it all out in the open, and now we have a very fulfilling sex life together." (married 13 years)*

of the surveys I conducted for research for this book, 25 percent of women reported having had troubles with pornography. And when we use it, just like men, our brains become rewired so that we start becoming aroused by a picture rather than by a person.

The Common Barrier to Intimacy: Dissociating During Sex

Whether your difficulty is from guilt over previous sexual encounters, a fear of sex, or fantasy due to pornography or previous relationships, all can lead to the same problem: dissociating during sex. For many women, sex doesn't bring them closer to their partners, because they're not really "present" while making love. Either they leave their bodies and think of something else because they really don't like sex or they fantasize because they can't get aroused otherwise.

Dissociating by "Running Away" from Sex

Clinical psychologist Jennifer Degler explains to a sexual abuse survivor how this dissociating works:

> Dissociation temporarily disconnects your mind from your body so that you won't be fully aware of what is being done to your body.
>
> You, like many abuse survivors, are finding that the dissociation continues even though the abuse has stopped, and it is robbing you of a great sex life. In order to enjoy sex with your husband, you have to be connected to your body — feeling, enjoying, and encouraging both his touch and your own body's sexual response. Sexual abuse trains us to not feel, enjoy, or encourage healthy sexual touch or our body's natural responsiveness to sexual stimulation.[1]

If you were sexually abused in the past, you may have hated the feeling so much that you tried to think of anything else during the abuse — and taught your mind how to separate from your body.

Today when you have sex, you still can't seem to "reconnect" your body and your mind.

Dissociating by Fantasizing

Dissociating isn't only due to negative conceptions of sex; other women dissociate by turning to pornographic images or to memories of other partners, because otherwise they can't get aroused. Perhaps the husband has never figured out how to make the wife feel good, or perhaps she has other issues, like past sexual baggage, abuse, or physical difficulties. She starts worrying about not being able to respond or to enjoy sex, so she does whatever she can to put herself in the mood. And frequently that involves pulling up pornographic images or fantasies seared into her brain.

I've received lots of emails and some brave comments from women saying, "I know I'm dissociating during sex and thinking about anything except what is actually going on, but I don't know how to stop."

Unfortunately, when you use fantasy to get you through making love, you're essentially conceding that sex is only physical, because you're not present in an emotional or spiritual way. I'm not saying that all fantasy is wrong; thinking occasionally about some great time you and your husband had last year is perfectly fine. But fantasizing about strangers or fantasizing about anything that would be better considered lust is wrong.

Not all of you have these sorts of dissociating problems, but based on emails I have received and responses to my surveys, there is much anguish about this topic. Let me explain what I mean by using a composite of some of these emails in the story of a woman we'll call Christy.

As a child, Christy was in a dentist's office playing in the toy box one day, waiting for her appointment, when she found a *Playboy* that some sicko had left there. She began to leaf through it, and many of those pictures made her feel very funny.

A few years later, she was at a sleepover with a friend when her friend decided to show her a stack of her father's *Penthouse* magazines. She began leafing through these too, and those funny feelings returned.

As a teen, she was date-raped, but she never told anybody. Nothing "bad" happened from it — she wasn't pregnant and she didn't get an STD — so she decided just to put it behind her. She was a Christian, and she wanted to forgive the boy, so she did. Forgive and forget, as they say.

In her midtwenties she married a wonderful Christian man. Before the wedding, they shared breathless make-out sessions, but they didn't go any further than necking. Then, on her wedding night, she froze. Instead of being excited like she was when they were engaged, she felt nothing.

Over time they continued to make love, with Christy desperately hoping her sex drive would return. But she didn't enjoy sex, and she found herself trying to think of anything *but* sex in order to get through it.

After a few years, she felt like a freak. Everybody else was enjoying sex, but she saw it as a chore. Surely she was capable of enjoying sex, wasn't she?

That's when the pictures started to come back. She remembered all those magazines she had seen and how they had made her feel aroused. She did some research on the Internet about this and found some inappropriate sites. And soon she had a whole bunch more pictures in her head to go along with the ones from her childhood.

a good girl dare

If dissociating has been difficult for you, rediscover his body. Tonight spend time exploring it — kiss it, touch it, run your hair over it. Memorize what his penis feels like. You're allowed to touch now — take advantage of it!

Now, the next time she had sex, she started thinking of those pictures. She found herself getting aroused. And she finally felt like she wasn't a freak! Her husband was happy because she was enjoying it.

But she was still separate from her body. She still was "running away" in her mind. Yes, her body was responding, but it was responding because of something she was thinking, not something her husband was doing. And over the years she got better at it. And he didn't know that anything was amiss.

Does that sound familiar to you? Many women are hurting like this, falling into several different categories:

Those for whom sex is painful or shameful

Those for whom sex just isn't fun, either because the husband doesn't know how to properly stimulate the wife or because they just have never bothered to figure out how to make sex work together

Those who were abused as children or teens

Those who were heavily involved with porn as children, often because someone else showed it to them

These women don't want to disappoint their husbands, and they don't want to feel as if there is something wrong with them because everyone else in the world seems to like sex but them. So they look desperately for some shortcut to arousal and find it in pornography.

Overcoming These Problems

While we may have different reasons for our difficulties connecting on a deep, personal level during sex, the solution to all of these problems is the same: go to God for healing, and then learn how to retrain your mind and body to feel, think, and respond differently to sex. Let's look at how to do that.

Healing Step #1: Experiencing God's New Creation

If sex has negative connotations for you, chances are you have either been hurt in the past or you have engaged in sinful behavior. Ask God to heal your heart from those scars. Confess any anger and bitterness you still have. Ask God to give you a new heart and a new mind when it comes to sexual intimacy.

Sometimes you can't pray through this healing on your own, especially if the problems are very deep-seated. You need a counselor or an older mentor who can help walk you through your healing.

Going to see a counselor doesn't mean that you're stuck going for the rest of your life. Some counselors will see people for a fixed time for a fixed purpose just to work through the problem. If sexual issues are hampering your marriage, counseling is worth the investment of time and money.

Maybe your situation is different because you don't feel guilt. You wish you hadn't fooled around earlier, but it's in the past. That attitude can be healthy if you've already taken the sin to God and dealt with it. But perhaps you haven't. And you can't have it both ways: you can't feel guilt-free while also revisiting those "positive" memories. Just because it felt good doesn't mean that it *was* good, and it's now having an impact on your marriage. You may have to go to God for a different reason.

Ask him to give you his mind about your past. By having sex outside of a committed marriage, you changed sex to be only about the physical and not about the relationship and the spiritual connection. Hand your memories over to God, agreeing not to keep unwrapping them when your sex life gets boring. Again, praying through this with a friend or mentor would probably be more helpful than doing so alone. James 5:16 says, "Confess your sins to each other and pray for each other so that you may be healed. The prayer of a righteous person is powerful and effective."

Healing Step #2: Give Sex a New Meaning

Now it's time to retrain your body! Jennifer Degler gives this promise — with a warning — to her clients: "You *can* retrain yourself to stay connected to your body during sex, but be patient with yourself because it takes a lot of practice!"[2]

Practice being naked together. Since healing can't be rushed, taking baby steps is the best route to enjoying your body anew. So learn that your body actually is fun. Lie naked together. Have baths together. Without any expectation that you will make love that night, enjoy your husband's body. Run your hands over it. Concentrate on the intimacy that comes from doing something you will only do with him. Don't think of this only as foreplay; do this separately from making love to get you more accustomed to being mentally present when you are making love. If you get him pretty worked up, you can also help him climax using your hands, for instance, so that you don't feel pressure to finish by having sex. Make the point of the evening be to help you feel how amazingly intimate it is to be naked together — and to appreciate how he responds to your body!

Play games to learn what feels good. Many women who don't seem to be able to be "mentally present" during sex, or who don't enjoy sex, like Christy, assume that their sex drives are dead — even those who desire sex a lot because porn has jump-started their libidos. They don't long for their husbands to touch them — they only get turned on by fantasy. If that describes you, let me reassure you that your sex drive is not dead! It has just been transferred somewhere else.

To defeat this pessimism, you need confidence that you *can* experience pleasure one day. Your body, after all, was created for this. Nevertheless, we don't all enjoy the same things, and so it's really beneficial to explore and figure out what you do like. Some women really love their breasts touched; others don't. Some find their ears or their toes erogenous zones; other women like to focus only on the genitals.

So let's play some games to learn about our bodies! Set the timer for ten minutes, and then let him touch you. Here's the deal: you're not allowed to tell him to stop at all — though you can ask him to move on to a different part of your body. Let him use a variety of things too, like a feather, an ice cube, his finger, his tongue. See what you like. This game also helps the men

a good girl dare
Forbid him from moving while you make him feel good any way you want. If he moves, you stop. That makes the feeling much more intense (and he'll be begging and crying by the end). Then turn the tables and let him do the same for you. This also helps each of you concentrate on how your spouse can make your body feel alive—and how you don't need anything else.

who may never have learned to appreciate the benefits of foreplay to see how aroused they can get their wives. Then do the same thing to your husband. Seeing the reaction you get and feeling the sexual power you have can be very erotic.

This process may take several weeks or months as you grow accustomed to relaxing, being present, and learning that your body can indeed respond. You aren't going to rewire your brain overnight. But the wonderful thing about being married is that you do have a lot of time to practice!

Healing Step #3: Learn to Be Emotionally and Mentally Present

It is a beautiful thing to be present with your husband body, mind, and soul when you make love. But if you have difficulty being present, here are some more ideas to keep your mind focused.

Pay attention to what is going on. If you find your mind wandering while you're making love, immediately stop that train of thought and replace it with this one instead. Ask yourself constantly, "What would I like him to do now?" It sounds silly, as if you're judging his performance, but that's not really the point. If you ask yourself, "What would I like him to do?" you'll start paying attention to cues your body is sending you, and you'll realize that different body parts actually do want some attention. Dissociation is the act of mentally leaving your body to think about something else. This technique pulls your brain back to the matter at hand.

When your breasts start to feel like they want some attention or your clitoris gets that almost painful feeling that it needs to be touched, tell him that. He'll likely find this very exciting, because he never will have seen you like this before. If you've used most of your intimate experiences in the past to think about other things, or to check out entirely, it means that you weren't as active physically because you weren't paying attention to your body. Once you start concentrating on what your body is feeling, you start moving a little more. To him, you're now much more engaged in the process!

And if something doesn't feel good, tell him that too. Don't just endure it, because for women, paying attention is the key to sexual arousal. You must keep your head in the game, and if he's doing something you don't like, it's hard to do that. In a polite way, redirect his hand or whatever else he's using to stimulate you.

Talk to him. If you want to stay present, talk. Tell him you love him. Tell him what you like. If you talk, you're forced to think about what's actually happening, and you're forced to stay in the moment.

Look into his eyes. You can't picture a different image if you're looking into his eyes. And the connection when you're doing that is really intense. If you talk to him, look in his eyes, concentrate on what he is doing, and banish distractions. You'll find that sex is much more intimate than it was before — even if you don't achieve orgasm right away. There's a big sexual high that comes simply from feeling connected to your husband, and many women, if you've been involved in dissociating during sex, have never experienced this. When you make love focusing on him, you're able to feel the love that truly connects you.

> **a good girl dare**
>
> Start your evening in bed together by reading Scripture or praying while holding hands. Even pray naked! Connect spiritually first, and the physical connection will be even better.

When He's the One Struggling with Images

While porn may no longer be solely a male problem, that doesn't mean males are dealing with it better. It just means women are lying down in the muck with them. When I surveyed men for this book, 66 percent admitted deliberately seeking out pornography in the past. This doesn't mean all were compulsive users, but it definitely is a temptation for the vast majority of men. Do their wives know? In the survey I did for this book, 43 percent said their husbands had sought out porn, while 7 percent said they didn't know. Many wives are simply unaware of their husbands' struggles.

One Good Girl respondent was totally ignorant of her husband's habit until the day of her seventh anniversary. She tells the story:

> My husband revealed to me that he was using pornography regularly and secretly.... It devastated me.... I thought we had

a marriage that was "perfect" in every way. Especially without secrets. It has taken a long time for us to recover. I struggle with the reality that he does not seem to have a strong sex drive like I hear other men have. He says he is insecure to initiate because there have been times I have not responded in the past. I don't want him to feel this way. There may be some validity to it, but I wonder if this is an excuse.

Here she is, years later, and she's still dealing with the fallout from her husband's porn addiction. He frequently turns her down when she initiates sex, so today they have sex once a month or less.

Unfortunately, this woman's story is not unique. But if your husband is involved with porn, it does not mean that your marriage is going to have an unhappy ending. Here's Anna's story to give you another perspective:

I was borrowing my husband's computer to watch a DVD, but when I put the DVD in, a video clip popped up (he had forgotten to erase the history that morning). I didn't think much of it at the time, but I made a mental note to ask him about it later when the children were in bed.

That evening I asked if he ever watches things on his computer or TV that are inappropriate. I told him I found a video on his computer. He wasn't sure how to answer. He figured he had two choices — lie again or confess and be free, which he had been praying for. He chose the latter and began to confess his struggle that he had had for many years (since high school). To say that I was "shocked" is an understatement!

I went to his parents (I confess, my reasons were partly to put Paul in a bad light, but also I was a wreck and needed support). I told his family and my family right away. My brothers right away unhooked our satellite, and they came over to talk and pray with Paul.

We also called our pastor. He came over right away and met with us, prayed, read the Bible, listened, and gave us the name of a Christian counselor, who ended up being extremely helpful.

It was very difficult at first to trust Paul. It was easier to trust him and to forgive him when I noticed the life changes in him.

He was broken before God and truly sorry for his sins. I know that in a marriage, love ought not to be conditional, but it sure was easier to love him again when I saw the spiritual growth happening in his life.

Through this experience, I have learned more about the importance of meeting my husband's physical needs (which are so different than mine)! I have a different attitude toward sex now than I did before. I still struggle with having the desire for intimacy as often as he does, but that's something I continue to pray about.

I don't doubt him today, though. Thanks to God's grace and mercy, our relationship has been restored and I am able to trust him.

God restored this couple's marriage, and if pornography is an issue in your marriage, he can restore yours too! Recovery, though, depends on both of you admitting how destructive pornography is. All too much sexual advice on the Internet or talk shows tells you that if he's addicted to pornography and you can't beat it, then you should join it. Watch it with him and act it out. That is a total misunderstanding of male sexuality. He's addicted to porn because he's addicted to fantasy. He isn't aroused by a relationship. You can't break that addiction by becoming sexier and more outlandish; in fact, if you do that, you'll cement the addiction, because you'll encourage him to act out those fantasies, and then you'll become an enabler of his porn habit. You are not responsible for his becoming addicted to porn, and having sex constantly will not break that addiction. He needs to decide it's wrong, he needs to go to God in repentance, and you both need to find a way to make love that forges a spiritual connection instead of just stretching the boundaries of what you do together.

Porn Wrecks a Man's Libido

Pornographic addictions are now one of the largest causes of divorce. It's wrecking marriages, but it's also wrecking men's libidos. In fact, it's one of the largest causes of men's reduced sexual interest. Danoah, from the blog *Single Dad Laughing*, wrote a powerful post recently begging men to stop looking at the airbrushed images of fantasy women. He believes one reason women are so insecure is that we notice what men want because we see them looking. But women aren't the only victims of men's wandering eyes. Men also hurt themselves when they look, as he explains in this insightful comment:

> We stop. We look. We comment. We joke. We implant those very thoughts into [women's] way of thinking. We make sure they know that we *agree* with everything the media has brainwashed us to believe beauty to be.
>
> I, for one, am done with it. I, for one, am taking a stand. I, for one, will no longer be stopping. I will no longer be looking. Why?
>
> Quite possibly for a selfish reason. I am a heterosexual man. *And, as blunt and uncomfortable as this may seem, I realized recently that I am starting to lose my attraction to women.* Over time, and after seeing enough of this concocted and concentrated hogwash surrounding me, I've almost completely lost my ability to truly *want* a "real" woman. Most of us have. We have somehow started wanting what we know we can never have. We want what we see on the cover of *Cosmo* and *Maxim*. We want what is displayed across calendars and centerfolds.
>
> And women know that. They see that. They feel it.[3]

No wonder so many men are suffering from lower libidos! Our pornographic culture is attacking them. All men are vulnerable, but those who use porn put themselves in major harm's way. Not all marriages experience this, but slowly and surely a man who is addicted to porn becomes less interested in sex with his wife. When he is interested, he tends to want to try more extreme things. And he also has difficulty making love without fantasizing.

A GOOD GIRL SPEAKS: *"At one time his sex drive was very low, and it made me feel like I wasn't good enough for him. I also found out that he was looking at porn. I felt like another woman entered our life, yet I couldn't compete with her (porn). I blamed myself, that I wasn't skinny enough, attractive enough, or good enough. It was a low time in our marriage. Once I confronted him and we went to God with it, our marriage was healed." (married 27 years)*

Even secular researchers are noticing this. Sex and relationship counselor Ian Kerner has coined the term SADD — Sexual Attention Deficit Disorder — to describe men who find that porn wrecks their sex lives. Kerner explains, "Just as people with ADD are easily distracted, guys with SADD have become so accustomed to the high levels of visual novelty and stimulation that comes from internet porn that they're unable to focus on real sex with a real woman."[4]

One twenty-nine-year-old Good Girl survey respondent has lived this out. She writes:

> My husband's past use of pornography has affected our sex life; thankfully, we have controls on the computers at home, so he doesn't see any here. I realized he was using it when he could go a month without ever having sex. I would try to initiate it, but he would be too tired. Most of that is in the past, but I still rarely initiate it because of the hurt and rejection I felt.

Understand That It Is an Addiction

What should you do if you're suddenly confronted, like Anna, with the fact that your husband uses porn? Here are a few thoughts. When men say, "It's got nothing to do with you," they honestly mean it. Men are wired, much more so than women, to be aroused visually, and so pornography is a huge temptation for them. Once they start watching, though, they tend to need more and more to get the initial high that comes with it, in the same way that an alcoholic needs more and more drinks to feel tipsy.

Porn changes the chemical balance in the brain, just like other addictions. That doesn't mean a porn habit can't be broken and that it isn't sin; it's just that many men *want* to break it but don't know how. They feel great shame about porn in the same way an alcoholic feels shame.

If your husband has a porn addiction, you're going to be angry when you learn. You'll feel disgusted, ashamed, and probably a little vengeful. But when you calm down, try, as much as you can, to also feel a bit of sympathy. Listen to your husband's heart. If he is repentant but doesn't know how to stop, help him. If he isn't repentant, lay down some pretty firm rules and an ultimatum. A marriage can't survive a porn addiction long term. It is cheating, whether he admits it or not. Using porn steals his sexual interest from you, transfers it to images of other women, and undermines the whole basis for your marriage.

Confront the Addiction

It would be handy if your husband could stop using porn all on his own, but recovery is rarely that easy. We don't ask an alcoholic to stop drinking when there is still a ton of alcohol in the house. In the same way, your husband can't stop his porn addiction without removing the Internet lure.

So either drop the Internet altogether or install filters. He may be leery at first, but make it clear that if he wants to stay in the marriage, he needs to take these steps. And please, try to do it in a loving way. Lecturing him will only drive him away. How much better to tell him instead that you want to work toward rebuilding your sex life and making it satisfying for both of you.

If he won't admit that his use of porn is a problem, then find a third party, such as a pastor or a counselor, to talk to together. He needs help, and so does your marriage. If he won't get it, then start talking to someone yourself to find a plan for healing. "I have never met anyone who has experienced sexual-addiction recovery alone," asserts Douglas Weiss, executive director of the Heart to Heart Counseling Center in Colorado Springs.[5] You need support as you work through this as a couple.

Do Not Be His Accountability Partner

Most men will need some sort of an accountability partner to recover, but you can't be that partner, because your husband can't be honest with you if he's tempted again. Instead, encourage your husband to find a godly man who can hold him accountable. Some computer programs can automatically send an email to someone of your choice if you visit a questionable website, so the partner can monitor your husband's web use.

Be aware, too, that your husband likely will fall in the initial period. It's very hard to break an addiction, and he'll be moody, twitchy, and angry. He can't become perfect overnight. Occasionally he's going to fall, whether it's at work where he still has Internet access or when he's in a hotel. When he does fall, he's going to feel even more like slime.

Have you ever tried really hard to lose weight? Do you recall how awful you felt when you scarfed down a forbidden donut? Giving in to the temptation of porn feels much worse. Just because your husband falls, though, does not mean that he isn't still moving in the right general direction. If he remains committed to breaking the addiction, forgive him, and encourage him to talk to an accountability partner about it.

The recovery process can go much more smoothly if you both are able to direct your anger in the right direction: toward the pornographic culture we live in and those who propagate it. Anna's husband, Paul, may have been addicted to pornography, but the original trigger that started the addiction was not his fault. He was sucked in. He found magazines in the ditch by his house when he was thirteen — and what thirteen-year-old is not going to leaf through magazines if he sees them like that? He wasn't seeking them out. He stumbled across them, and they excited something inside him, so he continued to look for more. Had that stranger not dumped those magazines in that ditch, Paul likely wouldn't have traveled down that road — or at least not as far down that road. Try to understand how your husband got sucked in, and then you can battle his addiction together rather than just being livid at him.

Rebuild Your Sex Life

God wants you to have a great sex life, and he wants to help you rebuild. Invite God into the process, and jump-start your spiritual intimacy. Paul notes that prayer went a long way in helping Anna rebuild trust:

> When we did become intimate again, it helped us a lot to begin with prayer so that we were able to bring God into our bedroom

to drive out the insecurities and hurt that Anna felt, so that she could feel comfortable with me again.

That's what prayer does. It clears the air, and it ministers directly to our hearts, giving us the healing we need.

Don't stop with prayer, though. Bring God into your bedroom completely to help you feel like sex is something holy, not something dirty. Read Psalms or the Song of Solomon while lying together. You may think this sounds corny, but honestly, when you are spiritually close, the sexual feelings often follow. One of the sexiest things you can do together is pray, because praying is so intimate (more on that in the next chapter). And it's the kind of intimate that is the exact opposite of fantasizing, so it helps keep those impulses at bay.

Starting Over with Your Husband

Pornography, fantasy, and masturbation go hand in hand. Males rarely have one without the other. So if a man tells you that he's addicted to pornography, it also means that he fantasizes and that he masturbates. It's gross to think about, but it's true.

To help your husband escape that cycle so that his physical desire is channeled toward you again is often a very long process. This is not going to be an easy road, but it is one you can travel together.

First, you have to give your husband the freedom to be honest with you. If you want to rebuild intimacy, he needs to be free to tell you when he's just not able to banish the images while you're making love. Because pornography rewires the brain, many men actually experience impotence unless they have extra stimulation (the images they're used to seeing). That's why a lot of guys, in order to have sex with their wives, start fantasizing about those images. Even if they desperately want to stop using porn, they're likely scared that they'll never be able to perform sexually again without it. Paul reports that it took three to four months before he could be intimate with Anna without those images intruding.

Help your husband get reacquainted with true intimacy. Using the same steps written above to help women break the negative associations they have with sex, spend some time, perhaps a few weeks, not actually making love. Just as we talked about earlier, lie naked together and get used to touching each other again. Look into his eyes. Let him experience the erotic nature of just being close to someone he loves. Explore each other, and take things very slowly so that he can see that he can become aroused just by being with you. If you try to go too fast, you can push him into fantasy again in order to "complete the deed." Instead, spend some time letting him discover that he can become aroused by being with you. This is much easier if there's no pressure, so spend time just being together naked, talking, kissing, and exploring.

Usually when we think of rebuilding sex lives, we think that we have to somehow compete with pornography. We want to be so arousing that he won't need it anymore, and so we go the lingerie route, or we decide to try new things. That actually feeds his addiction, because what he really needs is to experience the sexual high that comes from relational and spiritual intimacy, not just from visual arousal or fantasy. It's not that

A GOOD GIRL SPEAKS: *"I have recently really worked on giving to him — admiration, affection, and sex — and the difference in our sex drives is far less of an issue when I enjoy his pleasure. Before, especially through some of the hardest times of our marriage (including porn addiction and infidelity), he got angry when he wanted sex and I didn't, and I quit initiating after he had turned me down repeatedly."* (married 11 years)

you can never wear lingerie again; it's just that in the initial recovery period, the aim is not to be "porn lite" in your marriage; it's to help him channel his sexual energy in a different direction: toward you.

So take things slowly, and let your husband know that if he needs to take a break because his mind is wandering, it's okay for him to tell you that. You'd rather he be honest so that he can get his heart and head right and start again.

That's what we're aiming for: being able to be completely comfortable with one another, focusing on one another, and being present with one another. Once that barrier is lifted, we'll be able to experience the richness that God designed sex to be like.

CHAPTER 8

A Pure, Holy, and Hot Marriage!

If there are two words not exactly linked in the Christian mindset, they would be *holy* and *hot*. I don't think that's because God separated them; I think it's because we separated them. We don't understand how God designed sex to be passionate and how that passion, when properly channeled, is a good thing.

In chapter 7 we took a look at barriers to "holy" sex that some of us have: we have a hard time seeing sex in a positive light or enjoying our spouses because we're struggling with pornographic images or other flashbacks. But what does "holy" sex really mean? And is it possible to be holy and hot at the same time? Actually, I think that's the biblical view of sex. It's purity and passion together, and that's what makes it so wonderful!

Let's start with what "purity" and "holiness" mean in a Christian marriage context, and then we'll see how that leads to truly mind-blowing passion.

Holy Sex: Learning to Make Love

Most of us have had sex to say, "I want you." We've had sex because we want to relax, have fun, or experience fireworks. But too few couples have had sex to say, "I love you." What is really sexy, and what brings true bliss in the bedroom, is not *just* becoming multi-orgasmic. It's not being able to do sexual gymnastics, or being able to last for three hours at a time. It's something so much more profound.

161

It's that feeling of not knowing where your spouse ends and where you begin.

For those of you who are married, have you ever felt like you are saying, "I love you," when you have sex? Or has it mostly been about physical pleasure? Feeling love involves paying attention and thinking about your spouse while you are connected. One Good Girl, thirty-nine, opened a rather beautiful, intimate window into her life that illustrates this perfectly:

> Early in our marriage we were at a marriage conference where the speaker said that orgasm was a lot like imprinting. You know how little baby geese follow around whomever they see as soon as they are born? What they see first when they're born gets imprinted. And it's the same with us and orgasm. What we hear gets imprinted.
>
> So my husband decided (without telling me) that every time he orgasmed, and every time I orgasmed, he was going to say, 'I love you, Becky.' He wanted those words to become the erotic ones in our marriage. So no matter how hot the sex is, even if we're being rather raunchy, he always says, 'I love you, Becky,' at that exact moment. He uses my name. And now sometimes he just leans over to me during the day and whispers it in my ear, and it definitely gives me warm fuzzies!

Saying "I love you" when you're making love is such a simple thing. But it helps us focus on *why* we're making love. Look each other in the eyes. Say each other's names. Kiss each other, and that emotional and spiritual connection becomes much deeper.

A GOOD GIRL SPEAKS: *"It isn't about performance; it is about joining yourself in the most intimate possible way, sharing yourself deeply." (married 12 years)*

That's the connection you're looking for — not just physical pleasure, but feeling as if you complete each other. That's what speaker and writer Julie Sibert experienced after her house was almost burglarized. Coming home to fleeing thieves and a broken-in front door, she felt violated and scared. But that's not how the night ended. She explains:

I needed to make love. I needed to find reassurance in one of the safest places I know — my husband's arms and the truth of the one-flesh mystery.

When all else seems unsteady, plagued by uncertainty or disappointment, there is power in reaffirming oneness through sex. Raw vulnerability is allowed to find its core.

Literally and figuratively, my husband and I were saying that night that we are "in this together" — life's chaos, life's joy, life's journey, and even life's uncertainties. (You could even say we were spiritually taking a stand "for" our marriage and our family.)

You see, vulnerability is multifaceted. There is tremendous power when two people who love one another are truly vulnerable with each other. On the other side of the vulnerability coin, we discover reassurance when relationship calms the fear-based vulnerability we feel when our world is shaken. Hmmm. All that sounds a lot like what God desires we experience with him.[1]

When we're vulnerable with our mates, we feel a deep sense of connection because we vow that we are in a situation together. And that connection is very powerful. It's that urgency to devour your husband, to consume him, to be consumed by him, just so that you can feel even more connected. It's the hunger that God put in us to yearn for each other. And to feel that for your husband, you also have to realize how God feels about you.

Understanding God's Passion

It may seem strange to bring God into a discussion on passionate sex, but God did design sex to mirror his relationship with us. We are the bride being prepared for the bridegroom.

Renaissance poets expressed this quite well. Listen to what Shakespeare's contemporary John Donne wrote to God in his sonnet "Batter My Heart":

> *Batter my heart, three-person'd God, for you*
> *As yet but knock, breathe, shine, and seek to mend;*

> *That I may rise and stand, o'erthrow me, and bend*
> *Your force to break, blow, burn, and make me new....*
> *Take me to you, imprison me, for I,*
> *Except you enthrall me, never shall be free,*
> *Nor ever chaste, except you ravish me.*

Donne is asking God to overthrow him, to bend him, to break him, to conquer him. He's saying, "I'll never be chaste unless you ravish me." Does that sound like a nice orderly relationship in which no one ever loses control? Not to me. It's a tale of bending completely to another who physically overpowers you. That sounds a lot like passionate sex!

John Donne wasn't some pervert, though. He was expressing the same thing the apostle Paul expressed when he wrote in Galatians 2:20: "I have been crucified with Christ and I no longer live, but Christ lives in me. The life I now live in the body, I live by faith in the Son of God, who loved me and gave himself for me."

We are not alone; we carry God in our bodies, and we want more of him and less of us. "He must become greater; I must become less," John the Baptist said of Jesus (John 3:30). We yearn for God, and not just for his presence, but for a deeply intimate relationship in which he *does* overpower us, in which he *does* consume us, in which we no longer feel alone, but so imbued with him that we are finally complete.

That is how we feel about God and how he feels about us, and that is also what he made sex to be like. He uses sex as imagery for that deep hunger we have for a spiritual union with God. We hunger to be completed by God, and God made us so that we hunger in a similar way for each other.

Wanting to Devour You

In sex, we're not just desiring each other; we're expressing something of God's relationship with us. And in this, we're playing roles: we Good Girls are the brides, the ones who are being wooed. Our husbands are the bridegrooms, the pursuers. That's why all of us women, in the height of sexual tension, will at times long just to be "devoured," to be "taken," and men often experience the urge to comply! For men, it's saying, "This is mine." For women, it's saying, "I am not my own." It's actually a beautiful picture of how God longs to see us surrender. And it can only occur between a man and a woman. It can't work between two of the same sex, because the very illustration is meant to be between two very different beings: God and the church. There is no equality in sex.

That doesn't mean that there's not spiritual equality in our relationship, or equality in household tasks or any of those other things we debate when it comes to gender roles. But in sex, there is just *difference* — and it's that difference that's sexy, exciting, attractive, and intoxicating.

Celebrating the Differences!

That's also why we tend to feel most drawn to our husbands when we feel the most different, not when we feel the most similar. When we feel the most feminine, and he the most masculine; when we feel the most vulnerable, and he the most protective; when we feel the most helpless, and he the most knight-like — then we feel the most aroused by each other.

Celebrating our differences makes sense when you see that they are all part of God's spiritual plan. Think about this: when do you feel closest to God? Is it not when you recognize that you are definitely *not* God? When you decide to give him control, and you surrender; when you praise him for what he has done that you never could do; when you recognize that he is holy and you are not — that is when

A GOOD GIRL SPEAKS: *"Sex and making love are two different things. To be married and have a loving, patient lover who wants you to get as much enjoyment as he does is what it is all about! Wow!" (married 18 years)*

you are most drawn to your knees to worship and to pray. On the other hand, when you start trying to rationalize how God's preference for music or worship or politics completely mirrors yours, or you put God in a box and use him to judge others, you feel far from God. It's when you surrender and listen and realize that you need him that you are closest to him. *The difference is what is important.*

I've found that when I am most aware of the differences between God and me I'm most drawn to my husband too. That's the physical manifestation of a spiritual reality. Sometimes in church when I'm praising God, worshiping God, and recognizing that he is the great I Am, I need to take Keith's hand. I have spoken at marriage conferences with couples who always hold hands when they pray as a symbol that they are united before God. But I wonder if the relationship doesn't also go the other way: they don't only hold hands to be united before they pray; the very act of praying together makes them feel more united because they are recognizing their deep need for God, for difference, for joining with something outside themselves.

A GOOD GIRL SPEAKS: *"It gets so much better when you really know each other and love and trust. After twenty-five years we have such a hot sex life. It's terrific!" (married 25 years)*

Bringing God In

Unfortunately, one sector of the Christian church has this bizarre and dangerous belief that God and sex don't go together. They figure that if God were ever to think about sex, he'd arrange for us to do it like the chaste Mexicans, with a sheet draped over the women with a hole cut out so that only the absolutely necessary parts touch. They think sex God's way must banish all the carnal desire, messiness, and awkwardness.

But God designed sex with that messiness, awkwardness, and carnal desire! And I think he did it because our union is supposed to be messy and emotional and just a little bit out of control. As C. S. Lewis said of the Narnian Christ-figure Aslan — he's not a tame lion, you know. And our union with God isn't tame, either. The closer we get to God, the more intense our passions.

That's why sex isn't sterile. It isn't supposed to be, anymore than our relationship with God is supposed to be all neat and tidy and easily understandable. And so sex shouldn't be shameful before God. In fact, I think God probably laughs when we lose control when we're making love, when we surrender that little bit more, when we lose our ability to think clearly, even when we scream right before climax, because that's what we also feel when we draw close to him. Total vulnerability is part of an intimate relationship.

So sex with God on our side means lots of surrender and lots of fun! And the reason it's so stupendous is that it reminds us of that essential difference: while we may be one and we may be joined, we are not singular; we are completely different. We are different from each other yet drawn to each other; we are different from God yet drawn to him.

Speaking from experience, sex is even greater when you bring God into it. He cares about you being able to fully surrender and give yourself to your husband. He cares about how great it feels, because he made it that way. And there's no other time I want to make love with my husband more than after we've prayed together, especially for

A GOOD GIRL SPEAKS: *"It's not about how good you do it. It's the fulfillment of your love." (married 26 years)*

our kids. When I see my husband surrender himself to God and ask for God to work in our kids' lives, I need something else.

The spiritual bliss that we're supposed to feel from sex comes from this union that is built on physical desire, fueled by a friendship that brings trust and laughter, but culminates in beautiful longing for the other. So let's take that longing for the other and act on it.

Pure Passion: Intersection between Holy and Hunger

While theoretically the intersection between the holy and sexual hunger sounds intriguing and exciting, the practical living out of this passion can be a land mine for Christians. We want to build this spiritual union in which we deeply desire each other, lose control, and experience tremendous fireworks, but does it matter how those fireworks are exploded?

Yep, it does. The most common questions I'm asked through my website and blog are about specific sexual activities. Is oral sex okay? What about lingerie? What about sex toys? I know these are important questions, but sometimes they leave me rather sad, because I think women are focusing on the wrong thing: we're looking at specific physical acts instead of the relationship as a whole.

Personally, I do believe in freedom in marriage. God made sex to feel amazing as a gift, and he rejoices when we enjoy it. But before we flesh out that freedom, I want to offer a word of caution. These "extra" sexual practices have become more mainstream over the last few decades because pornography is becoming so rampant. All of this stems from the unhealthy sexual attitude that sex is all about pushing the physical boundaries and having more physical pleasure. One of the problems with getting *too* focused on these extra sexual practices, then, is that couples miss out on the beauty of just being together, especially early in marriage.

We even run into a danger of making sex into an idol. Take the verse that is often quoted at marriage conferences about giving to each other, 1 Corinthians 7:5, which says: "Do not deprive each other except perhaps by mutual consent and for a time, so that you may devote yourselves to prayer. Then come together again so that Satan will not tempt you because of your lack of self-control."

We like to focus on the "do not deprive each other" part of the verse to stress that we should be having regular sexual relations and satisfying our spouses. It goes right along with verse 4: "The wife does not have authority over her own body but yields it to her husband. In the same way, the husband does not have authority over his body but yields it to his wife." We belong to each other, so let's have sex!

A GOOD GIRL SPEAKS: *"Sex is better and more fulfilling as the years go by because trust builds, friendship grows, and transparency happens to allow for greater intimacy." (married 33 years)*

Yes, these verses definitely affirm that sex is good and that we should be making love regularly. After all, fasting from sex wouldn't work to drive us to God if we didn't also enjoy and yearn for sex. Yet we're often unwilling to look at the other ramification of that verse: *the fasting itself is part of a healthy Christian marriage.* In modern Christian writing and speaking on sex, we're far more comfortable debating what practices are and aren't okay and how to have the best sex possible than we are talking about how our devotion to God fits into our sexual relationship.

Sex has become all about how to have the most amount of fun, because God made sex! Yes, but he also made us to yearn for him, and even though sex mimics that, sex doesn't replace it. If you're already having regular and passionate sex, your intimate lives would be far more enhanced by spending time praying fervently together in bed without making love and then coming together at the end rather explosively than they would by pushing the boundaries of what's okay and what's not.

So, please, as you read this chapter, take that as its context. God wants us to enjoy our bodies. He wants us to feel completely one, to yearn for each other, to explore. But this should never replace our yearning for him, and as we learn to yearn for him, we likely yearn for each other more too. The key to a passionate marriage is not to be as sexually adventurous as possible, but to be as passionate about God as possible.

> **a good girl dare**
>
> Men love breasts—so show off yours! Grab some massage oil or moisturizer cream and rub it into your breasts slowly, while he's looking. Put on a real show!

As we come close to him, we'll experience more freedom and more energy in the bedroom.

How Do You Decide What's Okay?

Now that that's cleared up, let's turn to the parameters we've learned about to decide what activities are okay. Sex was designed by God to recreate in a physical way the longing that we have to be joined to him. That longing is wrapped up in other issues of us feeling incredibly loved and cherished, of us feeling amazing pleasure, of us becoming supremely vulnerable, of us being led. And in all of that, there is no coercion. There is no unhealthy fear. Thus, for a sexual relationship to be able to express that spiritual connection, it can't be something that's scary or domineering, because God does not express his relationship to us that way. It's voluntary, but it's also not tame. So here are some guidelines that logically follow:

> You're married. You're allowed to do stuff! Freedom is the theme of the Christian life (Gal. 5:1).

Sex should not be something that makes one person feel degraded or uncomfortable. It must always be done willingly. If you or your husband don't want to do something, don't do it, as long as you are still maintaining an active sex life with sexual intercourse as a part of that. In other words, you can say no to some things, but be careful about saying no to vaginal sex unless health issues are involved or you're taking some time to reacquaint your body with the good things that sex can bring after recovery from sexual abuse or trauma (see 1 Cor. 7:4 – 5).

Lust is wrong. If one partner is fantasizing about someone else, that's sin, even if the fantasy is being physically acted out with a spouse (see Matt. 5:28).

How do we apply these guidelines to specific acts? Let me comment on the most common questions I'm asked.

Oral Sex

Let's be honest here, girls: most men really like this. Most women really do too. While this may once have been considered an outlandish sexual activity, it's now pretty much mainstream. For instance, in the National Survey of Sexual Health reported in the October 2010 *Journal of Sexual Medicine*, 76 percent of women ages 25 – 29 gave sex orally to a man in the last year, and 72 percent received (versus 87 percent who had experienced vaginal intercourse). Now, just because most people do it is absolutely no reason to think that you should. After all, most people have sex before they're married too, and that's not morally right. I share those percentages with you not to tell you that you *should* have oral sex, but to explain to you that your husband is not a weird pervert if he's interested in it, and you're not a weird pervert if you're interested in it, either.

Nevertheless, some Christians object because it's focused on one person's pleasure rather than experiencing pleasure together, but I don't find that a particularly persuasive argument. Giving is a good thing, not a bad thing. Yet whole books have been written depicting anything that results in orgasm without actual intercourse as sin.

They rely on an account in Genesis 38 about a man named Onan. Here's the scoop: Judah, one of Jacob's twelve sons, in turn had a son named Er who was married to Tamar. Er was evil, and God killed him. In Jewish law, if a man died without an heir, the brother of the dead man was to marry the widow and have children with her, and those children would then receive the dead man's inheritance and the dead man's name. Onan was Er's brother, and he married Tamar. But he didn't want to raise and feed a child who wouldn't really be his own, so when he had sex with Tamar, he "spilled his semen on the ground" (v. 9). For this he was punished by God.

Doctrines have been built around this "sin of Onan," saying that this passage claims that any orgasm without the purpose of reproduction is wrong. I just don't see that in this story. The judgment from God on Onan wasn't about sex; it was about the fact that he wasn't fulfilling his duty, and he was thus using Tamar and treating her very badly. To apply that to something like oral sex in a marriage is an awfully big stretch.

Genesis 38 was not meant to be a treatise on sex. Song of Songs, on the other hand, was. And Song of Songs is full of play and fun and passion, involving all the senses, but nowhere does it actually talk about procreation. That's not to say that having a baby isn't a beautiful thing; it's only to say that the Bible does not present a constricting view of sex, in which the only permissible reason for having sex is to conceive a child.

> **a good girl dare**
>
> Tell your husband a fantasy—in as much detail as possible. If there's something you've wanted to try or always been curious about, tell him what you imagine. If you find this embarrassing, tell him while you're spooning or lying in the bath together so that you don't have to look at his face.

Ultimately, then, I think oral sex comes down to personal preference. Because sex is supposed to be something that connects you together, if you feel degraded or ashamed, it's not worth it. But if you want to try it, there aren't biblical injunctions against it. You can even make the case that Song of Songs 2:3, "His fruit is sweet to my taste," deliberately alludes to oral sex.

But what, exactly, does oral sex involve? When oral sex is performed on a guy, it usually involves his wife kissing, licking, and sucking his penis as she moves her mouth up and down its shaft. This doesn't have to be the whole sexual encounter, either. If you find the thought of kissing his penis attractive, but the thought of him ejaculating while you do it terrifies you, then simply use oral sex as foreplay.

When you're on the receiving end, oral sex usually involves your husband using his tongue to stimulate your clitoris — and even your vagina. It's really no different from him kissing your nipples or other erogenous zones. They're all part of your body, after all. Yet while this can be very enjoyable, many women balk at it because they're embarrassed. *What if I'm smelly down there? And what about all the hair?* The smell can be taken care of by washing, and there isn't actually hair on the clitoris or vagina; only around it. You can keep your hair clipped shorter around the labia minora (the inner lips where your clitoris and vagina are), and that may relieve some hesitation.

But if it's just not your thing, and you find the whole thought of it distasteful, then you don't need to try it. It's far more important to find things that you do enjoy and that you are comfortable doing and to do those things with as much gusto as you can muster than to try everything under the sun.

Anal Sex

While oral sex is practiced by the majority, anal sex is not, though its popularity is growing. Many Christians argue that the Bible specifically forbids "sodomy," although I think these passages are talking about male upon male relationships, rather than the act within a heterosexual marriage relationship (see, e.g., Lev. 18:22). I don't think the Bible actually speaks directly to the anal sex issue within marriage. Nevertheless, biblical injunction or not, I see anal sex in a very different category than oral sex.

First, anal sex can really hurt. It's also inherently more dangerous because of the risk of both tearing (fissures) and spreading disease. While the anus may be an opening in the body, the similarities with the vagina pretty much stop there. It's not like one is a front door and one is a back door; one may be a door, but the other is more like a sewage drain.

After all, they're anatomically very distinct. The vagina has many nerve endings; the rectum has virtually none. The rectum is part of the digestive system and was designed to absorb material, which is why it's so perfect for spreading disease. AIDS, for instance, spreads much more easily through anal sex than it does through vaginal sex. The vagina has a low pH to kill disease; the anus has a high pH. The vagina's cell wall is twenty-five to forty cells thick and is highly elastic; the wall of the rectum is one cell thick and is highly inelastic. If you are going to engage in any kind of anal play, you also have to be much more careful with cleanliness, since the anus obviously contains material full of bacteria, unlike the vagina.

Does this mean you can't have anal sex? I don't think the Bible explicitly forbids it, but I do believe it's becoming more popular because anything that pushes limits is now considered sexy. So if you feel tempted to try it, or if your husband wants it, ask yourself — why? Is it because you want to feel closer together, or is it because you've bought into what the pornographic culture says is sexy? If it's the latter, exercise a lot of caution, because it may feed into a view of sex that's a hindrance to intimacy rather than a help.

Sex Toys

Popping up all over my region is a chain of stores called Aren't We Naughty? While sex shops used to be lewd, dark places on back streets, these are bright, clean stores in strip malls. Sex toys have become mainstream.

Are they okay? Again, let me share my personal opinion here, rather than a biblical injunction, since I don't think the Bible directly speaks to this. Here's my problem with a lot of toys: many of them recreate body parts (specifically his) in completely unrealistic ways. Take the common vibrator, for instance, which is designed for clitoral stimulation. It vibrates very rapidly at just the right frequency to send many women over the edge.

A vibrator may feel good, but here's the problem: no guy can vibrate like that. He can't compete! And when you start to rely on a vibrator to achieve orgasm, achieving one with your husband can become increasingly difficult.

a good girl dare

Wake him up — with your mouth.

Similarly, many of the various rubber and silicone toys that mimic the penis do so in such large sizes that no man can realistically measure up. Men are insecure enough as it is about the size of their penis. Putting something inside you that's bigger isn't likely to help his confidence at all and could then put you in the awkward position that you may find you like something larger after all. Just stick to him, rather than comparing him to something unrealistic. It's much safer.

It's one thing to use a feather to excite someone or to put an ice cube in your mouth and then kiss him all over. It's quite another to buy an expensive toy that you use to give yourself a kind of pleasure he can't. Then he's left out of the sexual act for you — even if he's the one applying the toy.

I am not saying that all sex toys are wrong; I think it depends on the toy and the purpose for which it's used. I'm just wary of ones that do something to you that he never could, because that can make it much more difficult for you to respond sexually just to him. Some women who have had difficulty reaching orgasm during intercourse have turned to sex toys as a way to "train" their bodies. It's better to practice his foreplay techniques and learn your own arousal levels than to turn to a toy that practically guarantees you orgasm with *it* — but not orgasm with *him*.

Most of the internet literature on sex toys talks about women's sexual liberation as if orgasms are something that we are all entitled to. Yes, God created us to be orgasmic, but that doesn't mean he wants us to orgasm in any way and with anybody. Orgasm is part of a relationship, and when we separate the two, we make sex into something that is purely physical again. The sex toys aren't creating a connection between you; they're making you have almost parallel sexual experiences in which you both may be having good times at the same time, but you're having them separately.

Tread carefully with sex toys. Again, I don't think there are biblical injunctions against them; I think the context of the marriage relationship blesses just about anything. But I'd take certain sex toys in the spirit of "'I have the right to do anything,' you say — but not everything is beneficial" (1 Cor. 6:12). They aren't forbidden, but think and pray about using them before you add to your marriage something that could drive you into an unhealthy emphasis on sexual pleasure for its own sake rather than for the relationship's sake.

Lingerie

I love lingerie. It's pretty. Even the skimpy stuff can hide a multitude of sins, like stretch marks or a tummy or cellulite. Most of us feel more confident with something on rather than being completely naked, and the act of taking something off — slowly — is highly erotic to men.

So I say, jump in with the lingerie! Your husband is highly visual, and the only naked woman he is allowed to look at is you! Make it worth his while by building variety into what you wear to bed. You can even text him and tell him what to anticipate!

Lingerie gets a bad rap, I think, because it is associated with prostitutes or with role-playing. My friend Karen says one question that often comes up in her circle is when does lingerie become a costume? And are costumes bad? I think the answer to that has to do with how we feel about role-playing, so let's turn to that now.

Role-Playing

What if you have always fantasized about being a stowaway on a pirate ship? Or a girl in a harem (Esther, anyone?)? Is it okay to act out these fantasies? After all, even if the fantasy involves strangers, you're doing it with your husband, so does anything go?

Most of us fantasize. Whole books have been written of collections of women's fantasies. They're standard fare. So how do we approach them as Christians?

The traditional line Christians take goes something like this: If you are pretending to be anybody other than who you actually are, you are thus committing lust and bordering on adultery.

I think that's too hard-lined a stance. Let me explain. Role-playing usually revolves around one of three things: promiscuity, sexual acts, or a power relationship. Promiscuity is just plain wrong, and acting it out can fuel thoughts that are also wrong. Fantasies that involve making love with multiple partners or with a specific stranger aren't okay.

On the other hand, sexual fantasies that revolve around certain sexual acts may be fine. Usually when we want to try something new, we fantasize about it first, and some of us find it easier to try these out using some sort of role-playing or game. Again, as long as the sexual acts are agreed upon and voluntarily entered into, I don't think role-playing is wrong.

> ## a good girl dare
>
> Write out ten things you'd like to do in bed — and at least two have to be new things that you've always wanted to try. Stick them on cards and file them away. Have him do the same thing. Now every weekend you each have to draw a card and do what it says!

And when it comes to the power relationship, I'll give C. S. Lewis his two cents. Here he is, explaining why sex is not tame:

> Hence the roughness, even fierceness, of some erotic play; the "lover's pinch which hurts and is desired." How should a sane couple think of this? Or a Christian couple permit it?
>
> I think it is harmless and wholesome on one condition. We must recognize that ... in the act of love we are not merely ourselves. We are also representatives. It is here no impoverishment but an enrichment to be aware that forces older and less personal than we work through us. In us all the masculinity and femininity of the world, all that is assailant and responsive, are momentarily focused.[2]

Lewis is saying that when we make love, we cease to be just Tom and Sally, or John and Kayla, or Keith and Sheila. We become just Man and Woman. In a way, we stand for masculinity and femininity, for assailant and responsive, as Lewis says. That is why erotic play is often filled with such symbolism: the conqueror and the captor, the utmost surrender. The man takes; the woman gives.

The harm comes not in the role-playing per se, but in the purpose of it. It really depends on whether the role-playing reflects a prototype (like he's in charge in a variety of possible ways) or a specific scenario (like he's a stranger you pick up at a bus stop). Many couples, for instance, have some variation on a fantasy in which the woman is "forced" or "obligated" to do something. What it is really acting out is that urge that many women feel to be at someone's disposal, and many men would love to go along with this. It's not acting out a *scenario* as much as it is acting out an element of the marriage that mimics our relationship with God: God gives the orders and we comply. And sex is a mirror for how God relates to us. Of course, God does not hurt us, nor does he degrade, insult, or embarrass us, and these parameters should also be honored in the bedroom.

Couples who play games in the bedroom often do so to explore a bit more, but it is an exploration that is special, not routine. Most wives, for instance, would hate being "at their husband's disposal" every night of the week, but occasionally it might tickle their fancy. And so the role-playing is often an exploration of our more erotic side, to separate it from everyday sexual encounters.

Role-playing that explores relationship dynamics, or hunger, or exploring the body in new ways, then, is one thing; role playing that involves pretending to satisfy the whole football team is an entirely different story.

Again, none of this means you *have* to play games; if you love your sex life now and this sort of talk makes you raise your eyebrows in incredulity, then stick to what's working! No one needs to stretch any boundaries; but since many Christians wonder about which boundaries can be breached and which cannot, I felt it needed to be addressed.

Taking X-Rated Pictures

You know that porn is wrong because you're watching other people have sex. You shouldn't lust after others, and you shouldn't support sin in any way. But what about taking pictures of yourselves? If your husband wants to shoot some naked pictures of you, or you of him, or even some pictures of both of you together, is that wrong?

No, I don't think so, especially since men are so visually stimulated. You are married, and it is perfectly okay to love looking at each other's bodies and to become aroused at what you can do together.

But I do see two possible red flags: one is spiritual, and the other is practical. On the spiritual side, if he's been a porn user and he wants to recreate what he's seen elsewhere, then doing so could feed his improper view of sexuality. Yes, sex should be exciting, but if he needs to objectify you to become aroused, be careful.

Now what about the practical problem? You wouldn't want such pictures falling into anyone else's hands, especially your children's. If you do want to take pictures, I'd suggest having fun posing, let him look at you from all angles, look at the pictures afterwards, and then delete them right away!

Shaving

The latest trend in porn is the Brazilian wax, where women have no pubic hair at all. It's all been removed, so they look as if they're prepubescent. Is this okay to do?

I don't believe that there is a specific injunction against it, though again, I see two red flags: a spiritual one and a practical one. On the spiritual side, this trend was definitely started by porn. Twenty years ago, no one was talking about a Brazilian wax. Women may have shaved or waxed so that they looked good in a bathing suit, but the bikini line was the only concern. Today, many women remove all their pubic hair, and it's largely because porn has made this shaved look mainstream. If you or your husband want this, then ask yourself *why?* If it's because you really enjoy oral sex, and you find this makes it easier, then that is your decision. But ensure it's not because you're giving in to what the porn industry deems sexy — especially since it's a disturbingly perverted view of the female body, making us look like we're still little girls.

And let's not forget the practical. When you get rid of all the hair in very sensitive areas and then the hair starts to grow back in, it itches. Terribly. After being shaved in some rather intimate areas for episiotomies after delivering my babies, I would never voluntarily want to do that again. Besides, the vaginal area has a lot of bumps and ridges, and shaving can easily lead to nicks. Waxing can be painful if you do it yourself, and mildly humiliating if someone else does it. It's a lot of work to keep up. So think twice before going totally bare!

Masturbation

Masturbation is the dirty little secret in many people's backgrounds, and that's exactly how we see it: as something dirty. When we masturbate, we fantasize, and fantasy is lust. Therefore masturbation is wrong, isn't it?

Well, yes. And no. Let's go back to first principles with marriage again to figure this one out. Masturbation can be divided into two categories: (1) solo masturbation for sexual release, and (2) masturbation for sexual pleasure with our partners. The first category is how we typically view masturbation: it's done in secret when one is aroused and needs release. The compulsive pornography user, for instance, always masturbates to the images he sees (and usually to the images *she* sees). This kind of masturbation is definitely wrong, because it's pure and simple lust.

But that's not the only reason masturbating in secret is wrong. It also steals sexual energy from your spouse, and your spouse needs to be the only sexual outlet for you. God designed sex between two people, not for one person, and even though you are a sexual being, you are not supposed to act on that sexually except with a spouse.

One Good Girl, married fifteen years, knows this from experience. She writes:

> I basically refused my husband sexually for ten plus years. But, selfishly, for the last five plus years of that time, I was masturbating to orgasm pretty much daily. I am now at 150 weeks "clean," but we are still struggling in our sexual relationship.
>
> It occurred to me the other day that maybe one of the reasons I struggle so much when I do not orgasm with my husband

goes back to all that masturbation. It's kind of like how pornography affects people, how they become unable to have a healthy sexual relationship with a real person.

When we turn to masturbation instead of our husbands, it affects our ability to respond to them. Let's face it: a female orgasm is awfully tricky. You have to apply just the right amount of pressure on the clitoris for just the right amount of time, every now and then varying the rhythm. Most women, if they tried, could bring themselves to orgasm much faster than their husbands could (though it wouldn't be as emotionally — or even ultimately as physically — satisfying). And if you do this often enough, as this woman did, your body can start to crave stimulation that your husband can't give in the same way. You crave the shortcut to orgasm rather than the intimate experience you share together. Masturbation in secret, then, can start to deaden your desire for your husband.

Yet what if, in your marriage, your husband consistently refuses you? What about masturbating simply because you have a deep need that isn't being met?

Masturbation will not help the situation. It may offer temporary physical relief, but it will make you feel even more distant from your husband because you're not achieving the intimacy you want with him. And it could lead to a double life, like the one our Good Girl above lived. Things that are done in secret usually multiply, causing other things to be done in secret and pushing couples further apart. If you enjoy masturbation, for instance, you could start to look forward to the times when he's not home so you can be by yourself. Little can be more poisonous to a marriage. Yes, marriage is difficult when you feel sexually rejected, but the solution is not to turn to yourself, but to God.

Nevertheless, the problem masturbation poses to a marriage usually relates more to the secrecy than to the act itself. The secrecy cuts you off from your spouse and further eats into the spiritual union you should have. When secrecy and finding another sexual outlet aren't factors, though, I am not comfortable pronouncing the actual act as wrong. Many couples separated by business trips for long periods of time, for instance, engage in "phone sex," where they talk to each other while masturbating. They release tension and giggle about it afterwards. They're doing something together, they're each fully aware of what the other is doing, they're fantasizing about each other, and they're helping each other get sexual release — even if it isn't in a traditional way.

Other couples use masturbation as part of their sexual play in bed, with some major benefits. If you can show each other how you like to be touched, for instance, it's easier to pleasure your spouse. When health issues prevent or inhibit vaginal intercourse, masturbation can help you maintain intimacy and still experience sexual release — especially if you touch each other as well. When it is done within the marriage bed and you are not using masturbation to deprive each other of anything — such as intercourse or a sexual outlet — then it can be a tool for enhancing one's sex life. When you use masturbation so that you don't need your spouse, or when you prefer masturbation to intercourse and thus deny your spouse intercourse (when health issues aren't involved), it becomes a problem.

> **a good girl dare**
>
> Show him how you want to be touched by touching yourself while he watches. This requires a lot of trust (and vulnerability on your part), but he'll love it! And if he can see and learn how you like being touched, then he's more likely to be able to make you feel great.

Final Thoughts

This chapter is not an exhaustive list of all the sexual acts I'm frequently questioned about — there are just too many! But I hope you have a picture of how you can start to evaluate their benefits or hazards in a marriage: if it is harmful, hurtful, sinful, or coerced, it's wrong. If it enhances play, does not degrade, does not promote promiscuity, and is mutually agreed upon, it's not just fine, it's actually part of a pure, intimate marriage and something to be celebrated together. It's reflecting that hunger we have for a deep union, and it's part of what we were created to experience.

Now that we've dealt with these things, let's turn to the next important stage in our sexual journey: nurturing our friendship so we learn to laugh!

PART 4

relationship discovery: laughter

CHAPTER 9

Becoming
Best Friends

Early in our marriage, Keith and I watched a movie in which a fun-loving couple added the words "in bed" to the end of any Chinese fortune, giving that fortune an entirely new meaning. We decided the game sounded fun, so since then, whenever we've visited a Chinese restaurant, we've eagerly cracked open the cookies the instant the bill came.

We've saved well over 150 fortunes over the years, and here are just a few (you'll have to add the words "in bed" yourself):

You have the ability to be very persuasive.

Know the right moment and make your move.

You have both a lot of ideas and the energy to put them into action.

Nothing ventured, nothing gained.

It is time to help a friend in need.

You tend to draw out the talent in others.

Your present plans are going to succeed.

Be content with your lot. One cannot be first in everything.

The only man who never makes mistakes is the man who never does anything.

You possess an excellent imagination.

Use your talents. That's what they are intended for.

A focused mind is one of the most powerful forces in the universe.

Fight for it. You will come out on top.

You work best when meticulous attention to detail is called for.

The measure of time to your next goal is the measure of your discipline.

If your feet are firmly planted, you cannot be moved.

You can't expect to be a lucky dog if you're always growling.

No matter what mood we're in, if we find a "good" fortune, we smile. We even snicker over some of the ones that just don't work, like, "You have great entrepreneurial skills."

a good girl dare

Watch a movie tonight — naked under the blankets.

Having little inside jokes that can turn up at odd times throughout the week makes you laugh together and reminds you that you are connected in a very unique way to this person — and only to this person. It's a whole different kind of fun.

Building Fun into Your Marriage

And fun is what we need in our relationships. Without laughter, sex becomes far too serious. With laughter, we create shared intimacies and a closer bond. We need that closer bond to prevent sex from becoming, as C. S. Lewis said, a "false goddess." Sex isn't the basis for our relationship; it's the culmination of everything else, especially the friendship that we share.

That's one of the reasons, incidentally, why it's so important to save sex for marriage. That delayed gratification means that during your dating months and years you're learning to do things other than just make out. You take up biking. You play games. You listen to music. You find hobbies together. You serve together. You form common interests, and you talk about all kinds of things so that you are closely connected.

A GOOD GIRL SPEAKS: *"I find that our sexual relationship is like a thermometer in our marriage. If we don't spend much time doing things together outside the bedroom, we don't tend to do things together inside the bedroom (or whichever room)." (married 7 years)*

But then you marry, and often these things fall by the wayside because now you can actually *do it*! And so sex takes over, and if the sex isn't perfect, then you feel as if you've somehow failed.

You haven't. You're simply still on that journey toward increased intimacy, and the more that you can give yourself a break in the physical realm and keep working on your friendship, the more the physical side of sex is going to be fun too. And the easier time you'll have feeling a spiritual connection. You'll be able to relax and be able to give and receive much more easily. And relaxation is the key to a woman's sexual response.

Couples who focus too much on orgasm and not enough on friendship don't tend to have satisfying sex lives, because they've forgotten that it's not just about body parts; it's about the relationship. And when couples are trying to recover from pornographic addictions or from a "bad girl/bad boy" approach to sex, or even from a fear that sex is somehow shameful, the bedroom can seem so vitally serious. Connecting intimately both physically and spiritually is something that can take years for a couple to perfect. That's why sometimes it's important just to chill. If you've been married for a short

A GOOD GIRL SPEAKS: *"[Sex] takes practice, work, and a good sense of humor." (married 7 years)*

time, or if you're about to tie the knot, accept that sex is probably the main area you'll devote emotional and physical energy to in the first few years of marriage. Any problems will seem huge, because you were both expecting things to go like clockwork, and they likely won't. You have two options when this happens: you can sulk and blame, or you can throw up your hands, laugh, and say, "I guess it's going to take awhile to get this right!" I did the first. I so wish that I had done the second. And so, my dear girls, in this chapter I'd like to show you how putting a high value on friendship and laughter lowers the stresses in your marriage and smoothes the way for a much more fulfilling sex life.

Becoming Best Friends

Before we were married, my husband and I were once washing the dishes when I accidentally splashed him with water. He "accidentally" splashed me back. And within a few minutes a full-blown water fight had erupted, which I finally won because he was laughing too hard to fight back.

A GOOD GIRL SPEAKS: *"I think sex gets better the longer you are married and the more you know about your spouse. We had great sex then, but I think we have even better sex now. Now to get working on the dating part again ..."* *(married 17 years)*

Couples who are close friends are able to have fun together outside of the bedroom — and it's that fun that often feeds the more physical kind. You need to enjoy being together, to feel that the other person prioritizes your needs, and to feel as if you have something to share other than just genitals. Sex involves being vulnerable, and we can't be vulnerable with someone we don't love and trust. And so we have to create that relationship first so the physical can then thrive.

Developing Common Hobbies

People may tell you that the main causes for divorce are money issues, sex issues, and problems with the kids. These are all important, but I think there's something far more fundamental at work in all of these issues: we just don't connect. We've stopped being able to talk and solve problems, and the reason is usually quite simple: we've stopped doing things together. Two people can't solve problems if they don't first have a foundation of liking each other and laughing together. Before we can attack our marriage problems, we need to remember why we enjoy each other in the first place. We need to spend time together.

That's easier said than done, though, because most of us don't share our spouse's hobbies. Guys like tinkering with cars or computers, playing or watching sports, or playing video games. When we marry, they settle down into their hobbies, and we girls develop those of our own — crafts, watching TV, playing on the Internet, or organizing the house and cooking. Often couples find that the only things they actually do together are logistical — grocery shopping, errands, and caring for children.

That's what happened to a couple who are very important to me

—I'll call them Tanya and Mike. They were passionately in love with each other when they married. Their attraction was rock solid, but unfortunately they had little else in common other than the children who came in quick succession. Too early in their relationship they started to lead very separate lives. Tanya stayed home with the children all day, and then in the evening would occasionally convince Mike to watch them so she could have a "girls' night out" with old girlfriends from high school. Mike drowned himself in video games.

Soon they did absolutely nothing together other than have sex. They didn't even eat together most nights, since Mike would eat in front of the computer, and Tanya often ate with the children. I wasn't surprised when their marriage ended after less than a decade. Nothing was gelling them together.

What I'm amazed at, though, is the number of couples who think this kind of distance is inevitable. Nonsense! Tanya and Mike did not *have* to drift apart; just as easily they could have drifted together if they had made an effort to have fun together. And you and your spouse don't need to drift apart, either. After all, you have a brain and a body. That means you can think and move. So figure out some things you can do to move together! I hated gym class in school with such a passion that I used to fake asthma attacks to escape them. But that never meant I hated exercise; I just hated anything team oriented. So when my husband started playing squash with some friends, I decided it was worth a try. For five years, until our local squash club closed, we played squash several times a week. It helped us stay slim, and it was the impetus for loads of laughter.

Keith and I have taken ballroom dancing lessons too (though that took some prodding on my part). We've started cross-country skiing in the winter and biking in the summer. We have played board games with the children from the time they were old enough to graduate from Candyland. We still have hobbies we do separately, but we also make an effort to do things together.

> **a good girl dare**
>
> Apply some bright lipstick in the morning and leave marks on your husband's body that only he will see that day. Tell him you're branding him because he's yours.

Share His Interests

If you can't seem to find common ground with your husband, or if he doesn't sound enthusiastic about your new role as activities director, why not take an interest in what he already likes? If he enjoys hockey or football games, go with him occasionally. If he loves Sunday afternoon football, put some effort into learning about the teams and the rules and watch with him, even if you have to knit or crochet or cross-stitch at the same time.

My friend Lisa took up hunting with her husband, and every fall they head out to bag a deer together. Shooting Bambi may not be your idea of romance, but actually, spending a weekend in a rustic hunting cabin, with only a wood stove for heat so you have to snuggle, can be quite a bonding experience.

Kendria and Juan had been married for twenty years when Kendria started to feel antsy. They had been active in their California church, raised three great children, and led the youth. Gradually, though, Kendria confesses, they grew apart. Her life revolved around the kids, and his revolved around fishing and the gym. They had nothing in common anymore. When Kendria started to entertain thoughts of leaving, she panicked and took matters into her own hands. She explains:

> Last March our marriage suffered a huge blow. It was not looking good for us. Our church was having their annual fishing tournament, so I decided to go this year for the entire week and fish with my husband. I know it was the Lord! We purchased a boat, and in the four days on the boat and in the hotel, we really reconnected. And I won the tournament with a sixteen-pound catfish!
>
> I am surprised at how much I like to fish. I like the anticipation of the fish getting on my line. And I *love* the fight to bring the fish in the boat. I am surprised that I can and will bait my own hook! But I love the time we have to talk in between catching fish. It is so relaxing on the water. Now I understand why he loves it.
>
> My husband is proud of me for fishing. He brags all the time

about my fishing skills. When we've gone into bait stores, I have heard at least ten men say, "Man, I wish my wife would fish with me!" I didn't understand how much just going fishing meant to my husband and other men. I think they just want to be first in our lives and share their passions with us.

Spending all day on a boat waiting for fish to bite while handling worms and fish guts wasn't really something Kendria ever thought she'd enjoy. But she knew her marriage was in trouble because she and her husband were drifting apart. And look how that one relatively small thing — deciding to participate in his hobby — changed the whole dynamic of their relationship. Of course many guys pursue hobbies because they need their "man-cave" time — or time just to be a guy without women around. Don't interfere with this! But find a hobby that you can share together, even if it's not something you think you'd enjoy, and you may just find your relationship is stronger for it.

When you spend time together and invest in each other's lives, it is much easier to navigate the bumps in a relationship, because you have some strength to draw from. If all you're ever doing is ironing his shirts or figuring out who is picking up food tonight, problems will become magnified because you haven't developed a friendship.

Don't accept no for an answer in this realm of your life. You need to spend time doing something — almost anything — together on a regular basis. It doesn't have to be strenuous — you can even just place a book you like reading aloud to each other on your bedside table. Keith and I have read Dave Barry's columns and humor novels to each other at night. When you laugh so hard you're afraid you might pee, you're building great memories and a great friendship!

Sharing Our Thoughts

Spending time together will make you feel much more connected to your hubby — which will make you want to feel even more connected in other ways. But there's one more element we women need to really get in the mood. We have to be able to share our thoughts and hearts too. Fast-forward ten years after the wedding, and the following scenario becomes all-too-frequent: It's been a long, hard day. You've been wiping snotty noses, visiting the bank and the dentist, and throwing food on the table before chauffeuring to karate. The principal called today and wanted to talk about a bullying incident having to do with your six-year-old. The karate club says that your eight-year-old has great potential and should take an extra lesson each week. And your sister called; she and her husband are having problems.

The kids are now in bed and you want nothing more than just to relax and let all of those concerns fade away. You head into the bedroom, and there's your hubby, whom you adore, getting ready for bed. But you know from the glint in his eye that sleep is not what he's planning.

You smile and scatter your clothes in all directions, following him to the bed, praying that the kids stay asleep and don't bug you. He reaches for you and starts kissing you. And then — from somewhere deep within, you're not even sure where — you find yourself pushing him aside and saying, "Do you think Jeffy should take two karate lessons a week? He is really gifted, but I don't know if the teacher is just trying to get more money from us. And can we even swing it? When will we eat dinner as a family? But I know he really wants to do it. And then maybe he could teach his little brother to stick up for himself more when bullies pick on him. What do you think?"

Your husband sighs and rolls over as he starts to grunt monosyllabic answers to your monologue about karate, bullies, money, dentists, and schedules.

Then, when you're finished, you start kissing him again, but he doesn't seem interested. You're mildly ticked at him for being ticked at you, but you can't quite put your finger on the problem. So you give him a peck on the cheek and roll over and go to sleep. Maybe tomorrow night ...

Let's diagnose what's going on in this situation. Did you want to make love to your husband? Or were you pushing him away when you started talking?

From personal experience, here's my interpretation: you did want to make love, but you knew that you weren't emotionally or mentally ready yet because you had to get all this stuff that was inside your head out. As we've already learned, for women, sex is largely in our brains. If our heads aren't engaged, our bodies won't follow.

It took me awhile to figure that out about myself. I thought when I started talking instead of engaging in foreplay that I was somehow pushing my husband away. But I wasn't. My brain was just trying to relieve itself of all the pressure so that I could be present with him! *Talking was the foreplay.* I wasn't looking for my husband to solve my problems; I just needed to get the concerns out so that they weren't bouncing around in my brain like balls in a pinball game.

Now that we understand that, our evenings look much different. We'll often take walks after dinner to talk about the pressures I'm feeling or the frustrations I have so that they don't have to spill out right before bed. And Keith knows that for me that's part of warming up.

Maybe you're like that too. Explain to your husband that it's not that you don't want to make love; it's only that you may not be able to fully enjoy sex without that fifteen minutes of talking first to relieve the pressures of the day. When he sees what's in it for him, he may not become so prickly.

A GOOD GIRL SPEAKS: *"I made a private decision never to say no to him, and I've never regretted it. (Well, except for ten minutes here and there!) Because he knows that I will give if at all possible, he tries to pay attention to how my health is before initiating. This openness and self-denial on both sides has been a huge factor in us being best friends."* (married 2 years)

Sharing what's in your heart is a great start, but for most of us that's all it is: a start. We don't really feel connected unless we also hear what is in our husbands' hearts. Unfortunately, men often aren't as interested in sharing feelings as women are; frequently they'd rather just share body parts. That doesn't mean they don't have things to share; it's just that they like to share differently from the way we do, and we often disdain their ideas of "connecting." We women need that face-to-face time, which is why we get so ticked off when we're trying to talk to them and they don't look up from the video game. We like scrutinizing faces, watching laugh lines, and seeing ourselves reflected in their eyes. When we see eyeballs, we figure ears are listening. Without eyeballs, we figure we're being tuned out.

Not so fast! While women may like to communicate face-to-face, men often feel most comfortable and empowered communicating side by side. They're far more likely to open up and talk if they're also doing something else at the same time. So talk while you're walking, fishing, cooking, or driving. Don't demand that he sit across the table or bed from you and do nothing but talk for half an hour. That's likely not how he's made to share. Kendria, for instance, found that she and Juan hardly ever talked. But get her in that fishing boat, and suddenly he opens up!

Once you've developed that combination of spending time, sharing thoughts, and having fun, you'll likely find you're both far more receptive to spending more active time together at night. Sometimes cultivating that vital friendship, though, isn't easy simply because life gets in the way. Let's look at some of the common things that often undermine our friendship.

Defeating Exhaustion

In 2010 a National Sleep Foundation Survey reported that 25 percent of people living with a spouse/partner reported being too tired to have sex.[1] I'm actually surprised that the number's not higher. I remember when my daughters were little and I was so desperate to get at least six hours a night (even if it was broken up), that sex was far down on my priority list. It didn't mean that Keith and I weren't intimate; it's just that I was far more attuned to my need for sleep than I was my need for sex.

Whether due to children or work or school or just life, many of us are run so ragged that sleep looks awfully appealing at night. In fact, given the responses to my survey about sex, I think more women have rotten sex lives because they're too tired than because their husbands are distant. Exhaustion is our main problem. We may not think of exhaustion as a marriage issue, but it is. When we're tired, we don't have time to pay attention to our husbands because we're so desperate for time on our own just to relax or rest.

Recharging Your Batteries

So let's treat exhaustion seriously. What drains your batteries? Your job, talking to certain people, doing housework, running after kids, chauffeuring, scheduling? Minimize those things as much as possible. Get organized when it comes to errands and chores so they don't eat as much time. Stop calling your sister so much if she drives you crazy.

Yet we can't eradicate everything that drains us. Toilets still need to be cleaned. Homework still needs to be supervised. Work still needs to get done. So if you can't get rid of the stuff that makes you tired, add more of the stuff that gives you energy.

Don't let yourself come last in your list of priorities. Schedule time during the day to rejuvenate. Often we feel physically exhausted when the actual problem is that we just have too much on our plates and thus too much constantly going through our brains. Turn off the constant noise in your brain telling you to do more, and turn on the part of your brain telling you to slow down. You'll find you're less tired and much more in the mood than when you're always focusing on all the things you "should" be doing.

A GOOD GIRL SPEAKS: *"I'm too tired most of the time for sex due to children, home responsibilities and work.... When we're both frustrated, we negotiate an earlier bedtime so we can be intimate." (married 12 years)*

The biggest "should" in your life is about your marriage. You *should* be enjoying your husband. Are you? If you're too tired to enjoy him, then you have to cut stuff out and spend more time nurturing yourself. Growing your marriage is the most important responsibility you have, so stop allowing your husband to come last in your list of priorities.

Random Acts of Kindness

When we're exhausted, we naturally think most of our own needs. We're depleted, and we need to be filled up. Thinking that someone else may need something from us is the last thing we want to hear. But that kind of mentality only makes marriage worse.

Our son died five years into our marriage. Keith and I felt God carrying us through that time, but it took years until we were back on our feet and could laugh and smile and live large. During those years, a wise woman advised us to write down twenty things that our spouse could do for us that would make us happy. The rules were simple: the things had to be easy to do; they had to be free (or at least very cheap); and they had to have nothing to do with sex.

> **a good girl dare**
>
> Have a code phrase that means "I'm hot for you right now" like "Is it time for an oil change yet?" Work it into everyday conversation when you're with friends.

Coming up with twenty was a challenge, but we did it! They were small things, like "Kiss me as soon as I come in the door," "Give me a massage," or "Tell a friend that you love me when I can hear it." None of them took an inordinate amount of effort, but they all made us feel loved.

Then we switched lists, and we had to commit to doing two or three things on that list a day. It became like a game: which ones could we carry out next? And it forced us to come out of our own headspace and enter into each other's. It made us think that someone else had needs today too.

We all have different love languages, and it was important for each of us to figure out how to make the other person feel cherished.[2] But more than just figuring out what each other's love language was, we had to understand what little things fit in with each of those love languages.

When we're feeling remarkably close to each other, these things are easy to do. When we're walking through a bleak time because of grief, busyness, illness, unemployment, or infertility, these things become harder, because we tend to retreat into ourselves. Then we get angry because our spouse isn't meeting our needs — though any outside observer would instantly recognize that we're not exactly meeting his either. It's in those difficult times that it's even more important to challenge yourself to do acts of kindness. As we "act" kind, we tend to feel more tenderhearted and kindly toward our beloveds too.

If you think doing acts of kindness is hard when you're just exhausted, wait until you have children! Then a whole other level of stress conspires to rob you of your connection.

Putting the Marriage before the Kids

Pretty much every stage of parenthood provides its challenges: getting pregnant, being pregnant, caring for a baby, training a toddler, raising a teen, becoming an empty nester. Parenthood is busy and all-consuming, even when you're in the "just trying to get pregnant," or perhaps even "just trying *not* to get pregnant" stage. Birth control can put a damper on connection, since there isn't a perfect solution that allows total freedom but also doesn't kill libido. On the other hand, if you're trying to get pregnant, sex can lose its appeal too. It becomes all about ovulation. He doesn't like performing on a schedule, and you just want him to hurry up and do it so you can conceive.

The timing and size of your family are huge issues, and unless you feed your friendship, getting on the same page can prove awfully difficult. So keep talking, keep praying, and above all, keep working on having fun outside the bedroom. The more goodwill you build up in your relationship, the easier it will be to work through these difficult decisions and difficult periods in your marriage.

A GOOD GIRL SPEAKS: *"I never imagined that a day would come when my life was so physically exhausting that sex would become work — that I might not always be ready to go when he was. Five kids later though, we still make intimacy a top priority (and always have)." (married 5 years)*

All-Consuming Babies

As much of a challenge as preparenthood days are, though, parenthood can add a whole new layer of distance between you and your spouse. When a baby comes, Mom automatically becomes preoccupied with the baby — and understandably so. She's losing massive amounts of sleep — up to two months' worth in the first year of each baby's life, according to one British study.[3] Her husband falls far down her priority list.

Part of this is natural to us women — we develop a strong physical bond with another human being who is always hanging off of us. We get our cuddle time from a

A GOOD GIRL SPEAKS: *"There was definitely a strain in our marriage when we had babies. I was really tired and not very interested in sex, but he wanted me as much or more than ever. We worked through that stage of life, and our marriage is much stronger now."* *(married 12 years)*

baby and don't need our husbands for that quite as much. But don't give in to this tendency to retreat from your marriage. Your husband must always be your primary relationship — before your relationship with your children. Your husband was there first and will be there when the kids leave. And children fare best when their parents have a rock-solid relationship. *Do not let children displace your husband.*

Keep Your Bedroom to Yourself

Many parents opt for cosleeping, which means sleeping with the babies in bed (often called the "family bed" in parenting literature), because it helps Mom get more sleep (since she can breast-feed while lying there), and it builds intimacy and bonding.

In my husband's pediatric practice, he often talks to couples who cosleep, and almost inevitably he finds that it is the wife's choice, and not the husband's. The husband goes along with it because he feels like he must, but he's scared of rolling on the baby (a fear that is justified, as the American Academy of Pediatrics states)[4], and he doesn't like the new arrangement because he feels displaced.

Duane, a father-to-be, raised this issue in a *New York Times* parenting blog:

> As a father-to-be with a wife who really wants to co-sleep with our coming baby, I'm struggling with the idea. I have been through 100s of websites, and 98 percent are written by women saying how great it is and how happy it makes them. So far no one is really taking the father into consideration. From what I see, the father is left to deal with whatever the mother wants

and is left to the wayside. I feel that our bed is just that — *our* bed, for me and my wife. How do you not lose intimacy with each other when you have a baby/toddler between you? Does the father's opinion and feelings matter, or should I just shut up and do what my wife wants?[5]

Be careful about dismissing Duane out of hand, as many of the commenters did, claiming that he should understand that now the baby comes first. Commenter Kelly, for instance, condescended to say this:

> This just sounds like whining. Guess what? It's not all about you anymore. If your wife says she needs that baby next to her, I'd listen. She's a woman and the mother, and I'd say she has instincts about this beyond what you could possibly imagine. Both of you should trust them.

This idea that women know best when it comes to children, and men should just get out of the way and stop "whining," is toxic to a marriage. Parenting means that you have even more of a responsibility to work on your marriage, not less, because now more people depend on you.

When I asked about cosleeping on my Facebook page, I received dozens of answers from women, many of whom said something like this: "In your first year with a new baby, you're not going to sleep or have sex much regardless of where the baby sleeps. It's the lack of sleep that does it to you, not where the baby is. So bring the baby in bed if it helps you!"

Certainly in those first few months sleep is the main issue, and if Mama's tired, nothing's happening anyway. If

> **a good girl dare**
>
> Go on a braless scrubbing/ cleaning spree so he can appreciate the bouncing.

cosleeping helps you sleep, then go ahead, providing you have read and accept the American Academy of Pediatrics' warning. But think twice before you make it a habit to invite older babies and toddlers to share your bed perpetually. You need a place where you and your husband can be "just the two of you." Having kids in your bed will kill your sex life. As one Facebook fan admitted, "Kids were our birth control."

One cosleeping website I found dismissed the concerns about lack of sex with this comment: "Many cosleeping couples find that they are able to make love right in the bed while their child (or children) sleeps. How do you think families that live in huts, igloos, or other one-room structures manage to procreate? Simply have silent, almost motionless sex."[6]

Can you imagine telling your husband, "Don't worry, honey, for the next few years we'll just have silent, motionless sex!" I can't think of very many guys who would be enthralled with that, and yet all over women's media, this is being touted as what is most natural for families. Yes, you love your children. Yes, you want to comfort them. But never, ever let your children be an excuse not to listen to your husband's feelings. Your relationship with him comes first, not last, and that includes putting a priority on sex. It's hard to do that if toddlers are sleeping between you. Some women told me that they can just make love in another room if the kids are in bed, but I doubt that results in the same frequency as when you can just turn to each other when you're already lying beside each other. You're more likely to have sex if you don't have to work as hard at it — so don't put up barriers to intimacy with your husband.

A GOOD GIRL SPEAKS: *"Our differences created a rift that I felt guilty about, because it was I who didn't have the drive. But talking it out with him helped us both.... He was able to see that it wasn't personal; it was hormonal (after having babies) or stress/fatigue related; and I was able to let some of my feelings go. Not talking about them only made them grow. But sharing my heart with my best friend, my husband, allowed me to clean out those feelings of stress and guilt and made room for a sex drive. We now are more verbal during the day about our intents for sex at night and make every effort possible to avoid the common pitfalls (i.e., if he knows he's gonna get 'lucky,' he'll help more to put the kids to bed or finish the laundry — a score for us both!)." (married 13 years)*

When Kids Grow

The problem doesn't end when babies are out of the bed, though; even when they grow, kids can put a damper on your sex life. Here's a busy woman, married for fourteen years, who says:

> With four young kids and homeschooling, it is hard to feel like "doing it." We do talk once in a while to discuss this. We know that it takes work. I should initiate more often; I just don't have the energy at the end of the day.

Today this couple makes love less than once a week just because she is so tired. Ironically, sex would probably cure a lot of that tiredness! When we make love, we release hormones into our bodies that relax us, and we sleep better. We feel more connected to our husbands, so we don't carry around guilt that we're not being good wives — guilt that is, in and of itself, exhausting.

Life is so busy that you can always find reasons for ignoring your husband. Don't accept them as excuses. When you start to see yourself falling into a rut of exhaustion, overcommitment, or worry, it's time to turn more to your husband, not less. Don't live in survival mode.

Keep Everything in Perspective

Couples often have highs and lows in their sex lives. Sometimes you'll have the higher sex drive, and sometimes he'll have the higher sex drive. Rarely do married couples enjoy sex with the same frequency and intensity for decades. And couples who have a strong friendship find these things so much easier to navigate. When you're friends, sex drives return faster, because you want to give to each other.

So make this promise to yourself: *Even if I go through a sexual rut, and even if I don't always feel absolutely attracted to him, I will do my*

A GOOD GIRL SPEAKS: *"The first ten years was the hardest. It really took years for me to build up to having a drive at all. The next ten years have increasingly improved. I expect the next ten years to be even better." (married 19 years)*

best to increase the fun in our relationship. Commit to finding new ways of laughing together and expressing your commitment to each other, and problems you have in the bedroom will diminish. Then when things don't go well, just tell him, "Let's laugh about it and keep trying, because we have years to improve!"

And while you're at it, order Chinese.

CHAPTER 10

The Sex Circle:
Learning to Give

When a woman walks down the aisle, she's doing so because she firmly feels that the man she is facing is the man who will cherish her and make her feel loved for the rest of her life.

Maybe right now you don't have that kind of relationship. You've read everything I've written about friendship, and you're finding it hard to picture how to build a friendship with a guy who lives in front of the TV, never loads the dishwasher, and hardly seems interested in meeting you halfway. Yet our solutions to this supposed impasse often don't involve cherishing our husbands, either. They involve trying to *change* our husbands.

Here's an email I received asking a question that I think occurs to most wives at some point:

> Where does it say that everyone's appetites will be filled? There are a lot of things I want or would like to have but no guarantees I can have them just because I want them. It would be nice if we all had equal appetites, sure. But when one isn't as interested (due to lack of drive/stress etc., not withholding out of anger) why must they be the one who needs to fix their "problem"?... Why shouldn't the other be advised to control his/her urges?

In this chapter, I want to talk to the women who struggle with this issue. You may want me to say, "If he wants it a lot, it's his problem," but I can't do that. If he has a problem, then your marriage has a problem. And you can't change anyone else, anyway. What I hope I can do here instead is to help you to understand his point of view —

and show you a route out of this resentment and defeating attitude. I'm not laying the problem completely at your feet, but I do believe that the best hope you have of dealing with a difference in libidos is to work on yourself rather than on him.

Practicality, though, isn't my only motivation here. Plenty of women feel that marriage would be so much better if sex just weren't a factor — if we could just snuggle and talk and be good friends, maybe while sharing a box of chocolates. That may sound delectable to you, but that's not the way God made marriage. God made it so that in sex we reaffirm our commitment and we feel far more bonded. Sex isn't a negotiable part of the marriage; it's a vital part of it.

Yet God designed us so that we are very different in the way we approach sex. And the biggest challenge God has given us women is whether we will accept our husband's drive and jump in. God gave men an awfully big challenge too: he asked them to accept our need for emotional attachment and to open their hearts to us. We each have our own issues that God gave us to learn selflessness and surrender.

So let's turn to the lessons that we women need to learn. In researching this book, I conducted a focus group with several men, as well as large-scale surveys with both men and women. The women's responses didn't really surprise me; I'm a woman, after all. The men's responses weren't all that surprising, either. But what did hit me was the emotion behind them.

One very attractive man, married to an equally attractive woman, expressed an amazing level of hurt that his wife didn't seem to want sex more. "In just under a decade, she's initiated twice. Two times. That's it. Once every five years. How does she think that makes me feel?" Sure, she'll often agree when he initiates, but not always. "Sometimes I just want to stop asking. It's humiliating. What guy wants to get turned down again?" From the outside, they look like they'd be all over each other. But that wasn't the case.

Here was a man who adored his wife and kids, who took his responsibilities seriously, and who wanted his marriage to thrive. But he was left with this lingering doubt about whether his wife really wanted him. "When we do have sex, it's fantastic," he admitted. "Why can't she remember that and hold on to it, so that when I ask her, she'll actually want to?"

As I listened to his story, I wished that she was there to hear the pain. And over and over again, in the survey results, our Good Guys said something similar. Just listen to them:

> "I don't feel loved because my wife doesn't want sex. I feel like she doesn't want me personally."

> "You know there is a lack of interest, but you don't really know why. You start to think, *What is wrong with me?*"

> "I feel rejected, like my wants, needs, and desires don't matter."

> "It really hurts. I feel like a failure and a horrible husband because she almost never lets us have sex. It doesn't make sense, but it's how I feel."

Speaking as one who has done my share of rejecting, I found these responses rather humbling. Looking back, I could always see the many good reasons I had for saying no to sex, and if he was hurt, I thought Keith was exaggerating. But listening to these men speak, when I wasn't emotionally involved in the situation, I began to sympathize with the opposite sex.

Sex Is Men's Major Need

Often we can't hear our husbands' pain because we're so wrapped up in our own. We're tired, and we just don't want to be bothered anymore. We feel that they want only one thing and don't really value us. We feel under pressure to perform.

Yet for most men, being desired sexually is absolutely intrinsic to their sense of self-worth. When Keith and I were first married, we fought frequently about this. He would say, "I just want you to want me!" and I would yell back, "But I do want you! I want you as my husband! I want you to be happy! I want you with me always!"

A GOOD GUY SPEAKS: *"I'm not angry — but I could use more intimacy — I miss being as close to my wife as we could be." (married 30 years)*

What he really wanted was just for me to jump him. And I couldn't do that, because somehow it felt like lying. I really didn't particularly want to make love. Sure, I'd do it if he started it, but it wasn't like I was sitting there, engines ready to go, waiting to take off. I would much rather watch a movie, read a book, cuddle, or just about anything. I was still new at sex, so it didn't always work all that well. And I was so, so tired of him wanting it all the time.

More than that, I was tired of him not accepting me. He didn't accept me as I was. He wanted me to cheat, to lie, to betray what I was feeling. He wanted me to want to make love as much as he did — and how could I force myself to do that?

I remember countless nights early in our marriage when I would be too tired to make love, or too worried, too moody, too just-about-anything, and Keith would lie in bed for about fifteen minutes before he'd get up in exasperation and go do something else. He wouldn't end up falling asleep until the wee hours of the morning. I thought he was emotionally blackmailing me: if I didn't make love, he would endanger his own health by not sleeping! And I experienced it as rejection: *He doesn't love me enough to sleep in the same bed with me if I don't have sex first.* So I told him how I felt, and poor Keith tried to sleep. He really did. But sometimes his body was just too worked up.

In my survey, over and over again I read of other marriages with similar dynamics. One forty-year-old man, who makes love less than once a week, wrote:

> *It's been a big issue for many years. I usually withdraw. I lose sleep, and it impacts every aspect of me. My wife then gets mad at me for letting it impact me.*

He can't sleep. He's hurting. And then his wife gets mad at him for hurting — just like I used to seethe at Keith. I'd wonder, *Why is he so pathetic that sex matters to him so much that he'd risk his sleep — and his relationship — over it?*

Over the years, God confronted me with my selfishness, helping me to see my husband's point of view in a new way. For most men, sex is their ultimate love language. And when we diminish its importance, we're simultaneously asking *him* to deny *his* feelings. We're asking *him* to change. We're not accepting *him* for who he is, either.

Here's what a forty-year-old woman, married ten years, said:

> I have a really low sex drive due to medical issues (medication has helped, but not as much as we'd like). I probably want to about once a week. He wants to every day, multiple times! He says I'm just so dang sexy. LOL. But he does get frustrated if I never want to or he feels like I'm "giving in." We've talked about it a lot and tried different things, and I've found that if I say yes willingly if there's not a good reason for me to say no (feel bad, bad timing), and we take plenty of time for foreplay, my sex drive does catch up eventually and I can enjoy myself fully. That makes him feel like the king of the world, and now he can accept that I have a good reason to say no when I do. Our sex life has never been better! But it has taken us time to get to this point — if we weren't so committed to this relationship, I think it would have been a major issue.

She decided that if she didn't have a good reason for saying no, she would say yes. And she found that her sex drive often caught up! I love how he feels like he's "king of the world" — so much so that they've built up enough goodwill so that on nights when having sex really won't work for her, she can say no without it affecting their relationship.

Here's how another woman came to her epiphany of what she was doing to her husband:

> About five years ago, my husband was so frustrated with being turned down so many times that he told me that from now on it was up to me to decide when we would make love. He wrote a long letter that showed me that he felt neglected by me giving all of my attention and energy to our three kids. He felt he only got leftovers. We had removed the word *divorce* from our dictionary years ago, and he reaffirmed his commitment to me as a person, his wife and mate — but just couldn't live with the lack of sexual

connection and activity. He told me (in the letter) that he would *always* be ready if and when I was in the mood. That was one of the most tearful nights we've spent as I read his letter (sitting next to him), and we just held each other for the rest of the night.

In those next four years, he *rarely* initiated and just waited on me. God mightily changed my heart and my attitude. I began to take more initiative and got more interested in him and spending time with him (his primary love language). Our sex life has been changed profoundly. We are much more playful, and while we still have a few differences, it is *so much* better now.

In the last year or so, he has begun to initiate some too, and our sex life is beginning to be more mutual. God is *so good!*

In a way, I'm sad we waited so long to get this right.

This forty-eight-year-old woman, married for over a quarter of a century, didn't figure things out until well into the third decade of her marriage. Today they make love three or four times a week, and she rates every part of her relationship as "really great." Sex didn't just fix the physical side of her relationship; it impacted everything else too. They feel so much closer now. But take heed of her last sentence: *"I'm sad we waited so long to get this right."*

Don't Give Up!

What makes me sad is that so many women think that because they don't get aroused the way their husbands do, they therefore can't make love. They're somehow helpless. I know I felt this way, and it is a self-defeating spiral. Here's how one woman described it:

My husband of nearly twenty-two years has a very high sex drive. I had no idea before we got married that our sex drives wouldn't be the same — he says he wouldn't have married me if he'd known. (But really, how was I to know?) And in order to "turn him off," so to speak, and not have him asking twenty times a day, I gained weight. I thought that if I was fat he'd leave me alone — really his needs and the constant asking made me feel as though I had no other options. So here I am, obese and a huge disappointment to him. All because I have a low sex drive.

I ache for this woman because she is hurting so badly. She feels as if her husband doesn't love her, and as if she will never be enough, and she has ruined her own health in the process. They now make love a few times a month, and she rates their friendship and their physical life as "okay," but their spiritual connection as "not great." They're not connected because they're driving each other away with competing needs.

A GOOD GIRL SPEAKS: *"When we don't have sex very much, we are quicker to fight over little things. The stress level can be easily elevated." (married 3 years)*

How could this have been handled differently? I think many women feel like this: *He wants it all the time, and I will never be enough for him, so there's no point in trying.* Yet in general that's not true. Some men with sexual addictions may want sex too often and in too many kinky ways, but what really matters to most men is not only the *frequency* but also the *enthusiasm*.

At one point when I was recovering from my sexual problems in the first few years of our marriage, I made a commitment to make love to Keith whenever he asked. I was so proud of myself! I was a great wife! I was selfless! I was marvelous! I was amazing!

And then one day, after several weeks of what I thought was fairly frequent sex, my husband turned to me and moaned, "I just feel like we never make love."

I was incensed. So, surreptitiously, I grabbed a pocket calendar and started circling the days we made love. The next time he complained, I whipped out that calendar and told him, "You have nothing to complain about, buddy."

a good girl dare

Men love looking, so let him look! Tonight, after he's ready for bed, give him a striptease. Take off your clothes slowly and seductively (and throw off your underwear and bra while you're standing on the bed).

That led to a rather interesting — and heated — discussion. But finally I understood something. Men don't want to be placated. They want to be wanted. They want to feel as if we actually desire them, not just that we're willing to lie there while they get their jollies. Listen to this frustrated and sad Good Guy in his forties who has been married for more than twenty years:

We have what I call *obligation sex*. She gives me what she thinks she has to.... Believe me, you can tell if someone is into it or not. I just have to pretend she needs it to even get excited. Sometimes I am so needing it, but because I know she's not into it, I can't even get it up, to be totally frank.... I can't say I'm upset because I need sex, because then she gets very mad. So I don't say anything, and I just accept whatever she gives me, into it or not.

This husband's feelings of rejection aren't so surprising. Remember all the books talking about how important respect is to a guy? A man needs to feel like you're glad you married him, not just because you love him, but because you've looked around and have honestly concluded that he is the perfect one for you. You appreciate who he is and what he does.

Tied up in all of that is his sexuality. It's hard for him to believe that you're proud of him and that you're happy to be married to him if you don't also want him sexually. If you don't want him like that, then you really don't think he's a capable guy, a strong guy, an amazing guy. You just want to be married to somebody, but you don't actually respect *him* anymore.

One woman, who had once struggled with this herself, said this:

[One conference leader] asked the women to imagine our husbands not speaking to us for a week or two weeks or a month. Basically that's what we're doing to our men when we refuse them sex. It's their way of checking in on our relationship. It's their way of communicating with us. If we deny them that, we've basically ceased talking with them. After I heard that, I made a point not to refuse my husband except under dire circumstances — like a puke bucket next to the bed!

Sex is men's ultimate self-esteem issue. And the best way for wives to address it is by initiating sex every now and then.

Initiation Is the Key to a Man's Heart

Now, initiating sex may be the last thing you want to do for a host of reasons. You may be tired. You may be angry at him because he doesn't really pay attention to you, so why should you pay attention to him? You may be tired of sex because it just doesn't work well for you, and he has all the fun.

Let me suggest that if you start initiating, a lot of those issues will diminish in importance. Let's take just one: whether it feels good for you. If you initiate, you set the tone and the direction for what you do! Perhaps one of the reasons sex hasn't felt stupendous is because he has been rushing things. If you initiate, you can figure out what you want him to do. You can make sure the angle and pressure are right. You can control things a little better. So why not jump in with the express purpose of figuring out what's nice for you?

A GOOD GUY SPEAKS: *"Although my wife explains that she has little or no sex drive, it is still difficult not to take it personally and believe that she is not as attracted to me as when we first met. And then I wonder if she really cares about me if she doesn't make the effort to consider my needs." (married 8 years)*

One young wife, who has been married for just two years, finds that initiating helps her in other ways too. She says:

> I have this weird issue about being touched sometimes, and I know that my husband has a stronger sex drive than I do. I tend to initiate so that I am the one in control — doing the touching and being able to determine when we have sex.

When you have sexual issues, sometimes initiating can help you feel more comfortable — and more able to enjoy yourself.

Or, conversely, if you're tired of the stress of making sure that sex is pleasurable for you (because many couples get locked into this quest to make sure that she climaxes, for instance, and then sex becomes too goal oriented to enjoy), you can initiate so that *he* can feel good. You can throw yourself into making sure that he enjoys it, thus giving him a gift. And he'll feel ten feet tall. When sex becomes about him feeling good, but you're the one who initiated it, it's okay.

When he initiates it and you don't enjoy it as much, he can feel like a failure. It's just a different dynamic.

What about other problems? Let's say that you feel as if he is distant, and you're a little ticked at him. Part of the reason that he might feel distant, though, is because he feels as if you don't want him. Most men marry thinking that we will want them all the time, and when real life intrudes and it doesn't work out that way, they have nowhere to go but to retreat. I'm not saying it's right; I'm just saying that's what a lot of men do. So if you're feeling distant, why not take that first step toward repairing the rift?

A GOOD GUY SPEAKS: *"Our issue isn't necessarily who wants it the most but rather who initiates." (married 3 years)*

What counts as initiating? So let's go over the ground rules for what counts as initiating. Initiating does not mean saying, "I'm going to go read in bed. You have five minutes to join me." It doesn't mean just jumping into bed and pulling the covers up to your neck and saying, "We can tonight if you want," or "If we start now, we could be done by ten."

We women are always bugging men about how they need to romance us, bring us flowers, give us massages, and get us in the mood. But we don't seem to feel like we should reciprocate. We figure that since they're ready pretty much instantaneously, we shouldn't have to try to seduce them. But seduction tells your husband, "I really do want you. I really am excited about what we're about to do!"

Men are visual, so use that to your advantage! I know you may not always have the energy to pull out the lingerie drawer, but you can still get undressed slowly in front of him (or up on the bed leaning over him). You can grab him and start kissing him deeply, rather than waiting for him to make the first move. Or, if he's down on

A GOOD GIRL SPEAKS: *"It's come down to a lot of negotiations. There was a time when my husband said, 'You know, it's been almost a month.' I balked. No way. I counted back — sure enough. After that we had a specific contract (which days of the week). Now it's better, so … we generally have sex about two times a week. We intend for more — but that's usually what it turns out to be." (married 12 years)*

his computer and you're on yours, pop up on his screen and let him know what he's in for. It doesn't need to take a long time; just show some enthusiasm.

You may wonder if that's even possible. How can you initiate if you're not really "in the mood"? Read on!

Jump in. Part of our problem with initiating is that we have misconceptions of how sex is going to be. We marry with expectations that sex will be a glorious, rip-roaring fun, awesome experience. If night comes and we know that we're not going to be up for a glorious, rip-roaring fun, awesome experience, we women tend to feel like we're cheating if we make love now. We should wait until we're really "in the mood."

We feel like this is the honest approach. To make love when you don't actually feel like it seems somehow like lying. But it's not. I'm not talking about faking an orgasm here; please understand me. What I am saying is that he needs it in a way that you do not. And if you can give yourself to him, even if you don't particularly feel like it, you build incredible closeness in your marriage.

A GOOD GIRL SPEAKS: *"He so appreciates it when I initiate. It creates a unique closeness that lasts for several days." (married 27 years)*

We still need those rip-roaring good times. But they don't have to happen every time. Occasionally a quickie really is okay! And if you have too much on your mind and you just don't think you can relax tonight to enjoy it, then you can still challenge yourself to make it fun for your husband.

I'm not advocating making love no matter what — even if he's having an affair, he's into pornography, or he makes you feel dirty. Absolutely not. But marriage needs give and take, and sex is too vitally important to most men for us to never do any giving. When we don't consider his needs, our own libidos become the sole determining factor in whether we make love. We hold all the cards; men hold none. If we say yes, we do. If we say no, we don't. As one Good Guy respondent shared in frustration,

The one who wants sex the least ends up being the one who

controls the sex life ... and that makes me feel powerless, tempting me to withdraw from leading in any part of our marriage.

That may sound like a cop-out, but like many men, he's hurting; he has no control over something that is the key to his heart.

We women need to give up some control. We need to say occasionally — not every night, but consistently and regularly — "I want you, and I'm here." And if we get our minds in gear, our bodies will likely follow. We may not feel in the mood beforehand, but we can get in the mood if we decide to, because sex, for women, is all in our heads.

Let me give you a different analogy. You know how children adore hotel swimming pools? When our girls were very young, we'd sometimes take them to a hotel as a treat so we could all enjoy the pool. Keith and the girls would jump in and splash and play Marco Polo, and I would shiver on the top step, slowly dipping my toe down to the second step, all the while saying to myself, "It's so cold!" Little by little, I'd submerge myself more, tottering on my tiptoes so I didn't have to get wetter than necessary. And finally, after twenty minutes of wobbling, I'd count to three about seventeen times before diving in.

A GOOD GIRL SPEAKS: *"It starts in my mind.... I can choose to be 'in the mood' and my body will follow."* *(married 30 years)*

By that time the kids were ready to get out.

I didn't save myself from feeling cold; I was freezing anyway. I would have had a much better time if I had just dived in to begin with.

It's the same with sex. Many times we women lie in bed wondering if we want to have sex. The conversation in our heads goes something like this: *Do I want to tonight? I don't know. Does he? Probably. Is he lying there waiting for me to make the first move? Or is he already asleep? Nope, it doesn't sound like he's sleeping. He's probably thinking about sex. Should I do something? I'm not sure. It's 11:15 now, and I have to be up by 6:45. Will I be too tired in the morning if we make love? How long will it take?*

By the time we figure out if we really want to or not, we could be finished. And we would sleep better too.

Don't be a silly girl, hovering on the first step of the swimming pool, missing out on all the fun! Trust yourself that if you jump in, your body will follow. In fact, that's what Rosemary Basson, a University of British Columbia researcher, found when she interviewed several hundred women.

The conventional wisdom is that desire *precedes* sexual arousal. This works for most men. Men are often coiled springs of desire and easily aroused. Men often describe their libido as a drive similar to hunger or thirst. Twentieth-century sexologists assumed that women's libido was, if not identical, then similar — and that if women didn't feel desire, then something was wrong.... Contrary to the conventional model, for many women, desire is not the *cause* of lovemaking, but rather, its *result*. "Women," Basson explains, "often begin sexual experiences feeling sexually neutral." But as things heat up, so do they, and they eventually experience desire.[1]

> **a good girl dare**
>
> Grab him and lead him to bed tonight.
> Not by his hand.

So trust yourself! You don't need to be panting before you make love; that will come if your brain is in gear. And remember, too, that if you initiate, it's easier for you to influence the pace and the activity so that you make sure you enjoy it too.

Sex Makes Him Warmer toward You

A few years ago I was scheduled to be away speaking for a few days, and the night before I left I was rather distracted. So we didn't — you know. When I arrived home from being on the road it was midnight, so we didn't — you know. The next night I knew he was hoping for it, and normally it would have happened. I like sex too, after all. But I was tired and grumpy. So we didn't. And neither of us slept well.

The night after that I threw myself into it, we had a great time, and all was well. The next day he bought me flowers. Sex flowers.

And I thought, why do I get flowers on the days after we make love and not on the days after we don't? I started to grow angry. But after I came back to earth and realized that men are not actually women, I figured out what the issue was. Keith is a guy. Guys don't always think that deeply. Here is what was going through Keith's head: *I love my wife. I think I'll buy her flowers.*

But as a woman, this is what I assumed was going through his head: *She made love to me, so she needs to be rewarded. I need to withhold romance and affection when she doesn't perform and only give it to her when she does, so she starts acting the way I want her to.*

That's not what he was thinking at all! Here's the truth: women have surges of this hormone called oxytocin more frequently than men do. It's the bonding hormone. It's present when we make love, when we nurse our babies, and at many other times. It's part of what makes us affectionate and cuddly. Men experience their biggest surge of oxytocin when they make love, which is why they feel so close to us afterwards and so lovey-dovey the next day. It's not to be manipulative; it's because they honestly feel attached and affectionate. This is the way marriage works. When you meet his needs, he starts to meet yours. It's a give and take. But if you're waiting for him to be affectionate and romantic before you make love, it may never happen.

Friendship and Sex Form a Circle

We need to see this friendship-sex thing as a circle. Yes, companionship builds better sex. But here's something else to consider: *better*

A GOOD GIRL SPEAKS: *"A number of years ago, after countless arguments about why he needed sex so much and how I wasn't in the mood, I had a complete change of heart. I realized I am so lucky to have my husband want me and my body! My rejections were tearing away at his spirit. So I vowed never to reject again. Now we never argue about sex, I want it more, he's more responsive to my emotional needs as a response to my willingness and joy in the bedroom, and our marriage has greatly benefited from our increased lovemaking. I would encourage all women to see their bodies as something with joint ownership! It's not just mine, but his as well." (married 14 years)*

sex builds companionship. It all goes back to the adage, "Men make love to feel loved, whereas women need to feel loved to make love." You can't isolate what comes first: the sex or the friendship. Both are absolutely necessary.

One thirty-something woman found this out the hard way. Married twelve years, she reports:

> I've noticed that if I turn down my husband's request for sex more than once in a row ... he starts to withdraw from me in the ways I hunger for, especially communication. I truly believe he does this without knowing — he is not the type of person to hold a grudge. It's just when I don't meet his needs, he begins to feel like he can't meet mine. It becomes a nasty circle, because when this happens, I feel less and less like having sex.

How can you stop this cycle? Just realize that the cycle also goes in the opposite direction.

Listen, girls: often we women discount the sex and put more emphasis on the friendship. We feel that sex is a baser need, while friendship is superior. In doing so, we forget the missing ingredient: *men are more likely to feel lovey-dovey toward us when they also feel sexually connected to us.* When they feel as if we want and desire them, they're more likely to get excited about playing Monopoly as a family.

And that's what Sarah Kavanagh, thirty-nine, found when she promised her husband Colin to have sex every day for a month.[2] She told Britain's *Daily Mail* how her experience surprised her.

> I'd come up with the idea because, in common with so many couples, in recent years lovemaking had been relegated an item on my agenda.
>
> Unlike the heady days when Colin and I first met, now there is always something else that takes precedence — from work to domestic chores and even the simple pleasure of a full night's sleep.

And so she took things into her hands and decided to change their routine. By day three, Colin had already cooked two meals. In the first week they battled a bit with their own feelings that love-making had become a chore, but a week later they were starting to really enjoy that chore! Every interlude didn't last hours, either; sometimes they just shared a quickie. But the repercussions were experienced in other areas of their relationship.

A GOOD GIRL SPEAKS: *"As long as the sex is going well, everything else is going well. When the sex dries up, problems arise in all other areas of our marriage." (married 13 years)*

By day sixteen, she reported, "We're definitely a lot more tactile with each other, and have started flirting again." They even found that little fights were solved faster, because "it's hard to stay mad at someone you've made love to!" And when Sarah caught a cold by day nineteen, she found that Colin had suddenly developed a deep-seated desire to play nurse — a compulsion that he had never felt before.

Sarah wrote, "My friend has lent me a DVD I've wanted to watch for ages, so I put it on after dinner. Colin and I cuddle up on the sofa together to watch it — normally he spreads out on one chair while I take over another."

They cuddled more. He cleaned more. They touched. They kissed. They flirted. They laughed. And she felt more attractive (she even lost two pounds with all the extra exercise). The question is: why?

They felt more connected to each other because they were making love more frequently. And that connection spilled over into other areas of their lives so that they just plain had more fun together! Of course you don't have to promise to make love every day to your husband. But I do think that we Good Girls need a reminder to step up to the plate.

In one of the surveys I conducted for this book, 44 percent of women reported making love less than once a week. Only 21 percent made love three or more times a week. While we may begin marriage with the best of intentions, we don't seem to follow through. And our husbands are hurting because of it. Only 35 percent of husbands report being satisfied with the frequency of making love (while 5 percent say that they feel pressure from their wives to make love more). That's a lot of dissatisfied husbands.

Let's remember that maintaining regular sex — say, at least two to three times a week — has the benefit of boosting your friendship. It's a circle, you see. One thing leads to the other, and as each grows, you grow closer and closer.

If more women could realize what a big deal sex is for men, more marriages would thrive. Very few marriages where couples are making love several times a week are lousy. When you're making love, you're building goodwill. You're connecting. And it's hard to stay mad at someone you're making love to.

In fact, the respondents in one of my surveys who rated their spiritual connection as best and their friendship as best were also those who made love three to four times a week. Their average rating was 3.31 out of 4 for the spiritual connection, compared with 2.61 for those who made love once a month or less. Likewise, in the friendship department, the average rating was 3.72 for those who made love frequently, compared with 3.13 for those who did not. (Interestingly, those who made love every day had slightly lower ratings than those who made love three to four times a week, probably because they were also far more likely to be using pornography.) If you want to be close in other areas of your relationship, make sex a priority.

A GOOD GIRL SPEAKS: *"I can tell that he wants to have sex more ... he just doesn't always initiate it. And if there has been no connection outside the bedroom (emotional/spiritual), I find it hard to connect sexually. But I will say that when we do have sex, it seems as if our emotional connection is better for a while after being intimate."* *(married 12 years)*

Your marriage is your most important possession. Because of your marriage, you will live longer. You will be happier. You will have better adjusted, healthier children. You will suffer less abuse and less crime.[3] Invest in your marriage, and that means putting a priority on sex.

PART 5

putting it all together

CHAPTER 11

Hungering
for Each Other

L ast summer my husband and I escaped to The Couples Resort, a posh getaway near Algonquin Park in northern Ontario, while our daughters attended camp. Everything about that resort shouted "sex," from the logo of a couple intertwined to the king-sized beds and Jacuzzis.

The first day we played a lot of tennis and did a few other things to work up an appetite. We had heard that the food at this place was amazing, so I was salivating as they seated us for dinner.

To begin the evening, the waiter presented us with the tiniest little nibble to "whet your appetite." It was very tasty and very interesting, but it was only about a bite big. When the appetizers arrived, we found they were rather size-challenged too. Just enough was presented to seduce our taste buds.

While the appetizers were delectable, I was becoming mildly teed off. How about a huge Caesar salad or a really thick clam chowder? Sure, the food was scrumptious, but it was hardly enough to fill up a squirrel. And I was hungry.

But then it occurred to me that this resort was trying to make an *experience* out of eating. They weren't just trying to fill us up; they were trying to tease us for what was coming next. And because there was a lag of about twenty minutes between courses, by the time the next course came, we were ready for it!

Truck Stop vs. Resort

Too often we see sex like a truck stop diner instead of like that gourmet resort. Sex becomes utilitarian; we have it because we need to, especially from the male point of view. They're "hungry," so they need to "eat," so let's satisfy that craving so we can move on to the rest of our lives.

If that's our attitude, we're diminishing sex. Making love is not only about releasing physical urges, although it is about that. It's also the means to building deep, intimate connections in our relationships, and so it should be savored.

As women, though, it's hard to savor something when we view it from that utilitarian angle. Most women just don't get "hungry" for sex the way men do. Our bodies don't tend to yearn for it at regular intervals the way men's bodies are designed to do. If we think of sex as something just to satisfy a hunger, then it's all too easy to put it on the back burner. And what if your husband is hungry but you're not? Then sex becomes "just for him," and you feel used.

That's why we need to get out of the diner mentality about sex and get into the five-star restaurant mentality. Sex needs to be something that not only satisfies a physical need, but that *awakens* hunger. God created sex to be an integral part of our relationships, not just to satisfy a need but also to celebrate and reaffirm our unions. When we eat so we aren't hungry anymore, the purpose is to make the hunger go away so we can get on with our "real" lives. A resort, though, doesn't want to chase hunger away; it wants to awaken it, extend it, and celebrate the whole meal.

> **a good girl dare**
>
> When you get dressed tomorrow, put on a matching bra and panty set under your regular clothes. Text him and tell him what you're wearing.

As much as we want that resort experience, let me reassure you that I'm not arguing that each time we make love it has to be a profound experience where the earth moves. Life isn't like that. Each individual encounter may not be earth-shattering, but the sum total of the relationship should reflect that deep, intimate experience.

And when we make love in the context of a Christian marriage, with God at the center, our relationship does reflect that. What makes it stupendous isn't just our feelings during each sexual episode, but simply the objective fact that we are joining ourselves as part of an intimate, Christian marriage. That joining is blessed.

So sometimes you'll make love simply because you're anxious, on edge, or tired, and you need something to help you calm down. Sometimes you'll make love because you want to give him a gift even though you're pretty zonked yourself. Sometimes you'll have a quickie because the kids will be up in a minute and you're racing the clock. And sometimes you may even make love because you're incredibly aroused — and during that session you're thinking of something very hot that you and your husband did earlier.

None of that is wrong. In fact, all of it is pretty great! But sex, in the big picture, is about more than each of those things individually. It's also about expressing that deep connection, and while each individual encounter doesn't have to feel profound, some of them should. We should be moving more and more toward marriage relationships in which we can act out of a deep hunger. So how do we do that?

Whetting Your Appetite

The Couples Resort took something that could have been just physical satisfaction — food — and turned it into something to be savored. I think married couples could learn a lot about how to enhance our sex lives simply by studying how five-star restaurants make eating a luscious experience.

Food, like sex, is a physical hunger, but it doesn't have to be *just* a physical hunger or even primarily a physical hunger. It can be used to join relationships and forge intimacy. Sure, you could eat at a McDonald's drive through or a truck stop, but if you had the choice, wouldn't you rather do steak and potatoes with all the fixings? If we took a similar perspective on our sex lives — that it is a hunger meant to be stirred, an experience to be enjoyed, not just a need to be quenched — we'd experience and enjoy that spiritual connection so much more. So let's see how these rituals that make eating so much more meaningful can also make sex much more meaningful.

The Dedication

Before eating at a really fancy event, after the food arrives, traditionally guests have a dedication, in either the form of a prayer or a toast, or both. We lift our glasses and say something wonderful about our host or the reason for us being together.

> **a good girl dare**
>
> Every third time you make love, switch positions.

Who brought you together? God. God made sex, God likes sex, and God celebrates sex — in the right context. And marriage is the right context, so you're good to go! Part of seeing sex in its proper light and getting rid of any shame we may feel about it is inviting God in. This is especially important if you're still getting used to each others' bodies, or if you're going through a healing process from pornography, abuse, or a breach of trust.

But even if everything's A-OK, praying and reading Scripture together can actually make sex even hotter. As we remind ourselves of who God is, we frequently feel even closer to each other. If you don't believe me, listen to this:

> Like an apple tree among the trees of the forest
> is my beloved among the young men.
> I delight to sit in his shade,
> and his fruit is sweet to my taste.
> Let him lead me to the banquet hall,
> and let his banner over me be love.
> Strengthen me with raisins,
> refresh me with apples,
> for I am faint with love.
>
> SONG OF SONGS 2:3 – 5

Or how about this:

> "Come, all you who are thirsty,
> come to the waters;

and you who have no money,
come, buy and eat!
Come, buy wine and milk
without money and without cost.
Why spend money on what is not bread,
and your labor on what does not satisfy?
Listen, listen to me, and eat what is good,
and you will delight in the richest of fare."

ISAIAH 55:1 – 2

Those are both Scripture passages — beautiful, vivid ones about appetites. Appetites for God and for one's spouse. And the Bible has many more such passages. When we feel closest to God, we also tend to feel drawn to our mates, and so one of the best ways that you can make sex far more meaningful and exciting is to draw together spiritually *first*. If you're not used to doing devotions or praying together, it doesn't have to be a big production. Read a Psalm together. Pray together while you're lying entwined in each other's arms. Bring God in, and you'll find your physical intimacy far more meaningful.

The Setting

When my husband and I venture out for an anniversary dinner, we always head to a place with candles. There's just something about eating by candlelight that seems romantic — even if it's only that we don't notice our own imperfections. Food somehow tastes better on a lovely tablecloth, with the right music for ambience, and with candlelight flickering in your beloved's eyes.

The setting matters for sex too. Have you ever seen a movie where the breathless couple collapses into a bed of hay in a barn to make love? It's supposed to be all romantic, but when I watch that, all I can think is,

---

a good girl dare

Skirts make quickies easy! If you don't wear skirts very often, tell your husband that when you do put one on, it's a sign that you're willing. If you wear skirts a lot, pick a specific skirt. Tell him that when you've got that one on, he's welcome to hike it up when he wants.

"Wouldn't that be scratchy?" I have similar issues with the making-love-in-a-field scenes. What about ants crawling up places where you really don't want them?

Part of having fun together and feeling close is having a nice *place* to have fun, where you can relax, share, and talk, as well as roll around in the sheets. So ensure that your bedroom is a place where fun of all sorts can happen — and where you'll want it to happen.

Some bedrooms become a repository for "stuff." We don't know where else to put it, so it ends up piled in a corner by the bed. And since that bed is so deliciously large, with a nice big surface at a good height, why not sort laundry on it? Of course, chances are you won't actually get everything folded during the day, and you'll forget all about it until the evening, when you have to throw the laundry onto the floor anyway to climb into bed, but it's worth a try.

Let's be frank, girls: your bedroom should be the most important room in the house — more important than the kitchen, the living room, or the family room. The family functions well when the couple functions well. You will be a better parent if you and your husband feel intimate. And you won't feel intimate in a bedroom that's a mess. So don't use your bedroom as a storage room!

a good girl dare

Cook dinner in the slow cooker so it doesn't require last-minute prep. Then, when he comes home from work (or when you do), run upstairs for a quickie before dinner.

And that means keeping your work out of the bedroom too. Don't leave files from work around the bedroom, and banish electronic distractions. Keep it as a place for relaxation, so that when you're in the bedroom, you're together talking, not watching *CSI* before bed. When my husband and I watch a movie at night, we do it in the family room. Then we have to get up, turn off the lights, and retire to the bedroom. We're both awake. We're both climbing into bed at the same time. And then we can talk, snuggle, or whatever!

Your bedroom is for your relationship. Make sure it's conducive to that. Candles help. Comfortable pillows and a nice mattress help. A bed that doesn't squeak is rather important, especially as children age. I know furniture and bedding can be expensive, but don't scrimp on this area of the house. Make your bedroom a romantic oasis where you can escape into each other's arms, not a place where all the stuff in the house gets dumped, making you feel guilty every time you see it all. This is a place to reserve just for you and your husband and the sexual side of your relationship.

The Presentation: Making Him Drool

Have you ever had one of those molten lava cakes for dessert at a posh restaurant? You can buy them in the freezer section of the grocery store and then pop them into the microwave, and they're still yummy with soft, runny chocolate in the middle surrounded by spongy cake on the outside. But in a restaurant they're even better, because they come drizzled with cream and raspberry sauce and sprinkled with icing sugar, artistically arranged in the middle of an oversized plate, with a sprig of mint and a hint of cocoa. I'm drooling just typing this. The restaurant takes that same grocery store molten lava cake and turns it into a scrumptious work of art by presenting it so delectably.

Presentation with food matters, and it matters with sex too. Men are visually stimulated, and the best way to arouse the appetite is through the eyes.

My friend Terry posted this confession on her blog awhile ago:

The other morning as I was getting dressed, the husband said to me, "You need to go buy some clothes." I responded that I really didn't want to spend money on clothes. To which he responded, "Buy some clothes." That's all he said. He's a man of few words. I got a little concerned, because while I knew that I was well overdue for a shopping trip (aren't *most* moms?), I didn't think I was so horribly dressed as to be commanded to buy clothes and buy them now! Being the open-minded gal that I am, I decided to take a second look in the mirror. I was in my standard weekday uniform: jeans, T-shirt, and flip-flops. It was at this moment I noted my problem.

For the record, the problem wasn't the blue jeans per se. My husband rather likes the way I look in a pair of jeans. The problem was the lack of effort apparent in the T-shirt, flip-flops, ponytail, and no makeup that accompanied the blue jeans. I had become a carbon copy of the jeans, T-shirt, and Birkenstock™-wearing soccer moms typical in my suburban neighborhood. What's worse, I'd promised myself years ago that I would never do that.[1]

Terry brings up something we all need to think about. Men are visually stimulated. We may think that's stupid or silly or shallow, but they are. When it comes to whetting your husband's appetite, appearances do matter. Yet how many of us tend to look frumpy for the hubby?

a good girl dare

Throw a lingerie fashion show—with only him as the audience.

Often the only time we put effort into looking good is when we're heading out somewhere — to work, church, or even shopping. We take care to look attractive for strangers but not for our husbands. But think about this, ladies: who should you be dressing up for? Shouldn't it be for the one who is actually supposed to appreciate your body?

When I speak to women, I use a nightgown for a prop. It's oversized, it's flannel, and it leaves everything to the imagination. They say a little mystery is a good thing; that may be true, but a lot is too much. When I hold it up, everyone laughs, because everyone can relate to this hideous monstrosity. Of course, some people wear flannel like this because their husbands insist on keeping the house at fifty degrees at night, and to those men, I like to say, "If you want to turn the heat up in the bedroom, you might actually want to *turn the heat up.*" But what do you wear to bed? Do you take care to wear something attractive? Or do you look dumpy? If you look dumpy, you'll feel dumpy too.

When it comes to our appearance, what we women are most sensitive about is our weight. Let's get honest here for a minute. Women gain weight. We just do. We're not meant to be size 6 forever, and our curves are naturally pear-shaped after age forty. But that doesn't mean that we should just accept it and eat whatever we want. We owe it to ourselves, and to our husbands, to watch what we eat and to become active, even if it means just taking a brisk walk every night after dinner to talk with our hubby. You don't need to be superthin; and what makes a woman attractive is often her attitude. Dress in flattering clothes and feel confident, and some extra pounds won't matter as much.

While we're on the subject of naked bodies, let's not ignore texture. My hometown has two seasons: winter and construction. And winter is substantially longer. We all celebrate when the warm weather arrives, and we shove the hats, mittens, scarves, and winter coats away and replace them with cotton, flip-flops, sandals, and happiness.

And razors.

After all, when it's cold out, what's the point of shaving? No one's going to see our legs or our armpits until bathing suit season comes around, so many of us northern girls let ourselves go in the winter. That's a little rough on our husbands, in more ways than one. So use that razor! Buy some flattering clothes. Apply some lipstick. Kiss frump good-bye.

> ### a good girl dare
>
> Set a timer for three-minute intervals. When it goes off, change positions, no matter how much fun you're having. And you can't reuse a position!

Recently I was discussing grooming on my blog, and after several women made the point that God values the inside not the outside, and so we should never worry about appearance, one commenter vigorously disagreed.

> I have never understood the "letting myself go" [mentality]. Being ugly does *not* make you holier. And looking like a frazzled, overwrought, unkempt housewife on the outside does not make your heart godlier on the inside....
>
> My husband loves it when I dress it up for him, so I do that almost every day ... and it is not even all about makeup — which I only wear sparingly; it's about taking care of myself so I *feel* sexy. And when I feel sexy, I am able to come across as sexy.
>
> So I would say go one step further — put on a little skirt

(no panties) and clean the floor in that. Getting a white T-shirt wet (with no bra) while you are doing dishes and your hubby is watching you is bound to make him look.

Paint your toenails and tell him you like having them sucked, and I guarantee that will start some fun between you and *leave* a smile on his face. Husbands are not just there to provide a house and pay bills; they are a gift to have *fun* with. When did all these wives start forgetting that?

Good question! And I love this woman's attitude. So before your husband gets home tonight — or before you get home tonight — take that extra minute to apply some lipstick, brush your hair, and put on some earrings. Make that effort to look great for him — not because you're trying to compete with a supermodel, or because you're trying to compete with pornography, or because you're buying into our culture's take on beauty, but simply because you love him, value him, know that he's visual, and want to show him that you're taking time to prepare for him. You want to seduce him. You want to be beautiful for him. You even want to turn him on! What guy wouldn't like that?

The Appetizer

In a diner, the purpose of the appetizer is to start filling you up. In a five-star restaurant, the purpose is to prepare your mouth for the tastes that are coming next. We need sexual appetizers too — little things that start our own minds and bodies going in the right direction.

Those of us who waited to make love until we were married spent a significant amount of time flirting. We whispered, "I can't wait until we can...." We giggled at double entendres. We had breathless make-out sessions. But then we married, and for many of us that flirting all came to a standstill.

A GOOD GIRL SPEAKS: *"Sexual talking stimulates us so much and is a great foreplay method. It also helps us to stay close." (married 6 years)*

Part of the reason is that we no longer eagerly anticipated sex, but another significant factor is that we women can be reticent about putting a down payment on something in case we don't want to buy it later on.

That's why kissing is one of the first things to disappear from many new marriage relationships. We stop kissing our mates, because if we do, they often interpret it as a promise for what's to come. We figure the best way to make sure we don't promise something we won't deliver on is simply not to promise in the first place. One Good Girl admitted,

> I'm afraid to do too much touching because I'm afraid it will lead to sex. I don't get much satisfaction from sex, so I try to avoid physical affection.

Don't fall into this trap! We women don't build up a physical need for sex the way men do. We actually need a catalyst for sexual interest — whether it's physical foreplay or mental foreplay. Flirting and kissing are part of that. If we give up on those things because we're afraid we may not want to deliver later, it's almost guaranteed that we *won't* want to deliver later, because we're taking away our own tools to get us there!

One of the strangest mental flips you will have to make as a wife is that once you're married, sex is no longer something to run from. Here's how one woman described the difficulty in changing her perspective on how sex was quite the turnaround for her:

> I wish that in the months leading up to my wedding I had had some help in making the psychological switch from "chaste virgin" to "sexual wife." I engaged in the *act* of sex from my wedding night onward, but I did not make the mental switch. I was uncomfortable with my own sexuality for years. I have been married seven years this month, and it has literally been just the last three to four months that I have realized this about myself and finally made the change. It has made my sex life blossom so much, and I wish I had done it years ago.

Even if you weren't a virgin on your wedding night, you could still find this flip to thinking about sex during the day difficult. After all, when we have sex before we're married, shame is associated with it. No matter what our backgrounds before we were married, we need to think of the wedding as a clean break, the birth of a new person — because that's what it is. No longer are you only you; you and your husband have become one, and that means that you can view the physical side of your relationship in a whole new way.

So do little things to remind yourself to think about sex during the day, and let him in on it. Send him sexy texts to tell him what you're thinking (in fact, the act of sending them may be what gets you thinking about it in the first place). Make them X-rated, if you want and if you're sure nobody will see his phone. But if you're shy or worried about privacy, even texting "still tingling from last night," "I can't wait for you to get home," or "I have something in store for you," will remind both of you how much fun you can have together.

a good girl dare

When he's in a suit for work or church, take him up to the bedroom and sit him down. Strip naked (there's something very powerful for most men about being fully dressed in the presence of a nude woman). Make him feel really good any way you want while removing a minimum of his clothes (or even just unzipping).

If you flirt throughout the day and kiss your husband passionately when you're together again at the end of the day, it's not just him who starts thinking about plans for the evening — you do too! Now don't do this if you're regularly going to say no; that really isn't fair to your husband. Instead, flirt with the expectation that you *will* want to tonight. Have a great attitude about sex, and it's far likelier to be an attractive proposition to you. Spend your life running away from it, though, and you're not just magically going to flip on when you climb into bed at night. You have to feed your own sexual appetite and give yourself sexual appetizers by making yourself feel sexy throughout the day.

Spicing Things Up

Gourmet restaurants know that steak doesn't have to be served with peppercorn sauce. Fish doesn't need tartar sauce. Soup can even be made of fruit, mint can be served with meat, and flowers can be a garnish. The restaurant doesn't have to do the expected.

And that's true for married lovers too! You don't always have to make love at night when you're heading to bed. You don't even always have to make love in the bedroom! You can be creative and mix things up a little.

One of the biggest challenges of our modern lives is finding schedules that work for sex. With so many couples facing shift work scheduling conflicts, how can we relegate our sex lives to that hour between 10:30 and 11:30 when most of us head to bed? Even if shift work isn't a factor, many of us turn in at different times, depending on our sleep needs and preferences. So we have to get more creative at finding times to make love.

A GOOD GIRL SPEAKS: *"Quickies are okay!" (married 31 years)*

Some couples find that having sex first thing in the morning is easier than at night, because at least they're in bed together. Others use the time when children are napping or sleeping, regardless of the time of day. And when couples are first married and babies aren't on the scene yet, any time of day can work. Don't wait for night to fall and for both of you to wind up in the bedroom together. And if you're heading up to bed but your husband isn't following because he's watching television, maybe you just need to send him a signal that sleep is not what you had planned.

Even with kids in the house, a quickie during the day leaves you laughing afterwards. We women may not get that aroused (foreplay's often squeezed out when you're trying to beat the clock or be fast enough that the children won't realize you're not in the kitchen anymore), but he'll wear a smile on his face all day long. And then he's more likely to put in some time to return the favor later.

When it comes to making love, there are no hard and fast rules about the when and the where, as long as you're private. So be creative. You don't always have to serve things at the same time in the same place in the same way.

The Menu

In fact, you don't have to serve the same *thing* all the time, either. As wonderful as the food was at that resort, I still didn't want to eat the chicken every night. Sometimes I had the salmon. One night I had scallops. Naturally I sampled the steak. Food, no matter how good, gets boring if you eat too much of the same thing.

Be careful of the ruts in your intimate life too. We all hit them — when we're tired, when we're making love thinking it's "just for him," when we're preoccupied with something else. It's hard to feel a connection when sex becomes routine. My friend Christie Rayburn, who cohosted the television show *Marriage Uncensored*, once confessed to her audience that she and her husband Mark have a "three in a row — no-no" rule. They don't let themselves have sex three times in a row in the same position. They're always switching it up just so they don't hit that rut.

Here's how one twenty-nine-year-old woman, married eight years, described how she and her hubby keep things interesting:

> While my husband certainly craves sex more often than I do, we both have a policy to oblige the other whenever they want it. One thing that helps us in our sexual relationship is "topless TV" every night after we put our kids to bed. We snuggle together on the sofa to watch TV, but we both go topless. This started as my husband begging for more "breast time," but it has turned into my favorite part of the day. I think the skin-on-skin has produced bonding similar to a mom breast-feeding her infant! I also feel so secure and appreciated, and this snuggle time is what usually produces my desire to have sex with him.
>
> We also have a policy where I'm on top when we have sex before bed, and he has to be on top in the mornings before we get up. I only orgasm when I'm on top, and he really prefers that, but he always initiates in the mornings, so I make him be on top then. (I'm usually pretty groggy and may go back to sleep for half an hour afterward.) We don't have sex every day, but a few days a week we have sex twice, so it averages out.

Now that's a fun couple! And if they're being this adventurous and this open, you can imagine how close they feel. And for men especially, a bit of variation in the menu tends to help them feel closer to you. Here's how one Good Guy, married seventeen years, explains their problem:

> It's not so much the frequency, but the quality and character of the sex that I want. I would like us to be more adventurous, and she is way too conservative.

Now there's absolutely nothing wrong with the missionary position in sex; in fact, personally, I find that one the most pleasurable for me. But many guys want to try more than just that, and sometimes we women suspect that this makes them perverts. It really doesn't. It just means that they want to have fun, they want to have more abandon, and they want to feel a bit more vulnerable, all of which are healthy parts of sex. Sometimes these new things are easier to try when you put yourself in the driver's seat. If you're a little on the conservative side but you know your husband would like to try something new that you don't feel is sinful, then why not initiate it? It will make him feel so much better in the relationship. But more importantly, you'll probably feel more confident and better about yourself too.

A GOOD GIRL SPEAKS: *"There is more than one way to enjoy sex, and when both partners consent and do so out of love, you can really have a lot of fun with it." (married 23 years)*

Here's how one couple in their first decade of marriage worked this out:

> We sat down and basically made a contract. We designated how many times per week was our minimum. We made the policy that once we start we don't stop (if we get uncomfortable or frustrated about something, we deal with it, rather than shutting down and turning away.) ... We designated a regular frequency (about one time in five) would be a "his night" where we'd do the stuff he prefers, and an equal frequency would be "her night" where we do what I prefer. About one time in twenty we have a "fantasy night" where we take turns trying out things

we've wondered about or wanted to try but have been afraid the other might not be comfortable with. It's always okay to say no, but the intent is that on that occasional basis we're willing to go out of our comfort zones to try something for the spouse's sake.

No one forces anyone to do anything, and there's always a way out, but she's giving him back some control over something that's vitally important to him. She reports that her sex life today is much improved, and their friendship is really close too.

Sometimes we women steer away from more adventure in bed, because for us, the Old Faithful tends to work best. Men may be visually stimulated, so they enjoy a variety of views. Women, on the other hand, need to concentrate for our bodies to work like clockwork and achieve orgasm, so we can all-too-easily fall into a rut. We figure out what works for us, and we want to keep doing that same thing.

If you tend to orgasm best in one position, that's okay. But that doesn't mean you have to spend your whole sexual encounter like that! You can still spice it up. Start in a new position, even if you have to finish in Old Faithful (whatever that may be for you). Start in a different room. Do something different (like spending some time using your mouth or your hands to turn him on). As you do more things, you may find your body starts to respond unexpectedly too. And the confidence you'll get by seeing the effect on your husband will likely boost your libido as well. So every now and then, challenge yourself to be a little more adventurous. You just may find it's an awfully fun game!

The Celebration

Marriage is all about becoming one. But that "becoming" is a process — it doesn't happen overnight. Sure, it may happen instantaneously in God's eyes, but it usually takes time and effort for us mortals to truly feel "one": to truly become intertwined in every sense of the word.

In my focus group with husbands, one made a very interesting comment:

> When you're one, sex becomes a part of that, and you lose all the shyness you had at the beginning of marriage. Now we can do a whole lot more because it's not dirty; it's just expressing who we are together, and we're so much more comfortable.

Becoming one and feeling spiritually connected did not mean that their love life became more chaste; it meant that it became more adventurous, more fun, but at the same time, more comfortable and natural.

Experiencing that spiritual connection during sex is not only done by doing more sacred things; it is done by claiming more things that you do now for the sacred realm. Isn't that what God wants — to take more and more into his sphere? And as we grow closer together, we're able to grow in freedom together so that more is holy and right between us — even if it's also hot. In fact, *especially* since it's also hot, because sex is all about that urge to be together that reflects best the hunger that we feel for God. I can't think of a better gift God could have given to marriage.

a good girl dare

Talk sexy! When you're making love, tell him what you're thinking about, what you love, or what feels good — with as much explicit detail as possible.

CHAPTER 12

Moving Forward

I come from a family of divorce. My father left my mother when I was two. Today, looking at my extended family, I see how divorce has negatively affected nieces and nephews and even adults. As I can testify, those scars do not completely go away.

God is the only answer for our problems in the world today, whether they're in the tumultuous Middle East or in violent and hopeless public schools, prisons, or movie theaters. Our culture needs to come back to God.

But that task is so much harder when families fall apart. When marriages falter, adults turn to basic coping mechanisms rather than outreach. And children suffer such deep hurts that it makes it more difficult for them to experience the richness of healthy relationships. They're more likely to become involved in self-destructive and self-defeating behavior that in turn causes ripple effects for others.

Everything stems back to the family, and while this book may be about sex, I wrote it because I have a passion to see families stay together. And sex is a huge part of that. If Good Girls could just embrace God's idea of what sex is supposed to encompass and work on their friendship, their spiritual connection, and the physical fireworks, we'd end many of the problems families face before those problems even begin. We'd be stronger. We'd be happier. And we'd be far more energized and equipped to be great parents, great friends, and great neighbors.

I hope this book has given you the blueprint to create a great marriage — because a marriage that is having fun, regular, meaningful sex is not likely to be a marriage where affairs happen, disagreements grow, or bitterness thrives. You'll be too busy laughing and kissing and rolling around to do any of that.

And so, in this last chapter, I thought I'd give you some insight on where I think Good Girls are today when it comes to marriage, and then challenge you to aim even higher. Throughout the book, I've given you glimpses on a piecemeal basis of the research I did when writing this, but I haven't presented all the stats at once, because I wanted to focus on individual relationships, not on the big picture of what's happening in families today. But now that I've given you all the advice I can think of, I want to leave you this food for thought about where we Good Girls are and where we could improve. The numbers I'm going to share with you came from three surveys I conducted: the first one, looking at women's recollections of their wedding night and their satisfaction with sex now, had 1,011 respondents. The second, asking women about the frequency of sex and libidos, had 1,104 respondents. And the last one, asking men about the frequency with which they made love and their satisfaction with their sex lives, had 330 respondents.

The Good News

Let's start with the good news. First, I was surprised *not* to uncover the major libido problems that I'd been reading about in so much of the literature on sex. The standard line is that 30 percent of women have higher sex drives than their husbands — though many researchers think it's higher than that now.[1] Of the roughly 1,100 Good Girls who responded to my libido survey, only 24 percent reported having a higher sex drive than their husbands. And among husbands, only 18 percent said they had the lower sex drive (we'll look at the reasons for that discrepancy later).

Why is that good news? Well, God made us *in general* so that men would have higher sex drives. There will always be some natural variation, of course, but the differential should tend to go dramatically in the men's direction when it comes to libido. When too many men have lower sex drives than their wives, it may be a sign of relationship problems or pornography problems (on the part of either partner). The fact that we Good Girls fare a little better than most surveys of the general population is a good thing, though it's hardly consolation if you're one of the 24 percent!

Why are we likely to be lower? My sample was composed mostly of Christian women who take their faith seriously, since it was culled mostly from people who have been at the events I've spoken at, people who follow my blog, and people who follow me on Facebook and Twitter. Eighty-four percent of them defined themselves as "having a close personal relationship with God," so we didn't have a representative sample of the population as a whole. We were mostly talking to Good Girls. And the sexuality of Good Girls and their husbands, then, tends not to be quite as distorted as that of the general population.

Want some more good news? We're having a lot of fun! In our sample, 61.6 percent of self-identified "Good Girls" either usually or always reached orgasm with intercourse, compared with 52.1 percent of women who didn't profess a belief in Jesus.

PERCENTAGE OF MARRIED WOMEN WHO ORGASM DURING INTERCOURSE						
	Frequency					
Religious Beliefs	Never	Rarely	Sometimes	Usually	Always	Usually/ Always Combined
Christian	9.5%	10.4%	18.3%	43.7%	17.9%	61.6%
Non-Christian	13.8%	11.9%	22%	35.8%	16.3%	52.1%

Those who played by the "Good Girl" rules from day one also rate their sex lives the highest today.

RATING OF SEX LIFE TODAY					
Sexual Experience	On a Scale of 1–10 (10 being highest)				
	1–2	3–5	6–8	9–10	Average
Virgin when married	5.3%	12.5%	41.1%	41.1%	7.56
Had sex with husband before marriage	12.4%	12.3%	41%	35.9%	7.08
Had sex with husband and others	9.9%	16.9%	37.2%	35.9%	6.88
Had sex with others, not husband	10.2%	14.1%	33.3%	42.3%	7.26

Here's what I find most interesting about this chart. Those who rate their sex lives as best are those who were probably pretty committed to God when they married. They were those who were either virgins or had slept with others then met their future husband and made the decision to wait until the wedding. Those who rate their sex lives as worst today (although all are pretty good!) are those who had the most sexual partners before they married and who had already made love to their husbands. The message to take away? Practice before you're married does not make perfect afterward.

Here's another way to look at the data:

Religious Beliefs	RATING OF SEX LIFE TODAY				
	On a Scale of 1–10 (10 being highest)				
	1–2	3–5	6–8	9–10	Average
Christian	7.0%	13.5%	39.2%	40.3%	7.36
Non-Christian	15.7%	16.4%	39.6%	28.3%	6.38

When you're close with God, you're going to be closer with each other.

If that's true, then those who listened to God should also be the most likely to reach orgasm. Let's look at the rate of orgasm today based on one's sexual experience (or lack thereof) on the wedding night:

Sexual Experience	PERCENTAGE OF MARRIED WOMEN WHO ORGASM DURING INTERCOURSE					
	Frequency					
	Never	Rarely	Sometimes	Usually	Always	Usually/ Always Combined
Virgin	13.0%	6.4%	18.1%	45.8%	16.7%	62.5%
Had sex with husband already	10.3%	14.1%	17.5%	39.7%	18.4%	58.1%
Had sex with others and husband	8.3%	12.4%	19.4%	41.1%	18.8%	59.9%
Had sex with others, not husband	5.1%	12.8%	25.6%	41%	15.4%	56.4%

putting it all together

Here again, those who were virgins, the least experienced on the wedding night, came out on top (though the differences weren't as pronounced). Of course, they're also the most likely to state they never orgasm during intercourse, but that could be caused by the lack of sexual experience. So let's look at the rate of orgasm based on how long people have been married:

PERCENTAGE OF MARRIED WOMEN WHO ORGASM DURING INTERCOURSE	Frequency					
Number of Years Married	Never	Rarely	Sometimes	Usually	Always	Usually/ Always Combined
0–5	13.8%	10.1%	17.0%	43.6%	15.4%	59.0%
6–10	8.9%	8.9%	19.7%	45.1%	17.4%	62.5%
11–15	9.0%	9.9%	20.8%	42%	18.4%	60.4%
16–20	9.1%	11.7%	14.3%	42.9%	22.1%	65%
21–29	6.3%	9.8%	23.1%	42.0%	18.9%	60.9%
30+	18.4%	18.4%	18.4%	34.2%	10.5%	44.7%

Sure enough, the best years seem to be between years 16 and 20 of marriage, and then drop off as people age and health problems start to come into play. That's also true if you look at how women rated their sex lives:

Number of Years Married	RATING OF SEX LIFE TODAY				
	On a Scale of 1 – 10 (10 being highest)				
	1 – 2	3 – 5	6 – 8	9 – 10	Average
0 – 5	4.8%	14.9%	46.3%	34%	7.22
6 – 10	6.1%	14.1%	40.8%	39%	7.38
11 – 15	7.5%	11.3%	39.2%	42%	7.42
16 – 20	7.1%	13.0%	31.8%	48%	7.49
21 – 29	11.9%	14%	40.6%	33.6%	6.99
30+	22.4%	21.0%	30.3%	26.3%	5.92

We See Sex Holistically

Another sign that our Good Girls haven't completely given in to our society's more pornographic emphasis on sex is that we Good Girls don't rate orgasms as the be-all and end-all of sex. When we compare orgasm frequency to how women rate their sex lives, we can see that other factors are obviously at play.

Frequency of Reaching Orgasm During Intercourse	RATING OF SEX LIFE TODAY				
	On a Scale of 1 – 10 (10 being highest)				
	1 – 2	3 – 5	6 – 8	9 – 10	Average
Never	26.7%	19.8%	36.6%	16.8%	5.21
Rarely	24.8%	28.6%	35.2%	11.4%	5.06
Sometimes	7.5%	20.9%	47.6%	24.1%	6.66
Usually	3.3%	9.5%	41%	46.1%	7.86
Always	1.1%	5.2%	29.9%	63.8%	8.69

To me, this is one of the most interesting charts. Fifty-three percent of women who never experienced orgasm during intercourse still rated their sex life as 6 or more in satisfaction, while 6 percent of those who always orgasmed rated it as 5 or less. While the correlation is there, it isn't absolute.

I'd have to go back and ask detailed questions of my respondents to find out why the correlation isn't absolute, but based on the open-ended responses I received, I'd say the variation stems from three factors: (1) Some women may never orgasm during intercourse, but they do orgasm in other ways, and thus they enjoy their sex life anyway. They feel close to their husbands and enjoy their physical relationship. (2) Some women do orgasm frequently, but because of too much emphasis on pornography in the marriage or physical problems, they aren't able to really experience a spiritual connection during sex. (3) Women may orgasm, but there's another problem: they're just not "doing it" very often.

Let's look at that last possibility now, as we turn to the bad news in the surveys.

The Bad News

Looking at the data also shows that there's room for improvement. When it comes to porn, for instance, 25 percent of women reported having had a problem, and 66 percent of men reported seeking it out. But here's some more bad news: while 66 percent of men may have sought out porn, only 43 percent of their wives know about it. Even more interesting than women's ignorance, though, is men's ignorance. Only 9 percent of men thought their wives had ever sought out porn, though a quarter of all women admitted they had.

That's far too many couples dealing with the destructive effects of porn (even if they don't realize it), and I'm afraid that number is only going to increase. If you are a parent, install filters on your computer to stop your child from inadvertently coming across porn, even when they're not looking for it. Most porn addicts report that their journey into addiction almost always started by coming across something accidentally or being shown something by a friend. And don't stop with your sons — your daughters are at risk too. So get those filters and use them.

The other major issue facing couples is libido differences. Take our differences with initiation, for instance. On the positive side, only 8 percent of women reported never initiating sex because their husbands always do. Another 4 percent never initiate because their husbands always turn them down. But that means that about 90 percent do try to initiate, at least sometimes. That goes a long way toward telling your husband that you think he's awesome.

Nevertheless, many of us are initiating because our husbands have stopped due to our turning them down so much. One man, married eight years, admitted, "I have basically given up; it's not worth the pain of trying anymore."

That matches up with the numbers. Forty-four percent of women — and 44 percent of men — reported having sex less than once a week.

Could this be due to age? After all, people might make love less when they get older and health problems start, so maybe there's not really a problem with this lack of sex. So let's break it down by age:

	FREQUENCY OF SEX BY AGE					
	Average Number of Times Married Women Report Making Love					
Age	Almost every day	3 – 4 times/ week	1 – 2 times/ week	A few times a month	Rarely	Less than once a week (combined)
18 – 24	7.3%	30.9%	49.1%	12.7%	0%	12.7%
25 – 34	3.2%	21%	39.7%	27.1%	9%	36.1%
35 – 44	2.8%	19.1%	33%	33%	12.1%	45.1%
45 – 54	4.3%	10.2%	34.4%	28.5%	22.7%	51.2%
54+	0%	7.9%	27.6%	31.6%	32.9%	64.5%

Uh oh. That doesn't really help, does it? In fact, that makes it worse. In my category (ages 35 – 44), 45 percent of women make love less than once a week. Girls, there is something seriously wrong with that figure.

What if we remove the women who have the stronger sex drive and look only at the respondents who reported that the men have the stronger sex drive? That way we're only looking at marriages where the infrequency of sex is likely because the woman says no. Then here's what you get:

FREQUENCY OF SEX BY AGE, Men with the Higher Libidos						
	Average Number of Times Married Women Report Making Love					
Age	Almost every day	3 – 4 times/ week	1 – 2 times/ week	A few times a month	Rarely	Less than once a week (combined)
18 – 24	4.3%	36.2%	46.8%	12.8%	0%	12.8%
25 – 34	2.7%	23.6%	40.4%	24.9%	8.4%	33.3%
35 – 44	2.3%	21.1%	34.7%	33.7%	8.3%	42.0%
45 – 54	3.6%	12.4%	38.7%	29.4%	16%	45.4%
54+	0%	10.9%	29.1%	32.7%	27.3%	60.0%

The difference really isn't substantial, and all age groups of women still average out to 39.9 percent making love less than once a week. That tells me that many women are living in marriages where their husbands aren't all that happy.

When I started to see these numbers, I began to wonder what the men thought of them, so I decided it was time to survey not just Good Girls, but Good Boys too. I asked them how they felt about the frequency of sex:

	HUSBANDS' ATTITUDES TOWARD FREQUENCY OF SEX			
	Thoughts			
Age	"I don't think we have sex enough, and it really bothers me."	"I don't think we have sex enough, but it's not a big deal to me."	"I'm pretty satisfied with the frequency that we have sex."	"I feel like my wife wants it more often than I do, and I feel pressure."
18–24	0%	0%	100%	0%
25–34	30.1%	27.4%	35.6%	6.8%
35–44	45.4%	23.5%	27.7%	3.4%
45–54	25.3%	28%	40%	6.7%
54+	28.6%	31%	40.5%	0%

That's a significant minority of men who really are bothered by lack of frequency. But are these just sex maniacs who want sex all the time? Nope. The men surveyed showed that they weren't sex-crazed; they had legitimate grievances. Forty-six percent of men who make love just a few times a month are very bothered, and 71 percent who make love rarely or never are really bothered. If men have sex at least three times a week, they're much less likely to be bothered at all.

HUSBANDS' ATTITUDES TOWARD FREQUENCY OF SEX			
	Thoughts		
How Often Husbands Report Making Love	"I don't think we have sex enough, and it really bothers me."	"I don't think we have sex enough, but it's not a big deal to me."	"I'm pretty satisfied with the frequency that we have sex."	"I feel like my wife wants it more often than I do, and I feel pressure."
Almost every day	0%	11.1%	88.9%	0%
3–4 times/ week	15.4%	15.4%	66.7%	2.6%
1–2 times/ week	21.1%	32.8%	43.8%	2.3%
A few times a month	46.2%	26.9%	20.4%	6.5%
Rarely/Never	70.5%	18.2%	2.3%	9.1%

We can rationalize not having sex — I'm too tired, I don't want more demands, he isn't nice to me, he doesn't listen to my feelings — but none of that is going to help our marriages. You will always feel unsettled when your sex life is out of whack, because it is one of the main measures of your relationship. You won't feel as connected when you're not connecting sexually on a semi-regular, and semi-frequent, basis.

Listen to this frustrated and dejected man:

I have always seen sexual intimacy as the result of intimacy in general.... In the early years of marriage when we were very close and intimate in nonsexual ways, I would often initiate and was often turned down. I would try the spontaneous route. The planned route. Her drive and interest were low, and it hurt. My wall started to go up. We went for counseling. It would help for a few weeks and then be an issue again. We have fought through it, but I finally resigned myself to the fact that we will just be good friends and raise our kids well. Unfortunately, neither of us is feeling very fulfilled in our marriage, and the temptations to have needs met are great. [It is not that it bothers me that we don't have sex more]. *It is just that I have stopped caring.* (emphasis mine)

That man has been married for twenty years. He and his wife have sex less than once a month. And he is not alone.

We can always think of reasons *not to* have sex; I wonder why we women don't spend just as much time thinking up reasons *to* have sex, given how important it is to our husbands and how amazing it can be for us.

Of course, I'm not saying you should have sex just so that your husband won't feel so put out. That's hardly a very sexy thought anyway, is it? I also think it can be very hurtful to us women. Far too many Christian books give me the impression that "the wife's duty is to have sex, so drop your drawers and get to it." Saying that to a young bride who is nervous, a little ashamed, or hurting hardly helps. It can even cement into our minds this idea that "sex is only for him," when it's not.

And that's really what I've wanted you to understand from this book. Yes, men need sex, and it's intrinsic to their self esteem. But we need it too! God made sex to be an amazing stress reliever, commitment builder, connection builder, and laughter inducer. It's supposed to be one of the best parts of your life. If it isn't, then let's put those "go get 'em" abilities we women have to work. We women can hold down a job, get dinner ready, and chauffeur kids to appointments, all while putting on lipstick. We can micromanage many parts of our lives with energy and enthusiasm. How about applying some of that energy and enthusiasm to your sex life — not just so that your husband will be happy, but so that you can be happy too. And so that together you can discover all that God designed marriage to be.

If a survey were to be taken of couples in the midst of separating, I doubt that very many would report making love more than once a week in the preceding year, because it's hard to fight if you're also making love regularly. Sex is like relationship insurance; when you make love frequently, your relationship is far more likely to go smoothly in all other areas. You'll feel closer. You'll be more connected. When you're not making love frequently, it likely is a sign that you've let your relationship go. It's lower on your priority list.

I know that's hard to hear. I spent the first few years of my marriage in frustrated tears because I was mad that Keith wanted something I wasn't prepared to give. My marriage today is the diametrical opposite because we both learned how to give. And I found that when I stopped focusing on how I emotionally felt about sex and started looking at how he felt, I began to feel better about it. And lo and behold, it started to work a lot better too!

If you're one of those four in ten women who don't make love very frequently, do a thought experiment for me: I know you're tired. I know you're frustrated. I know you sometimes feel lonely in your relationship. But put those things aside for a second. Wouldn't you love to long to make love? Wouldn't it be fun to live with abandon, at least for a few minutes every few nights? Wouldn't you love to feel bliss, to feel his love, to laugh?

Make it happen! If you have sexual insecurities, that's okay. I did too. Deal with them! Talk to someone. Don't settle for the status quo. You aren't meant to have a blah marriage. You aren't meant to have a ho-hum sex life. You are meant to feel close together, to have a great time in bed, and to enjoy your husband.

Getting the physical side of marriage right may take some work, but it's a fun kind of work. And with the right attitude, we women can become the happiest wives who are married to the most satisfied husbands. That's what God wants for us, and that's what he'll help you do once you start getting excited about it. So jump in! Sex can be relaxing, intimate, and stupendous all at the same time. There's little else that's better in this world. So commit to yourself that you will work at having a marriage that is on fire: not just for your husband, but for you too. You are a beautiful creature. You were created for this. So, dear friends, go grab your husbands and have some fun!

Acknowledgments

For a book of this nature, the first person I need to thank is obviously my husband. But how exactly should I do that? I could say, "Thanks, babe, for showing me what great sex is," but he might find that somewhat embarrassing. I could say, "Thank you, honey, for not freaking when I told you what I was going to write," but that sounds trite. Perhaps something nice and neutral would be best, like, "Thanks for your support and for helping me with the research." But I really think I need something a little more personal, so let's go with this: "Keith, I love you! We've walked through so much in our marriage, and though many years were tough, they gave us the authority to speak on stuff like this. Thanks for sticking through the hard times with me. You are my best friend, and you always will be."

While Keith is obviously the biggest superhero guy in my life, two other men made this book possible. I know thanking one's agent in the acknowledgments section is akin to a beauty pageant contestant wishing for world peace, but in this case it is not an overexaggeration to say that this book would never have found publication without my agent, Chip MacGregor, of MacGregor Literary. Chip, I know it was a God-thing that we met. You helped give me confidence in myself again, believed in me when I felt that perhaps my writing days were behind me, and worked tirelessly to convince others that I was worth taking a chance on. Few have changed my life as much as you have. You're a great friend, and I appreciate all your encouragement.

And what Chip did for my writing, Eric Spath did for my speaking. Eric, you are amazing at what you do, even if you do email in sound bites. Thanks for having confidence in me and for helping build my platform. You're a riot and a really great friend, and I do appreciate your help. I'm looking forward to working with you for many more years!

Sandra VanderZicht, my editor at Zondervan, really went to bat for this book. She believed in it and believed in my voice. Sandy, thank you so much for the chance to write this. I hope I did you proud.

My children, Rebecca and Katie, were surprisingly not all that mortified when I announced to them what I was writing. Rebecca just said, "Now all my friends will know you're the cool mom," which I'll take as a tremendous compliment. Katie shook her head and admitted, "Yeah, that's what we've come to expect from you." I will try really, really hard not to do anything embarrassing for at least the next few weeks. But I can't promise anything.

My best girlfriend, Susan, was a constant as I was writing. I really appreciate your prayers and support, Susan, especially as you were walking through quite the ordeal yourself! And to Tammy and Evelyn, who prayed with me, thank you. To my reluctant rice-eating friend: your help and encouragement mean a lot to me. Thanks for being a sounding board to help me pare down this book to what really mattered.

To the guys who shared their stories, I know you want to remain anonymous, but I appreciate your help and your honesty. And to Johnny Rocket from Shine FM in Edmonton, who wrote a paragraph (which one shall remain a secret), that was an awesome breakfast at IHOP! Hollie, I feel your pain.

And now a special shout-out to so many who helped so much and whom I've never even met. To the faithful readers of my blog *To Love, Honor and Vacuum*, your stories helped so much. And to the thousands of people who answered my survey, thank you. Your words are in this book, and they make it richer.

To those who started thinking of me as the "sex lady" and launched me on this whole romp, my gratitude, even if I was a little credulous at first. Doug Koop of *Christian Week* and *Seven*, Karen Stiller and Bill Fledderus at *Faith Today*, and Drew Marshall, you pushed me in this direction. I hope you're pleased with the results.

Chuck MacKnee, from Trinity Western University, forged many of my thoughts on the Christian view of sexuality. Thank you for the interview you did with me years ago for that *Faith Today* article.

Sharol and Neal Josephson, Neal Black, and the other staff at FamilyLife Canada have provided great support and encouragement to both Keith and me as we speak into marriages. I appreciate our partnership.

I'd also like to thank my church family, who keep me grounded. To my pastor, Ernie Klassen, who helped me with some basic Greek and Hebrew questions, thanks! At Quinte Alliance Church in Belleville, Ontario, I'm not known as a speaker or an author; I'm known as that woman who leads youth Bible quizzing, and I love it. It is such a blessing to be part of a fellowship where I can just be myself and encourage my own kids and be blessed with the privilege of encouraging other kids in return. As I'm writing this, I'm gearing up for coaching our Eastern Canadian Team in the Bible Quizzing Internationals in Pennsylvania. I'm in awe of these ten kids' ability to memorize the Word, and I pray that God will keep that Word in their hearts so that when they grow up, they will have great marriages too! You guys give me something else to focus on other than writing, and you really are a huge part of the excitement in my life.

I also really want and need to acknowledge my two mothers. Cheryl, thank you for your love, your ability to laugh at your husband, your card-playing skills, and your son. You raised him well, and I'm grateful. And Mom, we spent so many years just the two of us. I know you were disappointed with the circumstances of my childhood, and I imagine the many nights you spent praying that God would help me make good decisions. I know you're grateful for what God has done in our family, and we're grateful for your prayers. And I'm sure that one day in heaven, you and I and Becca and Katie will have fun comparing speaking skills and stories with Grandma! I inherited some awesome genes from you. I hope that some of your wisdom has rubbed off too.

Finally, I want to thank God for giving me this ministry. As a child of divorce, I am thrilled and humbled to be used to strengthen the good girl's guide to great sex

marriages. My own marriage has seen ups and downs, and I wondered at the time why God would let such things happen to us. But he has brought tremendous good out of the things that we have walked through. I like to believe that this book is part of that.

Sheila loves speaking to groups of women. She's available for retreats, women's outreaches, and more!

Contact her to ask about her special "Girl Talk" night: Good Girls Talk about Sex, a funny yet practical evening that will strengthen the marriages in your church!

Or ask her about her different retreat packages.

www.SheilaWrayGregoire.com

Notes

INTRODUCTION: Who's a Good Girl?

1. William Mattox, vice president for policy of the Family Research Council, "The Hottest Valentine," *Mennonite Brethren Herald*, volume 37, number 4.

CHAPTER 1: How Good Girls Think about Sex

1. Linda Waite and Maggie Gallagher, *The Case for Marriage: Why Married People Are Happier, Healthier, and Better Off Financially* (Broadway, 2001). The discussion about commitment, sexual satisfaction, religion, and attitudes towards sex is found on pages 86 – 96.
2. Personal interview conducted on behalf of *Faith Today* magazine, December 2004.
3. Patrick Riley, *Civilizing Sex: On Chastity and the Common Good* (New York: T & T Clark, 2000), 32.
4. Tim Alan Gardner, *Sacred Sex* (Colorado Springs: Waterbrook, 2002), 49.

CHAPTER 2: How Good Girls Understand Good Boys

1. In 1973 author Marabel Morgan published *The Total Woman*, a book geared to Christian women and focused on how to have a happy, fulfilling life by recognizing your husband's needs. While she was ridiculed for many of her ideas — including greeting one's husband at the door in Saran Wrap — her book still became the bestselling nonfiction book of 1974. She believed that when wives catered to their husbands, everybody would be happier, and she encouraged women to free their sexuality up by focusing on their husband's pleasure. While she had a wide following, much of her writing is still considered quite controversial, since she seemed to ignore women's legitimate needs, thinking that most of those needs would be met if women just subordinated themselves to their husbands.
2. There's a bit of an urban legend about the origin of the "lie back and think of England" saying. Some think Queen Victoria was the one who first uttered it, but according to the Oxford English Dictionary, it first appeared in print in 1972 in Jonathan Gathorne-Hardy's *Rise and Fall of the British Nanny*. He quoted

Lady Alyce Hillingdon saying in 1912: "I am happy now that George calls on my bedchamber less frequently than of old. As it is, I now endure but two calls a week, and when I hear his steps outside my door I lie down on my bed, close my eyes, open my legs, and think of England." Her admonition was apparently used to tell other young British girls to buck up, grit their teeth, and get through the awful experience for the good of the country. Information taken from *http:// en.wikipedia.org/wiki/Lie_back_and_think_of_England*.

3. John and Stasi Eldredge, *Captivating: Unveiling the Mystery of a Woman's Soul* (Nashville, Tenn.: Thomas Nelson, 2005). Quotation taken from Stasi Eldredge talking with Beliefnet, "There's Something Fierce in the Heart of a Woman." Interview with Laura Sheahen, found on *http:// www.beliefnet.com/Faiths /Christianity/2005/09/Theres-Something-Fierce-In-The-Heart-Of-A-Woman.aspx*.

CHAPTER 3: Lighting the Fireworks

1. For more information about Fertility Awareness Method, and for temperature charts or cervical fluid charts, visit Christian Family Planning at *http://christian familyplanning.net/*.

2. Preventing implantation means that the sperm could meet up with an egg and conception could occur, but then the new embryo isn't able to implant into the uterus and isn't able to grow, so it gets "flushed" away in the next period. Many women are uncomfortable with the Pill because of this possibility, since they don't see the difference between the Pill and abortion. However, even physicians aren't in agreement about the science around how the Pill works, and most do not believe that the Pill prevents implantation; they believe it prevents conception. For both sides of the controversy from a medical standpoint, visit *http:// www.prolifephysicians.org/abortifacient.htm*.

3. Some hormonal contraceptive manufacturers claim that their products prevent implantation as a secondary benefit. For instance, Ortho Tri-Cyclen's website says: "Taking the Pill causes the lining of the uterus to change, which makes it harder for an egg to be implanted." They do not claim that this is the primary effect (the primary is still prevention of ovulation), but they do list it. From "How Does Ortho Tri-Cyclen LO Work?" *http://www.thepill.com/thepill/assets /How_the_Pill_Works.pdf*.

4. Sharon Kirkey, "Birth Control Pill Associated with Female Sexual Dysfunction, German Researchers Say," Canwest News Service, May 5, 2010, *http://www.canada .com/health/Birth+control+pill+associated+with+female+sexual+dysfunction+ German+researchers/2988974/story.html*.

CHAPTER 4: Beginning the Journey to Very Good

1. C. S. Lewis, *The Four Loves* (Glasgow: William Collins & Sons, 1960), 92.

2. Interview with Michael McManus, "No Way to Live: Cohabitation in Amer-

ica," *National Review Online*, April 14, 2008, *http://www.nationalreview.com/ articles/224058/no-way-live/interview.*

3. Taken from my "Wedding Night Survey," 1,011 respondents. Women were asked to rate their sex life today on a scale of 1 to 10. For the purposes of this chapter, a score of 8 – 10 was considered "great," a score of 4 – 7 was considered "okay," and a score of 1 – 3 was considered "lousy."

CHAPTER 5: From Fizzle to Sizzle for Her

1. "Women of All Ages Have Trouble Reaching Orgasm: Study," *Toronto Sun*, July 27, 2010, *http://www.torontosun.com/life/2010/07/27/14841776.html.*

2. Practicing cutting off the flow of urine helps you identify your pelvic floor muscles, so you can learn to control them better. But you shouldn't do this every time you pee or you run the risk of urinary tract infections because you may fail to completely empty your bladder. So try these exercises to identify the muscles, but once you've identified them, try the exercises when you're not urinating!

3. For more information on the treatment and causes of vaginismus, visit *www .vaginismus.com*, which features stories, in-depth explanation of the problem, warnings, and best of all, a detailed plan for recovery.

4. Tracee Cornforth, "Female Sexual Dysfunction: An Interview with Dr. Robert Taylor Segraves and Dr. Kathleen Blindt Segraves," August 29, 2009, *http://womens health.about.com/cs/sexualdysfunction/a/femalesexdysfun.htm?once=true&.*

5. Again, I am aware of the controversy of whether the Pill eliminates ovulation or prevents implantation. It seems clear that it usually does eliminate ovulation, but may also prevent implantation as a backup. Regardless, the hormones in the Pill do eliminate the libido surge women usually get every cycle.

CHAPTER 6: From Fizzle to Sizzle for Him

1. "Erectile Dysfunction (ED) Overview, Incidence of Impotence," Remedy Health Media, *http://www.urologychannel.com/erectiledysfunction/overview-of -impotence.shtml.*

2. Maggie Fox, "Impotence Plus Heart Disease Ups Death Risk: Study," Reuters News Agency, March 15, 2010, *http://www.reuters.com/article/2010/03/15 /us-heart-impotence-idUSTRE62E1SL20100315.*

3. My figure of 23 percent tends to be lower than most research on the subject, but as I explain in chapter 12, I think that is largely due to the different populations. My study was 83 percent Christian women who were active in their faith. It seems likely that in that subpopulation, male low libido is less of a factor, as we'll look at later.

4. Edward O. Laumann, Anthony Paik, Raymond C. Rosen, "Sexual Dysfunction in the United States: Prevalence and Predictors," *Journal of the American Medical Association* 6 (February 1999): 537 – 44.

5. "Low Testosterone Reference Summary," The Patient Education Institute, 2009, *http://www.nlm.nih.gov/medlineplus/tutorials/lowtestosterone/ur189102.pdf.*

6. Robert Rister, "Top Reasons for Low Libido: Sex Drive Killers," *Men's Health*, January 13, 2010, *http://www.steadyhealth.com/articles/Restoring_Libido_and _Sex_Drive_in_Men__a1147.html.*

7. Terry Hamilton, "Being Willing to Acknowledge When You're Wrong," *Breathing Grace: A Life in Bloom*, February 16, 2011, *http://terrybreathinggrace.wordpress .com/2011/02/16/being-willing-to-acknowledge-when-youre-wrong/.*

CHAPTER 7: Learning to Make Love, Not Just Have Sex

1. Jennifer Degler, "Reader Question of the Week: What Can I Do If I Check Out During Sex Due to Childhood Sexual Abuse?" CWIVES, October 18, 2010, *http:// www.cwives.com/?p=92.*

2. Ibid.

3. "Worthless Women and the Men Who Make Them," *Single Dad Laughing*, October 26, 2010, *http://www.danoah.com/2010/10/worthless-women-and-men-who -make-them.html* (emphasis mine).

4. Ian Kerner, "Too Much Internet Porn: The SADD Effect," *http://ca.askmen.com /dating/love_tip_500/566_too-much-internet-porn-the-sadd-effect.html.*

    Note: This is *not* a Christian resource, but I include it to show that secular counselors, despite years of recommending that couples watch porn together to reignite their sex life, are now admitting that it has negative effects, especially on men's libidos and abilities to respond sexually to their wives.

5. John W. Kennedy, "Help for the Sexually Desperate," *Christianity Today*, March 7, 2008, *http://www.christianitytoday.com/ct/2008/march/18.28.html.*

CHAPTER 8: A Pure, Holy, and Hot Marriage!

1. Julie Sibert, "Safe Sex: What Some Burglars Taught Me," Intimacy in Marriage blog, February 24, 2011, *http://intimacyinmarriage.com/2011/02/24/safe-sex -what-some-burglars-taught-me/.*

2. C. S. Lewis, *The Four Loves* (Glasgow: William Collins & Sons, 1960), 95.

CHAPTER 9: Becoming Best Friends

1. CBS News, "Survey: One in Four People Too Tired to Have Sex," March 20, 2010, *http://www.cbsnews.com/stories/2010/03/10/health/main6286161.shtml.*

2. To learn more about this concept, read *The Five Love Languages* by Gary Smalley (Chicago: Northfield Publishing 2010) or take his assessment tool at *http:// www.5lovelanguages.com/assessments/love.*

3. Gwyneth Rees, "Parents Lose Two Months of Sleep in Baby's First Year," *Daily Mail Online*, March 29, 2007, *http://www.dailymail.co.uk/news/article-445326/Parents -lose-months-sleep-babys-year.html.*

4. The American Academy of Pediatrics reports that the risk of sudden infant death syndrome (SIDS) is substantially higher in cosleeping families. Read their report at *http://aappolicy.aappublications.org/cgi/content/full/pediatrics;105/3/650.*

5. Lisa Belkin, "When Dad Doesn't Want to Co-Sleep," Motherlode blog, *New York Times*, May 13, 2009, *http://parenting.blogs.nytimes.com/2009/05/13 /when-dad-doesnt-want-to-co-sleep/.*

6. Carrie Lauth, "Cosleeping and Sex," *Natural Parenting*, February 1, 2011, *http:// parenting.amuchbetterway.com/cosleeping-and-sex/.*

CHAPTER 10: The Sex Circle: Learning to Give

1. Michael Castleman, "Desire in Women: Does It Lead to Sex? Or Result from It?" July 15, 2009, *Psychology Today*, *http://www.psychologytoday.com/blog/all -about-sex/200907/desire-in-women-does-it-lead-sex-or-result-it.*

2. Rachel Halliwell, "Could You Make Love Everyday for a Month? This Couple Tried ... But What Did It Do For Their Marriage?" Daily Mail Online, April 27, 2010, *http://www.dailymail.co.uk/femail/article-1269063/Could-make-love-day-month -This-couple-tried--did-marriage.html.*

3. Linda Waite and Maggie Gallagher, *The Case for Marriage: Why Married People Are Happier, Healthier and Better Off Financially* (New York: Broadway, 2001).

CHAPTER 11: Hungering for Each Other

1. From Terry at Breathing Grace, *http://terrybreathinggrace.wordpress.com.* That blog post has been archived now, but Terry has given me permission to share her thoughts from a few years ago.

CHAPTER 12: Moving Forward

1. Edward O. Laumann, Anthony Paik, Raymond C. Rosen, "Sexual Dysfunction in the United States: Prevalence and Predictors," *Journal of the American Medical Association* 6 (February 1999): 537 – 44.

Find encouragement — and challenges — for your marriage at Sheila's blog, To Love, Honor and Vacuum!

Do you sometimes feel like this marriage you signed up for has become a chore? Sheila offers insight and encouragement, sprinkled with lots of humor, to make your marriage thrive!

No pretensions — just real marriage. And real solutions. tolovehonorandvacuum.com

Also find her:

f facebook.com/sheila.gregoire.books

t twitter.com/sheilagregoire